D0203035

Gottfried Benn

PROSE, ESSAYS, POEMS

The German Library: Volume 73

Volkmar Sander, General Editor

Gottfried Benn

PROSE, ESSAYS, POEMS

Edited by Volkmar Sander

Foreword by E. B. Ashton

Introduction by Reinhard Paul Becker

CONTINUUM · NEW YORK

1987

The Continuum Publishing Company
370 Lexington Avenue, New York, NY 10017

The German Library
is published in cooperation with Deutsches Haus,
New York University
This volume has been supported by a grant
from The Marie Baier Foundation, Inc.

Library of Congress Cataloging in Publication Data

Benn, Gottfried, 1886–1956.
Prose, essays, poems.

(The German library ; v. 73)
Translations from German.
1. Benn, Gottfried, 1886–1956—Translations,
English.   I. Becker, Richard Paul.   II. Sander,
Volkmar.   III. Title.   IV. Series.
PT2603.E46A24   1987   831'.912   87-449
ISBN 0-8264-0310-7
ISBN 0-8264-0311-5 (pbk.)

Acknowledgments will be found on page 293,
which constitutes an extension of the copyright page.

Contents

PART THREE : POEMS

Translated by E. B. Ashton, Robert M. Browning, Alexandra Chciuk-Celt, Joseph B. Dallet, Babette Deutsch, Richard Exner, Franz Feige, Patricia Gleason, Michael Hamburger, E. L. Kanes, Max Knight, Christopher Middleton, J. M. Ritchie, Karl F. Ross, Gertrude C. Schwebell, Richard Sieburth, Vernon Watkins, Kerry Weinberg

Contents

Foreword

"German poetry's last internationally presentable figure"—this was one title bestowed on Gottfried Benn after his death in 1956, by a leading German news magazine. Earlier, in his lifetime, press and public had played guessing games with his Nobel Prize chances, popular dailies had placed him "at the top of our literature." He was "the man who exerted the greatest influence after the war" and "one of the grand old men of literary Europe."

These paeans were sung to an unreconstructed Expressionist, an esoteric thinker who wrote only to express ideas to his own satisfaction, an eccentric stylist whose mature prose was as popularly unintelligible as his youthful verses had been commonly unpalatable—in short, an author one would expect to be esteemed by the older sophisticates, shrugged off as a has-been by the avant-garde, and ignored by the public. Yet the public ate up Benn's books, and German youth hung on the lips of this bald, heavy-lidded purist and self-styled relic of a bygone age.

In part, no doubt, his magic lay in the promise of controversy. Dropping Benn's name among German intellectuals was enough, in the post-war years, to kindle a whole spectrum of reactions from angry red to mystic purple. He has been years in his grave, but eminent survivors of the German *hegira* of 1933 will still lump him with "a bunch of Nazi writers"—though Benn, unlike the rest of the bunch, had some violent Nazi attacks on himself to quote in reply, besides non-Nazi praise of his "confessions" of a later date: "They do not gloss over the refusal to emigrate," said a Professor Max Bense; "they defend it, and they complete this defense by defending his error. His submission is not to political change, but to error. . . ."

The poet Michael Hamburger, who translated Benn, compared him with "a man talking to himself in a room full of silly people. . . . Monologue is the only kind of communication which Dr. Benn thinks valid." . . .

A glance at the bibliography of publications about Gottfried Benn shows a strangely divergent history of the approach to him in Germany and elsewhere. In other countries he was unknown before Hitler (except to rare devotees such as Eugene Jolas, who tried for years to fit Benn into the *transition* movement of artistic revolt against the tyranny of form). The Nazi era brought him some ideological attention, largely because anti-Nazi polemics made him look like a pillar of the Third Reich. But only recently has he won serious recognition as a protagonist of modern literary trends.

In Germany, on the other hand, he was a noted modernist in the twenties, disappeared from view and almost passed into oblivion under Hitler, and then grew to amazing—and amazingly nonliterary—stature in the last five years of his life. Few of the hundreds of German essays devoted to him since he resumed publishing in 1948 explore his lifelong expressionism. Most of them stress the daring things he said, not the daring way in which he said them. Once upon a time he was an innovator—that's that; it does not seem to impress his present following. What does?

Probably the best, certainly the most thorough, non-German analysis of Benn's position in letters is found in Michael Hamburger's *Reason and Energy: Studies in German Literature*. The English poet ascribes Benn's post-war renaissance to "the interest aroused by the sole survivor from a great shipwreck." There is something to that, but it is no full explanation; others have survived the shipwreck without arousing such interest. Mr. Hamburger, after pointing out the "moral obtuseness" that let Benn "enumerate the misfortunes of his own family" in a work "in which he elaborates his anti-humanism," found it "peculiarly irritating to be asked for sympathy on one page, only to have it violently rejected on the next." But here, too, Benn would seem to deserve acquittal. For just what he did say in his preface to *World of Expression,* a book he called "a kind of reference work and primer on trains of thought in my generation"?

As an example of this generation I mention my family: three of my brothers died in battle; a fourth was wounded twice; the remainder, totally bombed out, lost everything. A first cousin died at the Somme, his only son in the recent war; of that branch of the family nothing is left. I myself went to war as a doctor, 1914–18 and 1939–44. My wife died in 1945 in direct consequence of military operations. *This brief summary should be about average for a fairly large German family's lot in the first half of the twentieth century.*

[Italics mine. E.B.A.]

The last sentence counts; and it is no plea for sympathy. What Gottfried Benn wanted and got from his German audience, in this and in scores of other passages, was not sympathy but *identification*.

There, it would seem, lies the key to the near-miracle of the old highbrow with the sudden mass appeal. The "world of expression" that Benn loved to discuss—a world understood, at best, by one out of ten of his readers—was hardly what spellbound them, nor is it apt to have been his complicated rationalization of their record, his philosophical defense of their "existential position." He had something more basic to offer: a sense of sameness. For here, however cryptic he might be in his writings, was a man who throughout his life, from Kaiser Wilhelm's time to Dr. Adenauer's, had shared the experiences, the actions, the reactions of the German people. . . .

The collapse, the "revaluation of all values," was a common point of departure for Werfel, Kaiser, Toller, and the rest of the politico-artistic vanguard. Each of them fought his private bout with despair, his own battle with nihilism. To Benn nihilism was "a sense of happiness." It absorbed him all his life—in avowal, in denial, in art, in the "world of expression," the only world acknowledged by the poet who attributed even artistic creation only to "the form-seeking power of nothingness."

Consciously or unconsciously, he spent the 1920s in a retreat from substance. It was the substance of his work that had caused his misbranding, and he withdrew to form: from the bald, unrhymed, ametrical language of his juvenile shockers to a glittering tide of poems in trochaic rhythms and short, flawlessly rhymed lines whose brilliance masked their punctilio—poems of which unfortunately only a few can be rendered in English, translation of all rhymed verse being a matter of luck. He fell back on tradition, on a deceptively deft employment of technological and scientific neologisms to conceal strict, classicist orthodoxy. In prose and in his philosophy he retreated all the way from asocial insurgence to a kind of atavistic tribalism—this, too, buried under avalanches of genetic and anthropological terms by Dr. Benn, who now made his living as a Berlin specialist for skin and venereal diseases. . . .

Paradoxically he was published, read, admired, promoted in the 1920s by a highbrow, humanistic, partly Jewish, dominantly liberal minority of Germans, while he, with the lowbrow majority, was inching toward the cult of disciplined violence, toward the primitives who were the sworn enemies of his audience. He was discovered and hailed by non-conformists abroad—as in the pages of *transition*—at the very time of his transition to the sternest of conformisms. He had given fair warning. "Is the individual case necessary?" he defined Dr. Rönne's dilemma; it was not Dr. Benn's fault if his reply was misconstrued. In "Primal Vision" he glorified "the tribe, the growth in darkness," sang of "mass in instincts," exclaimed, "Lost is the individual; down with the ego"—was he to be blamed for not being understood? When *transition* asked for views on "the crisis of man," he submitted "The New Literary Season," a 1931 lecture defending creative individualism against the literary commissars of Russia. It was not his fault if people drew the conclusion that Gottfried Benn would not embrace a different collectivism within two years. . . .

Was he a Nazi? He never joined the party—never considered joining, as far as is known—and never called himself what most Germans in 1933 called themselves every ten minutes. Why, then, his ardent declaration for the "new state"? His friends laid it to resentment of more influential and successful writers, leftists or Jews. Yet Benn always preached against art supporting the artist. He always scorned material success, and as for the other kind—he had sat in the Prussian Academy before 1933 and whatever he had written had been published (usually by leftists or Jews) and widely argued. The grudge theory may be correct, but it seems likelier to be doing Benn an injustice.

There is a touch of Luther's *"Ich kann nicht anders"*—"I cannot

do otherwise"—in what the Lutheran pastor's son replied to Klaus
Mann's letter: ". . . it is my people whose trail is being blazed here.
Who am I to exclude myself? . . . People means much! . . . [Europe]
whispers in your ear that the people are not behind Hitler. . . . A
great mistake! . . . Standing behind this movement . . . ready to perish, if need be, is the whole people. . . ."

Gottfried Benn could not exclude himself.

One of his poems of that spring became a hit, but not even the
title *"Dennoch die Schwerter halten,"* is adequately translatable.
"And yet to hold the swords"—*and yet, nevertheless, despite all*—
no English word or phrase conveys the Wagnerian overtones of
defying the world and challenging destiny which this *dennoch* caused
to ring in a majority of German ears in 1933. And in the body of
the poem readers found more: what "slept behind the millennia"
(i.e., "a few great men") and Nietzsche and "a few dying warriors"
and *Götterdämmerung* motifs, and *"dennoch".* . . . It was reprinted
over and over, finally in an anthology entitled *The Prussian Di-
mension: Intellectual Passages-at-Arms.* . . .

"The comeback is under way," he exulted. In the new year (1949),
book followed book off the press: *Three Old Men*—a playlet setting
the mood; *The Ptolemean*—the "Berlin story," including also "Wolf's
Tavern" and *Novel of the Phenotype*; the new poems; a selection
of old ones; the essays, titled *World of Expression.* The last-named
volume was not in print before the author's doubts were confirmed,
and this time the objectors were not the returned emigrants but the
lingering or resurgent half- or three-quarter Nazis who had already
envisioned Benn as their literary spokesman. Friends of long standing implored him to curb his "attacks on Germanism," begged him
to delete at least "Art and the Third Reich," the opening essay
which he had written in 1941.

Benn refused. He would not dilute his "doctrine of the world of
expression as the conqueror of nationalism, of racism, of history."
But he tried to dispel the publisher's fears for the book: "I could
imagine that it may even find a certain echo. . . . Something in what
I write must be jogging the world in its sleep."

The reception of the essays bore him out. He continued to be
criticized, but increasing plaudits indicated that he was striking

popular chords, that his instinctive rejection of totalitarianism as well as democracy, of war and of politics, of history and of humane ideals—a negation so comprehensive and at the same time so delicately balanced as to leave no philosophical approach but nihilism and no moral principle but detachment (*"Ohne mich,* count me out"*)*—was shared by multitudes of his compatriots.

In his next book he achieved the fullest measure of this identification. It was a political autobiography that he published in 1950— his and that of some 50,000,000 Germans. The *Double Life* of the title was his and theirs. He was "defending his error" and theirs. The first part, his 1933 declaration for the new state, was an intellectual version of a common experience, and so was the subsequent tale of his disillusionment, his silencing, and his resignation in the face of ruin.

In that second part of *Double Life* there is disingenuousness and special pleading; there are omissions and distortions of fact. But there is nothing, no argument, no evasion, no presentation and no misrepresentation, that would not make the average German reader feel he was hearing his own voice, or a voice he wished he had. Every word eased the general conscience. Beneath the cant that outraged foreign critics—"He wants one law for himself, another for those whom he dislikes," Michael Hamburger wrote indignantly—lay the simple instinct of moral self-preservation that has produced so many national cants.

In *Double Life* Benn spelled out a new pragmatism. What had been sensed in his earlier books was now couched in plain, easily understandable terms in an exegesis of the "Ptolemean" and his maxims:

> "Realize the position"—*i.e.,* adjust to the position, camouflage yourself, avoid convictions ("with a customer you keep your private views to yourself . . .")—but on the other hand, go right along with convictions, ideologies, syntheses in every direction of the compass, if institutions or agencies require it.

A great public need was filled by this canon that enabled men to live with themselves while surviving in our time. The premise of a senseless and intrinsically evil historic world obviated the passage of moral judgment upon one's superiors. It anticipated any turn in the political winds. It exculpated any collaboration with whatever powers might be ruling. True, it was a canon taken out of context, for Benn's next words show that he did not mean to preach "adjustment" for its own sake but in behalf of "artistics," of forms, of the expressive world. To the Ptolemean, forms alone count: "They are his ethics." But how few, in Germany or anywhere, can live by forms? How few can grasp artistics? To the many only the first half of the new canon made sense, and in *Double Life* it was the many to whom Benn was speaking.

"Never again shall I make a personal appearance," he had vowed in 1948. "Beyond fame and defeat, aloof from affirmation or negation, I have in the past years rounded out and concluded my inner image in some books. 'Silently the eon flows.' "

Yet he had always liked the platform, and by 1951 he felt ready to resume face-to-face contact with his audience. At historic Marburg University he delivered a lecture on "Problems of Lyric Poetry" that evoked echoes in the realm of European letters. T. S. Eliot, in Cambridge, quoted and discussed it at length—"and that," as one German paper noted proudly, "has not happened to modern German literature since the war's end, in so prominent a place and from such prominent lips." Benn spoke in Darmstadt, where he was awarded the Büchner Prize, one of Germany's top literary distinctions. At the Belgian resort of Knokke he spoke in French about mid-century German poetry. He spoke on Else Lasker-Schüler at the British Center in Berlin. He spoke over the radio. He spoke in discussions.

The young Gottfried Benn had offset the tendentious realism of *Home Front* with the explosive surrealism of the Pameelen dramas; now the aging one balanced the reminiscent philosophizing of his *Three Old Men* with the sardonic, semi-topical symbolisms of a new play, *The Voice Behind the Curtain*. He propounded a categorical imperative of his own: "To live in the dark, to do in the dark what we can"—the only kind of moral law he considered still possible. And he dedicated the play "to my wife, a generation younger than I, whose light, wise hand arranges the hours and the steps, and the asters in the vases."

He felt age creeping up on him. Medical practice grew too strenuous; he had to abandon it at sixty-eight. Never a coward, he faced and attacked the problem on two fronts: as a man of letters in an essay, "Artists and Old Age," and simultaneously as a man in a last, cautious, poignantly rejuvenating flight of fancy to a young poetess who had written a Ph. D. thesis about his lyrical style.

"Yes, in literature I have won through," he wrote at seventy, "and cabinet members and the Federal President and the Lord Mayor send me birthday greetings, but getting old means that everything one has done seems dubious in retrospect. . . . My wife is charming to the shabby old man." He died two months later, and the feuds that had been swirling about him, unabated, faded in the solemn chorus of eulogies.

They recommenced in a lower key. For once a man can no longer refute us, the issues shift, with his acts receding behind his effect on others, and Benn's influence, like his life, was paradoxical. The writers who sound most as he did decades earlier are either unlikely to know him (the French, for instance) or apt to bristle at his name. If they write poems, they jettison rhyme and meter; form, to them, is to be shattered, not to be sheltered in. Benn's themes bore them, and yet it is their work that seems to have fleshed out his "world of expression."

The aged Benn thought little of his successors. "They accept it as a given fact," he wrote not long before his death to a fellow Expressionist from the old days, Kasimir Edschmid, "that our generation exploded the language of the past century, ripped it apart, and that we rolled the stones farther, or tried to—and they don't know yet what it is in verse or in prose to move the pillars of Hercules even some worms' lengths. . . ."

Benn's influence, and the question of how much the *avant-garde* of the 1960s owes to that of the 1920s, will never be settled. His significance, however, is beyond question, and it is another paradox. The Germans like to call themselves "the nation of poets and thinkers," and Benn was both; even so, it was probably not as a bard that he appealed to them so strongly in his last years, nor as a sage, but as a German.

E. B. ASHTON

Introduction

In a series such as this, which presents the broad spectrum of German writing throughout the centuries, focusing on those figures who had a significant impact on the consciousness of their generation, who either embodied or provoked the literary, political, or moral tastes and styles of their contemporaries, a volume of selections from the works of Gottfried Benn serves an important purpose. It can be argued that no other writer of his generation reflects as magically and as painfully the cataclysmic shocks and the violent quakes which upset the social structures, the political life, and the literary and artistic traditions of his society between 1910 and 1950. As a young man, as a medical student, and as an army surgeon in the First World War, he found himself disillusioned with all the inherited values, taboos, and ideals which his father's generation had carried so naively and dutifully across that dangerous border between the nineteenth and twentieth centuries. More than that: he found himself increasingly haunted by a sense of disintegration and even decay in what had been perceived and accepted until then as "reality": "In war and peace, at the front and behind it, as an officer and as a doctor, among generals and profiteers, before rubber and jail cells, over beds and coffins, in triumph and decay, I never lost the trance-like feeling that this reality did not exist," he later wrote about those early years. To be sure, many of these concerns were shared in varying degrees by other young Expressionist writers at this time, but perhaps none of them broke as abruptly and mercilessly with traditional literary form and taste as Benn did in his first two volumes of poems, *Morgue* (1912) and

Söhne (Sons, 1913). They were received by critics and public with shock, dismay, even revulsion.

He was born in 1886 in the village of Mansfeld a few hours west of Berlin, the son of a Protestant pastor. His grandfather had already lived and worked in the parsonage as minister of this small congregation. Shortly after the birth of his first son, Benn's father moved his family to the village of Sellin east of the river Oder where a larger congregation offered him more challenging responsibilities and a better income. Here in rural Prussia Benn spent his boyhood years in an ambiance of peace and country bliss. He later wrote about this period in a passage that exquisitely reflects the charm and the simple joys of a village childhood before the turn of the century:

> A village of seven hundred souls in the northern German plains, a large parsonage, a large garden, three hours east of the Oder. . . . There I grew up among the village boys, spoke dialect, walked barefoot till the end of November, went to the village school, was confirmed together with the laborers' children, rode the haywagons into the fields . . . led the cows to pasture, picked cherries and nuts from the trees, made flutes from the twigs of willows and raided bird nests.

Although pastor Benn was a pious and conservative churchman, he was strangely affected by the socialist trends around the end of the century. He subscribed to the magazine *Vorwärts,* the leading journal of the Social Democratic Party in Germany. This was a peculiar political interest indeed for a clergyman who lived and worked among the families of Junkers and peasants in eastern Germany at that time. He was an amazingly liberal father who did not force his views on his children in matters of faith. Benn was not very close to him, and as he grew up he developed further and further away from the life style and convictions of his father. He never sympathized with the socialist tendencies of his generation; in fact he entrenched himself in a hardened anti-socialist position and in the 1920s he was to engage in loud and rather emotional public polemics with some of the Marxist intellectuals among his peers. In his early years as a medical student he turned away completely from the church and, unlike his father, he abhorred family life and avoided polite social contacts.

At the age of ten he entered the prestigious gymnasium at Frankfurt on the Oder, one of the finest institutions of higher learning in the area, where the world-famous historian Leopold von Ranke had taught in the early nineteenth century. Here the young boy had his first taste of freedom away from his father's parsonage and the confines of the village school. The Frankfurt gymnasium offered an excellent humanist program of classical languages, history, and literature combined with a good introduction to science and mathematics. He soon became engrossed in his studies which laid the foundation of a solid humanist education. His fellow students came mostly from the landed aristocracy of the area, and although the son of a pastor was not considered a pariah in their circles, young Benn remained quite conscious of a class distinction between himself and these young noblemen. He remained quite isolated but compensated for this with rather respectable scholastic achievements which helped him to cultivate an aloofness, a somewhat lonely personal independence. Many of his later solitary habits, his suspicion of human relationships, and his abhorrence of any form of social life may have been formed in these early years at school.

He graduated at the age of seventeen, and out of economic considerations his father urged him to complete a swift and goal-oriented university program leading to a career in higher education, if not in theology. His father enrolled Benn in the University of Marburg where he had connections which would help his son to gain financial assistance. Benn, now eighteen, leaped enthusiastically into academic life, taking courses which fed his growing intellectual appetites but which did nothing to prepare him, without waste of time and resources, for a career. He took courses in philology, poetics, and literary methodology, and he enrolled in a seminar on medieval poetry. From Marburg he sent some of his first poems to a literary magazine which featured a column where the anonymous texts were appraised by the editor. He waited anxiously for the critique of his poems, and when it appeared weeks later it was less than encouraging: "G.B.—friendly in their disposition but weak in their expression." In a speech at the University of Marburg ("Problems of Lyric Poetry," delivered August 21, 1951), Benn jested wryly that, while in the ensuing years he had gained fame as an Expressionist poet, he had received little praise for his friendly disposition.

After a few semesters his father grew quite impatient with him. He resented his son's reluctance to apply himself to a course of studies which would qualify him for a serious profession. In the middle of these unpleasant tensions between father and son, Benn's attention was drawn to an institution which was to end his indecisive search at Marburg by offering him the fulfillment of his strongest desire: the study of medicine. It was the Pépinière, the Imperial Academy for Military Medicine in Berlin. It was a medical school with a splendid tradition; some of the most distinguished men in nineteenth-century medicine such as Virchow, Leyden, Helmholtz, and Behring had been among its graduates. Another important aspect of this institution for Benn was that it charged no tuition, the only stipulation being that for every semester spent at the academy the graduates were to spend a year on active duty as military physicians. Benn was overjoyed; suddenly his most cherished elusive goal was within reach.

These years at the Pépinière between 1905 and 1910 were the formative years of his life. He received a thorough training in medicine, and in the extraordinarily stimulating atmosphere of Berlin he began to mature as a poet. He was able to serve only one year in the army after graduation, leaving active service in 1912 for reasons of health: he had dislocated a kidney during cavalry exercises. While working in one of the Berlin clinics in the following years, he immersed himself completely in the exciting literary scene of this metropolis. His first publications, *Morgue* and *Söhne*, established him as a radically new and provocative voice among the poets in Berlin at that time. The sounds and the images of these poems stood in glaring contrast to the lyrical tradition in Germany from Goethe and the Romanticists to the Neo-Romantic poetry (Rilke, Hofmannsthal, George) in the teens of this century. His frightening imagery grew out of the dissection rooms of modern clinics; these texts, which envision the probing work of surgical knives on corpses from the dangerous nether regions of the labyrinthine city, conducted the ultimate autopsy on the idealised self-image of man set forth in the conventional literature of the nineteenth century. These poems tumbled all the traditional concepts of human wholeness, beauty, and greatness from their pedestal;

they slit open the bellies of prostitutes, nameless coachmen, or a black man trampled to death by a horse, rummaged in their intestines, sawed off their limbs, and smeared the human form—that crown of creation wrought in God's image—with blood and pus. One of these pieces ("The Physician, II") begins with the brutal line: "The crown of creation, man, the swine." Another poem ("Man and Woman Go through the Cancer Ward," p. 187 below) conjures up the harrowing hopelessness and pain of patients dying of cancer; the stench of decay and the despair of death hover over these lines. The tone was cynical, irreverent, harsh; words crept in from the terminology of anatomy and the vocabulary of newspaper jargon; the rhythms were staccato: this was the audo-da-fé of bel canto in German poetry.

These years also marked the beginning of Benn's love affair with Berlin. After returning from the First World War, he was to live there with few relatively short interruptions until the end of his life. No European city at that time was as rich in contrasts, harbored as much glamour and as much misery. In those years Berlin was not only Germany's capital but its largest industrial center, where vast armies of laborers lived side by side with politicized intellectuals, actors, bohemians, artists, and writers. There were more theaters and museums, more bars and shops than in any other German town. In the 1920s a film industry was to emerge there that for a while fascinated the world with its creative genius, its innovative techniques, and its boundless imagination. Berlin had more prostitutes, more indigents, more millionaires, and more unemployed than any other German city of that generation. The young Expressionist writers and painters gathered in the many literary cafés, and Benn mingled for a while with this crowd and their hangers-on in the famous Café des Westens.

In the spring of 1914 Benn traveled as a ship's doctor to America. He earned so little money that he could not afford really to explore New York but spent most of his time sitting on a deck chair of his docked ship staring at the lights of Manhattan. But he did go to the Metropolitan Opera one night, and he heard Caruso who left an indelible impression. The moods of Manhattan, "the prairie fires of Broadway," are occasionally reflected in his writings in later years. Later that year he married his first wife, Edith Osterloh, but at the outbreak of the war he had to return to active duty. He spent two years (1915–1917) in Brussels as a physician in charge of a clinic for venereal diseases, treating soldiers and prostitutes.

During these years he wrote his first significant prose texts, the *Rönne* stories which appeared in 1916. Benn's early prose was as innovative and boldly original as his poems. The *Rönne* stories create a literary posture in which Rönne, a young physician who in most aspects is identical with Benn, becomes a mask for the author, a mouthpiece through which he expresses, filtered through reflection, his haunting experiences, his doubts and anxieties, his despairs and the occasional ecstasies which crowd his days and nights behind the front line in the strangely unreal city of Brussels, populated by the strange elements which gather at the periphery of the apocalyptic battles of the war: arms dealers, profiteers, military men of all descriptions, camp followers, adventurers, and demimonde types. The figure of Pameelen, who appears in his prose at this time, and, much later, the Ptolemean assume much the same function as media for the expression of the author's innermost experiences, fears, visions, provocative ideas, and rambling monologues.

In *Rönne* Benn begins to formulate some of the themes that will weave through all of his future prose in variations and mutations; they will gather momentum as the years go by and, like an avalanche, involve related materials and connected ideas and thus grow in breadth and in depth. Rönne experiences a sense of the disintegration of reality; something has gone awry in the relation between the world and man; consequently, the reality that once explicitly existed in relation to man has lost this significance and has thus assumed an uncanny reality unto itself. In the process it has lost its tangibility and familiarity; it has ceased to be transparent; all contexts have broken apart and only incoherent pieces of it can still be perceived. This fractured reality, which can only be rendered by the writer in fragmented, disjointed, though intriguing pieces, has turned into something distant, strange, forbidding, incomprehensible, odd, and frightening.

Man on the other hand has been raped by civilization, robbed of his primeval skills and instincts, emasculated by technology and comfort, and pampered by science. Culture has lost its life-giving and life-sustaining magical power over him; human beings have been reduced to consumers, to empty, run-of-the-mill clichés. Again and again from Rönne to Pameelen to the morose patron in "Wolf's Tavern" and to the Ptolemean, the hollow specter of contemporary man is exposed, void of content and substance, stripped of dignity, lobotomized by ideologists, manipulators, and advertisers. In his lecture commemorating the fiftieth anniversary of Nietzsche's death, Benn hurls the ultimate indictment against contemporary humanity: "Human beings don't exist anymore—only their symptoms." These ideas began to take shape in *Rönne* before the backdrop of wartime Brussels. They continued to spawn and to proliferate in his mind and in his writing to the end of his life, and as his bitterness and his nihilism grew, so did his disillusionment with the redeeming powers of science, his contempt for the mirage of progress, and his pessimism about popular concepts of history.

Late in 1917 Benn returned to Berlin and opened a practice in his area of specialization, the treatment of venereal diseases, which he conducted until 1935. His daughter Nele had been born in 1915, and his wife now moved to Berlin with the child but rented a separate, rather comfortable apartment. Benn spent much of his time in his office and in the small apartment attached to it where he read and wrote in his leisure hours. His contact with his family was regular and cordial but apparently somewhat distant. When Edith Benn died in 1921, his daughter was raised by friends in Denmark where she grew up as a Danish citizen and later became a successful journalist.

By that time he had established a literary fame of sorts, limited to Berlin and its sophisticated circles of writers, critics, and publishers. Outside of the city his name was known only to a handful of people interested in avant-garde poetry. He entertained few but very close friendships with other Expressionist authors; his important relationship to the eccentric and flamboyantly talented poet Else Lasker-Schüler dates back to these years.

This period until 1935 was also marked by the advent of the Third Reich and marred by Benn's entanglement with the new state. His involvement with National Socialism lasted exactly one year (1933–1934), but no matter how one looks at this aberration, it was embarrassing and damaged his reputation among the other writers of his rank who distanced themselves immediately from Hitler and his fascist society.

There cannot be the slightest doubt that, unlike most other Expressionist writers (Johannes R. Becher, Ernst Toller, Bertold Brecht, and others), Benn was a totally unpolitical person during the twenties. He had no political instincts, no political passions, and compared to Brecht he appears naïve, uninformed, and out of touch. By nature and preference and perhaps tempered by his years among the military, he had developed into a rather conservative man with an emotional rather than a rational dislike of the political left. After his *Collected Prose* had appeared in 1928, he became embroiled in a noisy controversy with two Marxist writers (Johannes R. Becher and Egon Erwin Kisch) about the relationship between literature and politics and the political role of the writer in society. Benn had always been adamantly opposed to the politicization of literature. The attacks of his two critics were triggered by a glowing review of his prose volume. He was enthusiastically praised and favorably compared to the writers of political propaganda material which, according to the reviewer, had taken over the German literary scene. Becher and Kisch reacted sharply and aggressively to this review, and Benn felt cornered and unfairly attacked. He lashed out at his critics bitterly, venting louder and more emphatically than ever his deep-seated aversion to the Left. He strongly resented the Marxists' anti-art position and what he perceived to be their arrogant intellectual intolerance.

Unbelievable as it may appear today, Benn knew practically nothing about National Socialism when Hitler seized power in 1933. Of course, he could have been informed; after all, the fascists had been playing a gradually increasing role in the political chaos of the Weimar Republic since 1923. But he was not. It is well documented by people who knew Benn during these years that he, like so many of his fellow countrymen, had closed his eyes and ears toward the unpleasant political upheavals, the street brawls, and the growing violence of the decade. This is upsetting—a contradiction considering the fact that he was an intellectual, a writer who should have been in touch with the political developments of his society, who should have had his finger on the pulse of the dangerous eruptions occurring around him; but the fact is that he didn't. In this regard he is part of an unfortunate tradition in German intellectual and literary history from Goethe and the Romanticists to the beginning of the twentieth century. That he allowed himself to be taken in by the vulgar and demagogic propaganda of National Socialism, even for a moment, appears to be incomprehensible but has to be accepted as a matter of record. He was neither familiar with the party program nor had ever read *Mein Kampf.* He had never had any personal contacts with politicians; he had never attended any political meetings. All of this is even harder to understand when one realizes that all his life he was a voracious reader of newspapers; he subscribed to the *Vossische Zeitung* and almost regularly bought one of the many Berlin dailies. His reactions to the events of 1933 were purely emotional and not at all rational. He had always harbored a deep resentment toward the turmoil of the many splinter parties in the German Parliament. Their fruitless and unproductive bickering and quibbling was extremely obnoxious to him and led him to view the concept of democracy negatively. After a decade of hopelessness and squalor, hate and fear, economic depression and general despair, Benn, along with many other Germans, wanted to believe that the events of 1933 finally offered a ray of hope. For a while he shared the mood sweeping the country, the feeling that the chaos and tumult were going to end, that instead of empty words, unworkable deals, and hollow promises there was finally going to be action, a determined new course, a strong and firm leadership.

During the first months of the new regime, he thought he heard sounds among all the noise which he considered not uninteresting; he thought he saw indications of potential change which were not unwelcome to him. In addition, he felt attracted to the rigorous anti-Marxist stance of the new state and to some of its vaguely formulated ideas of "discipline," "elitism," "genetic health," "race," and "national rebirth." They seem to have appealed to him since they coincided with some of his own long-standing prejudices and apparently confirmed his pessimistic and cynical ideas about the cultural decay of his society and the waning biological and psychological substance of the individual in the twentieth century.

Whatever his reasons may have been, for about a year he went public with his support for the new state. He wrote three pieces for radio and the press in which he endorsed a number of hair-raising fascist doctrines: "Art and Power," "Breeding I and II," and "The New State and the Intellectuals." When Thomas Mann's son Klaus asked him in a letter to reconsider his alliance with Hitler's regime, Benn answered him in a radio address filled with pro-fascist statements and invectives against those who had "cowardly" fled the country.

Benn's sympathy for the Third Reich quickly evaporated as he began to understand the true objectives of National Socialism. He reeled back in horror, appalled by the brutality and vulgarity of the new power brokers and the moral bankruptcy of their programs. He made his final break with the new government after June 30, 1934, when, during the "Night of the Long Knives" in connection with the Röhm-putsch, over one hundred dissidents and suspected enemies of the state were executed without trial. This was one of the first mass murders of the regime, and Benn was filled with revulsion and disgust. On August 27, 1934, he wrote to his friend, the writer Ina Seidel:

> I live with my lips pressed tightly together, inwardly and out-wardly. I can't go along with this anymore. Certain events have pushed me over the brink. What a horrible tragedy. The whole thing begins to look to me like a third-rate theater that constantly announces a performance of *Faust* when the cast hardly qualifies for a potboiler like *Hussar Feaver*. How great seemed the beginning, and how dirty it all looks today.

In the following months Benn lapsed into progressive depression. After his short fling with the new hopes, his returning alienation from contemporary man, his frustration with science and technology, his nausea over the corrosive effects of civilization on culture became deeper and more irrevocable than ever. The government classified his writings together with those of most other Expressionist authors as "degenerate art." His early poems and his revolutionary prose texts of almost two decades previous were banned from circulation. Even his medical practice became problematic. By now all physicians had been organized in the *Reichsärztekammer* (National Chamber of Physicians) which strictly controlled their professional activities. They had to fill out copious questionnaires, the most important criterion being proof of Aryan heritage. Late in 1933 Benn was struck from the list of physicians authorized to issue certain medical certificates. In *Double Life* he later described how his professional life began to deteriorate after this. He had even fewer patients and his income dropped below a tolerable level.

In order to escape his growing uneasiness in Berlin and to secure a regular salary, he rejoined the army, sponsored by some of his former influential military friends. He was transferred to what largely amounted to a desk job in Hannover. A farewell letter to Ina Seidel expresses the despair and the resignation which enveloped him at this time:

> On January 1, 1935, I am going to leave my apartment, my practice, my whole life here in Berlin and I am going back into the army. . . . I don't know to what place they will send me. My future is uncertain. . . . But morally and economically I cannot go on living like this, I have to cut myself loose from all my ties here. It is an aristocratic form of emigration. Not an easy decision! Last November I applied for a position in my field of specialization—after all, I have lived in this town . . . for thirty years. My application came back a few weeks later with the blunt comment "No openings."

Although it took him a while to readjust to military life, he felt quite safe and content during these two years in Hannover. The army, whose senior leadership was still notoriously stubborn in its disdainful passive resistance to the party and its gang of upstart policymakers, provided him with a sense of stability and protection from government harrassment. He grew fond of his quiet life in the provincial peace of Hannover but never stopped missing the hubbub and excitement of Berlin. In his evening hours he sat in cafés and taverns drinking his beer and reading stacks of newspapers and magazines, and on weekends he frequently made excursions to the surrounding countryside. He felt at home in his sparsely furnished apartment; he spent much time with his books and slowly he began to reappraise his intellectual position. After a while he started writing again, projects which he knew were unpublishable for years to come.

In his returning mood of cultural pessimism and amidst his increasing fear of the complete decline of Western culture, he wrote "Wolf's Tavern" which reflected all these old concerns of his in a new and more urgent light. In a passage at the beginning of this text, Benn draws a compelling portrait of himself at this time of growing isolation, increased government pressure and withdrawal from people around him:

> I had taken an apartment at the back of a house, all the windows overlooking the court. On purpose! For one thing, I can't stand light, can't stand being drenched in strong natural rays; but then, too, in order to hide from both men and women. "Always polite" was my slogan, "but few appearances and never without preparation." I had no telephone either, to make appointments impossible. I went to the usual parties, clinked glasses with the men, ran through the standard gossip with the ladies, and never let the flower girl pass without buying the bunch in season for the lady on my right. I don't think anyone thought of considering me improper. Of course, there was a lot of calculation and superstructure in all this, yet that was my own business.

The lonely and contact-shy patron sits at his table, sipping his wine and subjecting the types which fill the tavern to his devastating cynicism in an acid and revealing stream of consciousness. His polemic against the consumers of the culture industry is biting and, as so often in his satirical analytical passages, filled with black humor:

> This was what had chased me through all the countries that this race inhabited, through all its social stratifications and professions. I surveyed their current cultural values, their so-called theaters, and the lobbies alone condemned the whole epoch. An audience that has to recuperate from the terrors of tragedy by strolling for twenty minutes along counters laden with ham sandwiches and brandy bottles and then goes back to carry on is ripe for the guillotine. By their metaphors ye shall know them! I eavesdropped on their minor characteristics, on what sufficed to satisfy their minds: a pilot is a Marshall Blücher of the air; a Pomeranian backwoods village with a duck-pond at the back of a stable is a Venice of the North. Then, too, I heard their songs—yes, the linden is their tree all right, sweet and heartfelt and, what's more, you can make tea from its flowers.

In 1936 a volume of his *Selected Poems* appeared on the list of a prestigious publishing house. It contained the new poems he had written in Hannover together with some of his earlier ones. It was to be his last publication during the Third Reich. Although the government censorship office had insisted that five of his earlier poems be excluded from the volume because of "obscenity," massive and vicious attacks were launched against him by the two most influential party magazines *(Das Schwarze Korps* and *Der Völkische Beobacher)* soon after the book came out. He was labeled "a swine," "a pervert," "a fag," "a Jew-boy," and his poems were described as "filthy slime." A year later in a book by the SS author Wolfgang Willrich *(The Cleansing of the Temple of Art),* he was excoriated for his association with the "Jew-girl" Else Lasker-Schüler. He became very frightened and withdrew completely into the grey, monotonous daily office routines of the military medical administration. In 1937 he was transferred back to Berlin where he continued to absolve similarly dreary duties. But he was grateful and excited to be able to live in his favorite city once again and to resume contact with some of his friends. He was delighted that one of his oldest and closest friends, the Jewish publisher Erich Reiss, was still in town. They met often and exchanged their thoughts and fears about the growing catastrophe that was engulfing their country. Because of the immense influx of people into Berlin and the virtual stop in the construction of housing, it had become extremely difficult to find adequate, much less attractive apartments. A friend of Reiss's, a real estate broker, was able to help Benn find a new apartment in Bozenerstrasse, the house in which he was to live, except for a brief interruption during the war, until the end of his life.

Early in 1938 he married Herta von Wedemeyer, a sophisticated aristocratic woman whom he had met during his tour of duty in Hannover. She came from an old military family, her father having been killed in the First World War. She was a very quiet person, shy and retiring. Benn felt attracted to this tall, slender woman, and he was grateful for her warm, low-keyed presence in his life after seventeen years of bachelorhood.

In March of 1937 he was kicked out of the *Reichsschrifttums-kammer* (National Chamber of Writers) and was put under strict prohibition against writing. What this meant practically was that he was forbidden to publish from now on. Thus, at the age of fifty-two, he was forced into obscurity and silence. Writing now became an intimate, very private, and forbidden act in which he indulged obsessively and in secrecy. In the next few years he began to learn to live a "double life," a dialectical existence between inside and outside, between a disintegrating reality and almost hallucinatory phantasies of regression to primeval beginnings, to antediluvian forms of life and states of being.

Living once again in Berlin during these years, in this city which he cherished above all others, registering daily in his nerve ends its myriad excitements and irritations, nurtured his creative energies. A few years earlier he had written in "Primal Vision" about his chaste and sensuous romance with this town:

Three of these rooms faced the street, a fourth the backyard. A night club opened on the yard; I often listened to its seductive themes. Sometimes music rang out at night when I entered my bedroom. I would open the window, turn off the light, and stand breathing the sound. For long times I would stand gazing into the night that held nothing for me anymore, nothing but the dusk of my heart, an aging heart: vague air, greying emotions, you give yourself only to fall a prey—but giving and falling prey were very remote. Into the other rooms fell the red glow of the city. Not having seen Niniveh on its jasper and ruby foundation, not having seen Rome in the arms of the Antonines, I viewed this, the bearer of the myth that began in Babylon. A mother city, a womb of distant ages, a new thrill by tap dance and injection.

When the war broke out in 1939 Benn's professional activities remained unchanged for the next few years. He continued to work in the medical administration drafting reports on the growing suicide rates in the army and issuing medical certificates for the pension applications of crippled veterans. However in September of 1943 the administrative section of which he was now in charge was transferred to the small town of Landsberg in far-away provincial Prussia. He later wrote to his friend Thea Sternheim about the change from Berlin to this confined and isolated place:

I took my wife along and got her a job as a typist, we lived in the marvellous barracks high above the town and we were well fed. . . . There was nothing left to do any more, I had more time to myself than ever in my life, I read and I wrote—actually these eighteen months were the most peaceful and happiest time of my life. (August 12, 1949)

He was able to put his thoughts and his literary projects back in order, and he embarked on one of the most productive periods in his literary career. The hardships of the past years had given a new clarity to his thought. During this relatively short period he achieved a maturity in his craft and art which led him in the final decade of his life to the height and perfection of his artistic abilities. Unquestionably, the marble prose of "Block II, Room 66," which later appeared in *Double Life,* ranks among the clearest, most disciplined, and most lucid German prose of his generation. In addition, in these months he wrote the *Novel of the Phenotype,* some of the finest pieces of the cycle *Static Poems,* and many of the essays in *World of Expression,* such as "Pallas" and "Induced Life."

Parallel with his literary prose from the early thirties on, Benn turned again and again to the essay, a genre in which he honed his peculiar prose style of provocative, arrogant formulations and of far-flung heterogeneous associations which constitute collages of encyclopedic fragments of information from paleontology, anthropology, biology, psychiatry, history, the classics, and medicine. His essays reflect the wide range of his growing intellectual interests, and they are the experimental medium for his brilliant and virtuoso craft of formulation. Although his basic stance as a thinker is that of a scientist, and although he constantly draws upon the vast pool of scientific insights, fact, and ideas, his method of argumentation is far from scientific. His thinking is subjective, speculative, emotional, provocative rather than rational, synthetic, or empirical. He always states personal positions; he is given to elaborating his own preconceived ideas and prejudices; and he is not above citing unscientific or pseudoscientific sources to bolster his arguments. Dieter Wellershoff in his penetrating study *Gottfried Benn: Phänotyp dieser Stunde* (*Phenotype of This Hour,* 1958) traces the origins of much of Benn's thinking and establishes the deep impact on Benn of such serious and fascinating ideas as C. G. Jung's "collective consciousness" and Ludwig Klages's "cultural pessimism." But on the other hand the early twentieth century was awash with wild and phantastic anthropological and paleontological theories which were disguised as science or solid scholarship but were bare of any proof and often stood in glaring contradiction to established scientific facts. Wellershoff shows that Benn's recurring idea of "progressive cerebration," the theory that the human brain constantly increases in volume as man sinks lower and lower to the level of a dehumanized automaton bereft of culture and moral dignity, has its roots in just such murky "scientific speculations around the turn of the century. His yearning dreams of regression from the deteriorating reality and the devastations of civilization back to untold human cultures which flowered and perished hundreds of millions of years ago are based on the fanciful theories of such obscure authors as Eugen Georg *(Forgotten Cultures)* and his French mentor, Edgar Dacqué.

This technique of weaving together unrelated materials and iconographies, of forging and forcing disparate references and allusions into new and often surprising or bewildering contexts, also marks the style and structural character of Benn's literary prose. Wellershoff offers a superb characterization of this elusive, brilliant, and often baffling quality of Benn's mature prose:

> The summarizing surveys, the surprizing synopses, the unifying views of phenomena which are separated in space and time, the countless allusions which conjure up unexpected analogies, the accelerated change of perspectives, the genesis of thoughts by association, the turbulence of themes, the love for the remotest, most curious detail, the effective text-montages out of lyricisms, newspaper jargon, idioms, meditations, and statistics, the aspect of parody and travesty which prevades everything—this is a free and deliberate play with the elements of a disintegrating historical world. (p. 82)

This developing and changing configuration of ideas, concerns, and obsessions, often preformulated or simultaneously articulated in his essays, constitutes the heady and rich intellectual framework of his literary prose from its beginning to the more disciplined and form-conscious mastery of Benn's last years. The early experiences of disintegrating reality merge in the tumultuous and unsettling decade of the Weimar Republic into a growing pessimism toward culture and history and into an increasing preoccupation with irrational philosophies of life. Benn begins to view the unfolding events in Europe during the Third Reich in the light of Spengler's *Decline of the West*. Progressive cerebration is compensated by a flight into the archaic dawn of mankind. The more uncompromising his rejection of the outside world became, the more powerful the role of the unconscious within him. And as the outside world lost its dependable reality, the rising tide of phantasm and the flood of images from within assume the concreteness of a vicarious reality. His wallowing in prehistoric chaos, in speculations about prelogical and collective consciousness, shifts in the last decade of Benn's life to its opposite: a need for concrete approaches to a new consciousness, a reaching for form, a quest for and an expression of a "static" existence. The "static," permanent, balanced quality in works of art and literature now appears to him as the transfigured contrast to the senseless amorphous process of constant changes and mutations in life and history.

Benn and his wife were still in Landsberg in 1945 when the Eastern Front collapsed and the Russian army began to move quickly toward German territory. Most Germans never held a realistic view of the outcome of the war with Russia. The government stepped up its propaganda during the last months: the German army was never going to let the Russians cross German borders. Capitulation was absolutely unthinkable. When the end finally came panic and confusion broke out. Hundreds of thousands of people, soldiers and civilians, fled west before the advancing Russian army. It was an extremely cold winter, people carried their belongings on their backs or carted them on the congested icy roads. The death rate among the refugees, especially among the children, was staggering. The horrors of this trek west in the winter of 1945 have become legendary. Benn and his wife made their way back to Berlin in this caravan of hysteria and despair. The final paragraph of "Block II, Room 66" gives a description of this journey; it opens a view into a cold grey hell of those horrible weeks.

Soon after they returned to Berlin Herta Benn became ill, and at the beginning of April Benn sent her to a small village on the Elbe. He hoped she would be safer there and better able to recuperate.

The following weeks turned into an inferno for Benn. The Russian army encircled Berlin and began to take the city block by block in tough and furious street battles. All communication with the outside world was cut off, and Benn lost contact with his wife for several months. His situation in Berlin was precarious; the Russian military immediately began to search the city for Nazis and suspected war criminals. Benn was arrested and interrogated several times, but the fact that he was needed as a physician saved him from detention. He was busy treating Russian soldiers for venereal diseases and was able to survive on the occasional gifts of food and cigarettes some of his patients gave him for his services.

In June, he had the first chance to contact his wife, but the woman he had sent to bring her food and some money was intercepted by the Russian troops and never reached Herta Benn. Late in July, shortly after the American army had moved into Berlin, he received the first news of her and it was tragic. Sick and despondent, fearful that her husband was no longer alive, she had committed suicide. In the fall of 1945 Benn was finally able to get out of Berlin to visit her grave. In November of that year he wrote to his friend Else Kraus:

> Nothing in my life has ever devastated me as much as that day in that miserable village, in that kitchen where she had been living for months waiting for me, on the floor where she lay in a corner on a potato sack over wood shavings, where she had injected herself with morphium.

On May 2, 1946, he turned sixty, a melancholy and depressing day for one who had long felt uneasy about aging and about his own old age. Celebrating this day amidst the rubble and ruins of Berlin, surrounded by famine, hopelessness, and despair, rekindled his pessimism about his own destiny and that of his generation. In 1949, in his preface to *World of Expression,* he wrote with sadness and bitterness about his generation ravaged by two world wars. He cites his own family as an example: three of his brothers were killed in World War I, a fourth was seriously wounded twice, a cousin was killed in the battle of the Somme, the son of that cousin lost his life in the last war, and Benn's wife died as a victim of that war.

A tragic family chronicle, and yet a chronicle which is typical for a German family of that generation.

He had no way of knowing in that dark and hopeless spring of 1946 that fame would finally come during the last decade of his life. Not the kind he had known until now. In the twenties and since, his notoriety had been limited largely to Berlin and to a few circles in other large towns where people followed the activities of the avant-garde. But now after ten years of enforced silence and obscurity, this final decade was to bring him the kind of national and international fame that would secure him a place in history.

At the end of 1946 Benn married for the last time. One day a colleague entered his office, a dentist by the name of Ilse Kaul whose practice was located in Benn's neighborhood. She came to get her typhoid shots required by the military government. For a while they both had misgivings about entering a serious relationship because of the considerable difference in their ages: Ilse Kaul was then in her early thirties. Their marriage turned out to be a stabilizing and encouraging force for both of them. Benn thrived in this association with a woman who brought light and hope back into his life, and he probably invested more of himself in this third marriage than he ever had before.

At first the precarious peace after the fall of the Third Reich did not bring much relief to Benn. He was still not allowed to publish. The military government, which took strict control of all aspects of public life, began issuing licenses to newspapers, magazines, and publishing houses only after careful scrutiny of their political past. Individuals in public service, teachers, professors, artists, and authors as well as people on the management level of industry and commerce were subjected to similar investigations of their past political affiliations. In Berlin and in the American, British, and French occupation zones of West Germany, Benn remained blacklisted for the next two years. His comeback, therefore, did not at first occur in Germany but abroad. In 1948 the Swiss publishing house Arche published the slim volume *Statische Gedichte (Static Poems)* which contained 43 poems from the years 1937 to 1947, finally breaking Benn's twelve-year silence. They caused a sensation quite different from and infinitely greater than the upheaval his first publication of poetry had unleashed. The reviews in the press and on the radio were unanimously enthusiastic. By comparison the few other postwar lyrical voices appeared weak, derivative, full of self-pity, and without a new substance or a new élan.

The new Benn texts that were now either resurrected from his files after years of obscurity or were to be written in the remaining years of his life constitute the first entirely new, uniquely original tone in German lyric poetry since Rilke and Brecht. And with this new and commanding presence all of a sudden a new and challenging standard of artistic quality, a new criterion for lyrical relevance, was established in German poetry against which every new talent and poem of the post-war generation could be measured. Benn's poetry had matured considerably since the explosive revolutionary years of *Morgue* and *Söhne*. His language had expanded into all layers and facets of contemporary German, utilizing the terminologies of many areas of specialization, the lingo of the modern media, as well as the cryptic words of ancient religions and cultures. In Benn's usage the German lyrical language, which had emerged so pure and homogeneous from the Romantic tradition, became a linguistic landscape pock-marked with heterogeneous elements, at times harsh, sober, and even alienating, at other times smooth and laden with intoxicating aromas and scents. It was in this lyrical language which knew no boundaries of expression that he was now able to formulate many of the ideas and images that in the past years had crowded and sometimes obscured his prose. They took on a new and transfigured life in his disciplined verses, distilled by his intellect, mystified by his passion. In these magical verses his old yearnings to regress from the ravaged present back to a wholesome, innocent, vital animal existence with its wisdom and rich instincts take on a luminous transparency and convincing power. Here the longing to be liberated from the tortures of consciousness, or the eloquent laments about having to bear a brain (the painful curse of cerebration) sound persuasive, make sense, and touch common human experiences and sentiments.

Many of these poems are so deeply rooted in Benn's unique intellectual and poetic iconography and have grown so inseparably into the ideomatic textures of his language that they seem to elude the translator's grasp. This volume offers in its selection of Benn's poems the rare luxury of presenting two or more translations of some of those texts whose enigmatic qualities, like a faceted stone, show more than one surface and more than one aspect. To have several versions of such texts allows for the exquisite possibility that more than one facet of the texture of these poems will become visible.

In the beginning the great fame which now began to come to Benn was puzzling and bewildering to him. After all, he had been an extremely private man all of his life, and as he grew more and more into a public figure during those last years, he had to guard himself increasingly against intrusions upon his private sphere. This last decade is more carefully documented than any other part of his life. He himself disclosed a great deal of details about his person in the many prefaces to texts which had been waiting for publication since the late thirties and in the new prose of his final years. There was an onslaught of interviews and personal approaches by fellow writers, literary historians, and admirers. There were innumerable conversations on the basis of which his partners afterwards carefully documented every view, feeling, and observation he had expressed. In the volumes of his letters almost two thirds date from these public years of his life.

At first he had hesitated somewhat to accept the new celebrity status with all of its implications. When the prestigious Munich magazine *Merkur* solicited contributions from him, he vented, in a famous letter of July 1948, all of his uneasy feelings about the way in which he had been treated as a writer:

> The wings of fame are not white, as Balzac says; but if, like myself for the last fifteen years one has been publicly referred to as a swine by the Nazis, a halfwit by the Communists, an intellectual prostitute by the democrats, a renegade by the emigrants, and a pathological nihilist by the religious, one is not particularly keen on pushing one's way out in front of that public again—all the less if one does not feel any inner bonds with it.

Finally, in the fall of 1948, the German publishing house Limes managed to obtain permission to print Benn's works in Germany. The publisher, Max Niedermayer, had to struggle long and tenaciously to overcome the obstacles which the Allied authorities and the post-war German bureaucracy had placed in the way of Benn's comeback in Germany.

The first publication was the dialogue *Drei Alte Männer (Three*

Old Men), which bore the notation: "This is the first book of Gottfried Benn to appear in Germany after a twelve-year interruption." Next came the German edition of *Statische Gedichte*, followed in short succession by his new prose, such as *The Ptolemean* (containing "Wolf's Tavern" and *Novel of the Phenotype*) and the volume of essays *Ausdruckswelt (World of Expression)*. From now on until his death in 1956 new publications of Benn's works appeared every year.

When he was granted a pension in 1953 after the many years of service as a military physician, he gladly closed his medical practice and withdrew completely into an active but very secluded life of writing, editing, and reading. Early in 1956 Benn became very ill, although most of those friends and acquaintances who helped celebrate his last birthday were unaware of how sick he was. He was hospitalized for a few weeks but was soon released without improvement and without a clear diagnosis of his ailment. There followed a short stay at a sanatorium which did not produce any measurable positive results either. He returned home, weakened, in great pain, his face marked by suffering and insomnia. He died a few weeks later on July 7, in the town that he had loved above all others, and, as he had once wished, on a day

> ... in summer
> when everything is bright,
> and the earth is easy on the spade.

R. P. B.

Part One

PROSE

The Birthday

Sometimes, for an hour, you are;
the rest is what happens. Sometimes
the two worlds surge into a dream.

Gradually a doctor had come to be past twenty-nine, and the sum of his impressions was not such as to arouse especial feelings.

As old as he was, though, he asked himself this and that. An urge to know the meaning of existence came over him repeatedly: who fulfilled it? The gentleman who was walking vigorously, an umbrella under his arm; the market-woman sitting in the evening breeze under the lilacs, after closing time; the gardener who knew all plants by name, cherry laurel or cacti, and that the red berry on the dead bush was last year's?

He came from the North German plains. In southern lands, of course, the sand was light and loose; it had been demonstrated that the wind could carry grains of it around the globe. Here a grain of dust was large and logy.

What had he experienced? Love, poverty, and x-ray tubes; rabbit pens; and recently a black dog in an open square, straining about a big, red organ that swung between his hind legs, calmingly and winningly, as children stood by, ladies' eyes sought the animal, teen-agers shifted position to see the event in profile.

How had he experienced all this? He had brought in barley from the fields, in harvest wagons, and everything was big: the shocks, the baskets, the horizon of the horse. Then a young woman's body had been full of water, calling for discharge and drainage. But hovering above it all was a faint, doubting As If: as if you were real, space and stars.

And now? It would be a gray, meaningless day when they buried him. The wife dead; the child weeping a few tears—a teacher by then, probably, obliged to look at copybooks in the evening. Then it would be all over. The influencing of brains by and through him would end. The preservation of energy would take over.

What was his first name? Werff.

What was his full name? Werff Rönne.

What was he? A doctor in a whorehouse.

What time was it? Twelve o'clock. It was midnight. He was thirty years old. A thunderstorm roared in the distance. Clouds burst into May woods.

Now, he said to himself, it is time to begin. In the distance roars a thunderstorm, but *I* happen. Clouds burst into May woods, but *my* night. I have northern blood, I'll never forget that. My forefathers guzzled everything from troughs and stables. But I, he encouraged himself, am only taking a walk. Then he searched for something metaphoric to tell himself and failed, but this he found significant and portentous: perhaps imagery itself was already escapism, a kind of illusion and a lack of fidelity.

Silent blue mists driven inland from the nearby sea enveloped Rönne next morning as he walked to his hospital.

It lay out of town, far from any paved road. He had to walk on ground that was soft and pervious to violets; loose and watersoaked, it swayed about his feet.

Out of gardens crocus hurled itself at him, the matitudinal candle of poets, the yellow variety that had been the epitome of loveliness to Greeks and Romans. Was it any wonder that it transported him to the realm of the gods? In ponds of crocus juice they bathed, sheltered from intoxication by wreaths of blossoms. Saffron fields by the Mediterranean: tripartite stigma; flat pans; sieves of horsehair over light, open fires.

He egged himself on: the Arabic was *za-fara*, the Greek, *kroké*. Corvinus came to mind, the Hungarian king who knew how to avoid saffron stains while eating. Effortlessly the dyestuff occurred, the spice, the flowering meadow and the Alpine glen.

Still yielding to the delight of such extensive association, he noticed a glass sign with the inscription "Maita Cigarettes" illuminated by a sun ray. And now—via Maita—Malta—beaches—shiny—ferry—port—mussel-eaters—corruptions—there ensued a bright, ringing, gently splintering sound, and Rönne swayed with happiness. But then he entered the hospital: eyes inflexible, unshakably resolved to connect today's sensations and feelings with his existing stock, omitting none, linking every one. He envisioned a secret construction suggestive of armor and the flight of eagles, a kind of Napoleonic fancy, such as conquering the hedge he lay behind. Werff Rönne, thirty years old, established, a physician.

Ha, not so simple today. Straddle, and down from the chair, Miss—that thin blue vein running from the hip into the hair, we'll remember that! I know temples with such veins, slim, white, weary temples but this I'll remember, this snaky little twig of violet blood! How? Well, when the talk gets around to small veins, I shall stand fortified, especially in regard to surface veins: at the temples?? Ah, gentlemen!! I have seen them on other organs, too, thinly winding, like a sprig of violet blood. Would you like a sketch, perhaps? It went like this—shall I go higher up? The opening? The great ventricular vein? The heart chamber? The discovery of the circulation of the blood—? A wealth of impressions faces you, does it not? You whisper: who is this gentleman? He stands absorbed? Rönne is my name, gentlemen. I collect such little observations now and then, not uninteresting, but of course quite insignificant—small contributions to the great structure of knowledge and the cognition of reality, ha, ha!

And you , ladies, we know each other, don't we? Permit me to create you, to drape you in your essentialities, your impressions within myself. The lead organ is uncracked. It will demonstrate its memory. Already you rise . . .

You address the part you love. You look into its eye, animate, inspire. There are scars between your thighs—an Arab bey. Those must have been large wounds, opened by the depraved lips of Africa.—But you sleep with the white rat of Egypt whose eyes are pink; you sleep on your side, with the animal along your hip. Its eyes are glassy and small, like red caviar pellets. At night the animal gets hungry. Over the sleeper it climbs to a plate of almonds on the bedside table and softly returns to her hip, sniffing, alert. Often you wake when the cool, thin tail snakes across your upper lip.

For a moment he probed into himself. But he stood powerfully, as memory picture followed memory picture and the threads between them rustled hither and yon.

And you from the lupanar in Aden, sweltering between the desert and the Red Sea. At all hours bluish water trickles down marble walls. Clouds of incense rise from trellises on the ground. You know the love of all nations on earth, but you long for a humble cottage on the Danish Sound. Come last flushes, a billiard table, boys in light suits playing before it—and you in a brothel in the path of war, between harness and leather, daily riven a hundredfold by unknown members, or by lumps of clotted blood and dung.

Transfigured he stood before himself. How he was playing it up. Playing? Rainbowing! Greening! A May night utterly ineffable! He knew them all. Face to face with them he stood, clean and natural. He had not weakened. Strong life pulsed through his head.

He knew them all, but he wanted more. He wanted to explore a most hazardous field; there probably was, or had been, a conscious life without feelings, but our likings—he distinctly remembered that sentence—are our heritage. In them we experience our lot: now he wanted to love one.

He looked down the corridor, and there she stood. She had a birthmark, strawberry-colored, running from her neck over one shoulder and down to the hip, and in her eyes, flowerlike, a purity without end, and about the lids an anemone, still and happy in the light.

What would her name be? Edmée, that was enchanting. What else? Edmée Denso, that was supernatural; that was like the call of the coming new woman, the imminent, longed-for creature that man was about to create for himself: blonde, and with the lust and skepticism of sobered brains.

Well, now he loved. He sounded the feeling within him. Exuberance had to be created against nonexistence, lust and pain to be forced out into the bald, gray light of high noon. But then there must be oscillation too! He was facing strong sensations. He could not stay in this country. Meridionalities! Exaltation!

Edmée, a flat-roofed white house in Luxor or the Cairo palace? City life is gay and open; the light is famous, a limpid glow, and night comes suddenly. You'll have innumerable fellah women to serve you, to sing and dance for you. You'll pray to Isis, touching your forehead to pillars whose capitals bear the flat heads with long ears on their corners. You will stand in sycamore gorges among wading birds.

He searched a moment. Something like Coptic had arisen, but he was unable to bring it to light. Now he sang again, the happy tender heart.

Winter comes and the fields green; a few leaves fall from the pomegranate bush, but the corn shoots up before your eyes. What will you have: narcissi or violets the year around, poured into your bath when you rise late in the morning; or do you want to roam at night through little villages along the Nile, when the bright southern moon casts large, clear shadows on the crooked streets? Will you have ibis cages or heron houses? Orange groves, flaming yellow and clouding the city with sap and vapor at noon, or a chiseled frieze from Ptolemaic temples?

He stopped. Was that Egypt? Was that Africa around a woman's body, gulf and liana about her shoulders' flow? He searched here and there. Had something been left behind? Was there anything that could be added? Had he created it: glow, sorrow, and dream?

But what a curious ferment in his breast! An agitation as if he were drained out. He left the examination room and went through the hall into the park. It drew him down, down on the lightly-mown grass.

How this has tired me, he thought, by main force! Then it struck him that pallor was the fruit, and the tear was pain—: tremors! Gaping distance!

The park glowed luxuriantly. A bush on the lawn wore fernlike foliage, each frond large and fleshy as a deer. About each flowering tree the earth lay like a closed bucket, watering it and surrendering itself. Sky and blossoms: softly, out of eyes, came blueness and snow.

—Sobbing and more, ever nearer, Edmée, to thee! A marble parapet rims the sea. Meridionally gathered lilies and barks. A violin opens you, all the way into your muteness—

He blinked upward. He trembled: against the lawn a radiance stormed, moist, from a golden hip, earth mounting the sky. Spread on the shadows' edge, light struggled. Back and forth played the tongue of enticement; out of its plumage a shower of flowers escaped from the magnolia into a breeze that brushed by.

Edmée laughed: roses and bright water.

Edmée walked: on narrow paths, between violets, in a light of islands rising from osmium-blue seas—in short, of rock and star. Doves, rock-pigeons, chopped silver with their wings.

Edmée grew tanned, a bluish oval. She played before palms, she had loved much. She carried her nakedness like a cup, coolly flexing her enkindled stride, the hand on her hip heavy, harvest-yellow under grain and seed.

In the garden mingling ensued. No longer did the flower bed riot with colors; the humming of bees no longer ochred the hedge. Extinct were direction and cadence: a drifting blossom halted and stood in the blue, like the hinge of the world. Treetops gently dissolved, chalices shrunk, the park submerged in the blood of the disembodied one. Edmée sprawled on the ground. Her shoulders smoothed, two warm ponds. Now, slowly, she closed her hand about a shaft, the ripe abundance, brownishly mown, on her fingers, under great sheaves of transfigured lust—

There was a swell in him now; now a tepid escape. And then the structure became confused as his carnal ego melted away—:

Steps resounded over the slope of a valley through a flat white town; dark gardens enclosed the alleys. On crumbling sills and architraves, scattered over a Florentine landscape and representing gods and mysteries, lay drops of bright blood. A shadow swayed among mute members, among grapes and a herd; a fountain plashed in splintering play. . . .

A body lay in the grass. Fumes washed up from basements; it was mealtime, pipe smoke and bacon rinds, the bad breath of one dying.

Up looked the body: flesh, order, and preservation summoned. He smiled and hardened again; withdrawing already, he looked at the house: what had happened? What had been mankind's way thus far? An effort to bring order into something that should have remained play. But after all, it had remained play in the end, for nothing had reality. Did he have reality? No; all he had was every possibility. He bedded his neck deeper into the may-weed that smelled of thyrse and Walpurgis. Melting through the noon-day, his head pebbled, brooklike.

He offered it to the light; irresistibly the strong sun trickled into the brain. There it lay: scarcely a molehill, brittle, the animal scratching inside.

But what about the morel quarter, he asked himself soon after. Behind the palace with the laurel-ringed pillars, alleys plunge precipitately, house leaning on little house, down the slope.

One-eyed men hang about snail wagons. They put down money. Women pry up the shells. A circular cut, and the pink flesh hangs out. They dip it in a cup of broth and bite. The woman coughs, and they move on.

Soothsayers, aided by thought transference, ring incessantly, shrilly, addressing ladies especially, and carry batteries.

Gypsy women before pushcarts. Rays, flattened, purple and silvery, their heads chopped off, are split in half, notched, and hung up to dry between other fish, thin, crooked, copper-glistening.

There is a smell of fire and stale fat. Countless children are relieving themselves; their language is alien.

What about the morel quarter, Rönne asked himself. I have to face it! Come on, down! I have sworn I'll never forget this picture of summer beating a wall with shrubs of flaming plumage, with rushes or taut, blue, stinging flesh—beating against an un-streaming wall the damp blue vine!

He raced down. About the cavernous alley flocked little houses, undermined by long narrow caves spewing forth bone: young and lusty, old and creaking, the groins girt high.

What was sold: wooden clogs for want, green dumplings for the ego, schnapps for pleasure, necessities of body and soul, salve boxes and Holy Virgins.

What went on: small children close before kneeling women, just off their breasts; rough voices, down and out over charred stone; a gentleman digging inconceivably far into his pocket; skulls, a desert, bodies, a gutter, treading earth, chewing: I and you.

He fled deeper into the alley. But there, a small monument, erected to the founder of a boys' club—the human soul, the community system, the longer life expectancy and the city council, flaunting full beards and population increase. Reconstruction unfolded: abilities were tested and re-tested, investigations carried on and results determined.

Where had his South gone? The ivied rock? The eucalyptus, where by the sea? Ponente, coast of decline—where the silver-blue wave?

He raced into a dive, battled drinks, hot, brown ones. He lay on the bench to let his head dangle, because of gravity and blood. Help, he cried, exaltation!

Chairs—objects for gentlemen with knees bent forward and desiring support for the rear surfaces of their legs—dried dully, northern fashion. At tables such talk as "Well, how's it going," waggish and manly and about the lower parts of the anatomy, ran honorably through time. No death hurled the bleary-eyed barmaid hourly into nothingness, at the stroke of the clock. Shopkeepers scratched with their feet. No lava over the dead rubble!

And he? What was he? There he sat among his sensations; the rabble was what happened to him. His noon was mockery.

Once more his brain welled up, the dull course of the first day. Still between his mother's thighs—thus he happened. As the father pushed, he rolled down. The alley had broken him. Back: the whore screamed.

He was about to go, when a sound happened. A flute chimed in the gray alley, a song, blue between the shacks. A man must be walking there, blowing it. A mouth was active in the sound that soared and faded away. Now he was starting again.

Out of the blue. Who asked him to play? No one thanked him. Who would have asked when the flute was coming? Yet like a cloud he came, appearing for his white moment and already disappearing into all the gorges of the sky.

Rönne looked about, transfigured, though nothing had changed. Except for him: he was blissful up to his lips. Plunge after plunge, thunder by thunder, rustling sails, flaring masts, the dock stretching, roaring between small basins—great and glowing, the *harbor complex* approached:

The light rises over the rocks, casting shadows; the villas shimmer, and the background is mountain-filled. A black spindle of smoke darkens the pier while the tiny local boat fights the crinkled waves. On the swaying gangplank bustle the *facchini:* "Hoyoh—tirra—hoy," ring their voices; the full tide of life flows. The ship's belly points to tropical and subtropical regions, to salt mines and lotus rivers, to Barbary caravans, to the very antipodes. A mimosa-fringed plain yields reddish resin, a slope between chalk marl, the rich clay. Europe, Asia, Africa: bites, deadly consequences, horned vipers, and the whorehouse on the quay meet the arrival; silently in the desert stands the sultana-bird.—

It still stood silently when the *olive* happened to him.

The Agave was beautiful, too, but the fine-oil-bearing Taggiaska came blue-black and melancholy before the Ligurian Sea.

Sky, seldom clouded; roses casading; through every bush the blue gulf—but the endless bright forests, what a shadow-weighted grove!

When the cloth was spread around the stem, there was work to be done. A mixture of horns, claws, leather, and woolen rags; every fourth year one had eaten. But now men otherwise devoted with suspenseful zeal to the bowling game were cutting treetops, abruptly engrossed in the fruits.

The weevil in touchwood. A wood-nymph, flaring out of the myrtle. A small press is turned, a slate cellar crossed in silence. The harvest nears, the blood of the hills, round the grove, bacchantically, the city.—Came *Venice,* and he flowed across the table. He felt lagoon, and a relaxation, sobbing. At the muffled sound of the song from the old days of Doge Dandolo, he scattered into a zephyr.

The stroke of an oar; a breath drawn; a barque: support for the head.

Five iron horses given by Asia, and around the columns rang a song: sometimes, for an hour, you are; the rest is what happens. Sometimes the two tides swell into a dream. Sometimes a rustling: when you are broken.

Rönne listened. There must be greater depths. But the evening came fast from the sea.

Bleed, rustle, suffer, he said to himself. Men looked at him. Yes, he said, their freckles, their bald necks with hair stubbling over the Adam's apple—under my crucifixion; I will go to rest.

He paid quickly and rose. But from the door he glanced back once more at the darkness of the tavern, at the tables and chairs of which he had suffered so and would suffer again and again. But there, from the shaft of the centerpiece next to the leaky-eyed woman, a large, legendary poppy glowed with the silence of lands untouchable, russet, dead, and consecrated to the gods. There, he felt deeply, his way would now lead forever. A yielding came over him, a surrender of final rights. Mutely he tendered his brow, loudly its blood gaped.

Darkness had fallen. The street received him, above it the sky, a green Nile of the night.

But over the morel quarter the sound of the flute rang once more: sometimes the two tides swell into a dream.

A man decamped. A man hurled himself into his harvest, to be bound by reapers offering wreaths and verse. A man drifted out of his fields, aglow under crown and plumage, immeasurable: he, Rönne.

(1916)   *Translated by E. B. Ashton*

Alexander's March
by Means of Flushes

It is winter, severe frost, in the mornings almost a little hazy with cold. As the geography textbook puts it, a pale, delicate haze accompanies the sun at a distance extending to the orbits of the nearest planets: it is the Zodiacal Light, appearing in pyramid form like a shimmer of the Milky Way. Something of this pale and delicate haze appears far away in the morning, especially during the hours before noon, when the flaming sun slowly rises over Gneisenau-strasse.

It is the time of the solstice; something about tropics is going on. Say what you will about the problems of evolution, in any event a Gregorian year is drawing to a close. You get older; temples turn gray. Nothing abnormal, no specific phenomenon: air gets into the medulla, anatomically speaking, in some families as early as the twenties, in the present case in the thirty-seventh year.

It is Christmas Eve; the case in question is alone but not quite forgotten. Quite unexpectedly a messenger brought him a small package. A sloshing inside, as of water, was traced to a small tri-angular carton, a fantastic glass jar, a fairy tale name—in other words, to a perfume evoking Punjab and Asiatic subtlety, with place designations like "Champs Elysées" adding detail, and "Mouchoir de Monsieur," moreover, strongly influencing the whole *milieu*. Could not the notion strike for an instant—might not the recipient momentarily succumb to the illusion of being the *monsieur* so abstractly adverted to: a gentleman, a member of the communal sphere, so to speak, carrying in his jacket the cambric handkerchief he had taught himself to use discreetly, with well-attuned calm and without exaggeration? Somebody sounding, whose approach and measured

entrance one looked forward to? A not insignificant center of this
or that grouping, and, to complete the picture, a social figure casually exuding the entire complex of modern civilization, a sediment
of the age and a reflex of its manifold phosphorescences? Like a
flatulence it hung over him, reddening the organs of his face and
neck, and he went on groping through this and that.

This is Rönne, a doctor, of medium height and healthy constitution, left eyelid drooping slightly, usually disgruntled, dyspepsia
in the brain, a tendency to gain weight and perspire. In his youth
he had gathered all sorts of impressions on his own, also combined
with revealing moods, elations, evanescences; now these had become rarer. What can impress, what is to be revealed, everything's
got worms inside—that was one of his sayings. Wherever you looked,
things were a public nuisance: Faust became So-what, Don Juan
manufactured pessaries, Ahasuerus learned to fly gliders, the myth
of Man was crying for execution.

Formerly, perhaps, one had at times been thinking, too, in a way,
but a certain something was always so quickly encountered. No
matter what the starting point: the Hegelian business manager of
cosmic reason or the manifestation of smallest changes in the ma-
turing social reconstruction, the synoptic or the causal-genetic method,
the individual or the catastrophic approach—even about these preliminary questions there was only indecisive gabble. As far as he
was concerned, Rönne would gladly forget it; he did not mind; he
was ready to grant everything—but what followed so closely after,
this obtrusive insistence on amalgamation, this propensity for results implying such a fatal urge for security, this was what he could
no longer share.

Rönne had spent the past year pretty much without impressions.
To be sure, after a spring that was no spring and a summer full of
excesses, he had sometimes felt somewhat dizzy late in the year,
even structurally unsteady. Then an autumn day would dawn over
Berlin, a consecration of blue, an illumination of things hidden; he
would soak up the light and feel in the back of his neck a kind of
minglement, a nearness from far away—and there were odors that
relaxed, too, and odors that weakened: southward, of fruit markets,
heavy and umbellar.

However, he had spent the past year not only without impressions
but completely withdrawn. He regarded public figures as vulgar,

ridiculous scum pursuing a fame they paid for and betting on the idiocy of their grandchildren. A tenor's trip to Riga seemed a far-reaching scandal to him. The newspaper jungle rustled, offices got up steam, photographers had a high time, residents of noble and distinctive bearing were involved in such utterly dubious matters as tone scales, creation, and the world once more—ah! The world once more that was the means whereby the naive and those who bore themselves well were to be brought to their knees. Creativeness: this lack of skepticism, this substitute for a resigned perception of death, this last great fetish in the talons of vultures, waved before cadaver-blue continents! He, Rönne, had a patient in the Latvian city, an engineer, probably employed in some enterprise, whom he had once treated and who had impressed him as a quiet middle-class gentleman. That was *his* relationship with Riga, and to his mind a far cheaper and less equivocal one than the fogginess of those lacquered buffo roaches.

Or a politician's tour of the villages—could there be as much shamelessness anywhere else under one skin? Those eternal "decisive moments" and "world-historic instants," before lunch already, and at the grand opening of a men's room—this communal divination, this latrine demonry—that one cranium could be designed to shield such quantities of cerebral garbage from the influence of the weather! it was a miracle of nature, a true miracle of nature, considering the usual cool reserve of inorganic matter toward the organic hoopla. Something in Rönne was crying for purification. Somewhat voluminously he made for the window: there was snow, the sweet sleep of colors, the deep uninseminability of whiteness—snow and stars, the emptiness of the universe.

Or, if life required conversation with an engineer, principally about progress in Diesel engines or something else with axle and torque—certainly plenty, granted, but what was so urgent about it, after all—improvement, the great motive for sleeping, or elaboration of culture, the great motive for sleeping with? But what was his concern, anyway; those were trains of thought, rather— and Rönne shivered and virtually felt himself shrink. No hallucinatory warmth, no hyperemia; dark was the room, cool the night round the house in the snow. Mutely into the distance he gave one of those unmoving glances, at the eye full of tears, at the dark, wounded countenance of life.

Had anything happened at all since the dawn of the world? He was in the mood to doubt it. Alexander's march, for instance, had that happened? A thousand missiles and the tragedy with the battering-rams—plenty, granted, but here he stood, a little man, middle-class background, not much family and slight effect: did any part of these connections exist for him, carry him, animate his planes, or even those of his patients, the customers of yesterday? What about it, where were they, were they rising anywhere—not a chance, empty, dropped off, literally wiped out—*how should there be an exchange?* Rönne, looking into the night and devoid of flushes, and those traceless nonentities, so-called personalities, spasms of nothingness, whooping-cough of the void—? Life was a matter of hours, full ones and empty ones, that was the whole of psychology. The institutionally construed, recollectively delivered, social personality, the empirical phenotype with the balanced blood pressure, was facing the other: the staccato type about to crack the sphygmometer with acute hyperemia, the expansive type with simultaneous vision, the shifty-eyed hallucinator. Cain and Abel, Klante and Zoroaster, laughable nuances of the same buffoonery—but some day it must be decided, Rönne cried; comprehensive ideas, perspectives of dimensions are coming over me—let's go and conquer the world, march with Alexander by means of flushes: there is Balerm the Saracen city, a flake on white rock, with arabesques senselessly pressing; there is the Barbary blood, the Gobi gull, plunging and numbed by a dream.

(1924)   *Translated by E. B. Ashton*

Primal Vision

A matchless clarity came over me as I saw I had passed the peak of life. I scanned the day, one of the unpeculiar days in the recurrence of time—early November, slightly chilly, in the street tokens of autumn haphazardly expended by the tepid earth.

I noticed a lightness that moved me. It probably was how things were, myself included, all of us transparent in the cadence of the world. A coming and going, an urging and denying, and, in between, untouchable, the way of existence. The source beyond comprehension, the end a myth, the here and now an evaporating puddle. Far and detached the years of youth, the stormy features, the malady of the great flight. Far and detached that brush and countryside— "we'll go to the woods no more, the laurels have been cut."

From the century when Antiquity was aging comes a strange report. It looked to people in the Roman Empire as if the rivers were becoming shallower and the mountains lower; on the sea one could not see Mount Etna as far away as before, and the same was told of Parnassus and Olympus. The universe as a whole, said the observers of nature, was on the decline. This downward trend in space was what I felt so strongly. Everywhere one saw daylight between the trees, and shouting and screaming were heard where once one had had to listen for any sound. My eyes ranged over the topography, and in curiously plastic fashion space covered me with a nearness from far away.

So it was in the country, when I went on Sunday excursions, and in the city, where my home soared above all else. Above the decade, today, after the war's end; above the forty years since Nietzsche, the starting point of instinctual psychology; above the hundred

years since the first gas lamp burned in the city, in the famous year
that gave Europe a continental railway net, transatlantic steamers,
the telegraph, photography, improved microscopes, and the means
of inducing artificial sleep.

Yes, this city—truly not made of dew and bird song, but rather
swarming with material bustle—how light and soundless it is in
my room! Outside, if anyone noticed, what life and strife, what
chaos, what *paradoxa:* Antiquity and experimentation, stages and
neuroses, atavisms and ambivalence! Epic bizarrerie of the moment:
collectivism, yet even fruit barges incorporate, and roadside stands
pay dividends; five proletarians sleep in one bed, but the brace of
griffons must resemble madame's face, perfumes come from truffles,
and dishes from palm marrow. In the Land of Singers and Sages
every fifth grade school pupil is too poor to breakfast before morning classes, but the Dahlem institutes spend millions on a board-
inghouse for visiting foreign scientists. The starry skies: moon rockets,
missile flights to the stars, and the last horse-drawn cab rolls from
Wannsee to Fontainebleau with the family following, bag and bag-
gage, in a dogcart; two waiters, in tails and white tie, walk from
Brandenburg to Geneva to lay a wreath before their union mem-
orial; three Hindus approach on a bicycle trip round the world—
all surely items worth mentioning, fraught with reality, but in my
rooms they become soundless and mute.

Three of these rooms faced the street, a fourth the backyard. A
night club opened on the yard; I often listened to its seductive
themes. Sometimes music rang out at night when I entered my
bedroom. I would open the window, turn off the light, and stand
breathing the sound. For long times I would stand gazing into the
night that held nothing for me any more, nothing but the dusk of
my heart, an aging heart: vague air, graying emotions, you give
yourself only to fall a prey—but giving and falling prey were very
remote.

Into the other rooms fell the red glow of the city. Not having
seen Niniveh on its jasper and ruby foundation, not having seen
Rome in the arms of the Antonines, I viewed this, the bearer of the
myth that began in Babylon. A mother city, a womb of distant ages,
a new thrill by tap dance and injection. What the monastic eras
poured into horal books and corollaries, the centuries of rationalism

into speculations and cosmogonies, was now throbbing in the movements of chorines: in the murmur of their knee joints they revealed the existential cast of whole series of nations. And the same unknown Something pulsed before me in the city's flesh and stone. It ripped foundlings from the fields and spewed forth community blocks from its bowels; it smeared forests with concrete for a mankind engaged in multiplication. A human mass that had more than doubled its live weight in the past century, was increasing further by twelve million individuals a year, and would put on another hundred per cent in less than a hundred years. Result: giant centers, overpopulation, bread dearer than children's flesh, melons into garbage, potatoes into the flower bed—this was what the world was coming to, far beyond me and my time, beyond my rooms and this hour of standing in the November night, in the silence facing the red glow.

After years of struggling for knowledge and ultimate things, I finally had come to realize that there may be no such ultimate things. In part, this discovery was due to my encounter with an elderly gentleman who had convivially accosted me one evening—a fellow townsman of mine, an ear specialist with his own hospital, and a medical colonel in the Bavarian army, as he pointed out in his first sentences. He talked about mutual acquaintances, some young men who had often been at his father's house—drones, good-for-nothings, penpushers, sots—all long since gone and forgotten. Years ago he had met one of them again and would, he said, have helped him to a newspaper job, if the fellow had kept the appointment instead of appearing at his home several days late, totally inebriated. The ear specialist "had him shown out," as he put it, and after a few more weeks the man had succumbed in delirium.

Thus the medical colonel awakened the past and was, indeed, the dead man's superior in living standards, attire, scope of activities; he surpassed him considerably in resonance, hospital ownership, and military rank; in fact, he eclipsed everything about him—but did this mean that the friend of his youth had died wholly unfinished, useless, without a symbol? Did the course of his life not even suggest the enormity of life, its immense urges and intoxications, its indifference to individualities, its carnal disintegration? He, too, after initial years of surely angelic purity, had gone down in this rhythm; did the one before me cut a wider swath, did the ear clinic serve him as a vehicle of more mysterious experience? I wavered, could not bring myself to say yes. Life, having been fully operative on the deceased, must have marked even this human form, however far beneath the medical colonel. At the moment, to be sure, I could not tell the mark.

An idea took shape in me: it was the unity of life that I saw here, to be defended from attack. Life seeks to preserve itself, but life seeks also to perish—more and more clearly I perceived this chthonic force. When I thought of the animal kingdom, of the genus, of the origin and death of species, it was true that inundating oceans had carried off whole racial segments in short order, geologically speak-ing, and that volcanic eruptions had smothered great animal com-munities under a downpour of ashes; but the actual extinction of species, the passing of biological forms, had never been caused by these geological incidents. The extinction of species, as well as the spontaneous emergence of new ones at the same time, impressed me more and more as a paleontological fact due to a single under-lying cause. Thus butterflies and other honey-sucking types ap-peared at the same time in the Earth's history as flowering plants, certain sea urchins and crustaceans appeared along with the reef-building corals they would live in symbiosis with—and their even-tual simultaneous disappearance was unrelated to elemental events, not visibly connected with environmental changes, baffling expla-nation, to be interpreted only as a phenomenon from within. It seemed to express a fading formal tension, an aging, a decrease in numbers and living space on the one side, and an unfolding presence on the other; there seemed to be a polarity of the formative drive, an inner tension between formal features. In scales, balanced by gods, existence seemed to rest: now there was more water around, now more land, here a coral, there a bivalve in repose at the base, rising and falling about the figure of man who exuded animals and split off plants—he, inescapably subject to forces of further crea-tion, of the scalebearers, and of their distance. To these, then, the late inebriate would also have succumbed, and in great associations his series of forms sank into a premature grave.

A trivial occasion, a purely personally motivated line of thought—yet the experience induced me to take a closer look at my com-panion, this gentleman at the peak of his era, the leader of broad strata, the carrier of the positive idea, the causal-genetic thinker. I saw him before me with his instruments, his otoscope, his pincers, germ-free and nickel-plated—way behind him lay the Moorish epoch, the age of the herniotomists and lithotomists, the Galenic darkness, the mysticism of the mandrake. I envisioned his hospital, spick and span, a very different thing from the herb gardens and distilleries of the medieval urine watchers. Tangibly his sonorous and voluminous voice enveloped me in its suggestive and hypnotic charm, completely dislodging the memory of those spells and incantations of the Cimbrian priestesses I had been reading about, who practiced their so-called healing art in white linen garments girt with a bronze belt. Only when I reflected how long mankind had survived just the same, although till recently obstetrics had been carried on underneath the clothes, in secretive obscurity—when I considered how long it had survived despite all plagues and leprosies, despite epidemics, worms, and the bacteria which our representative had only for a relatively short time risen to combat effectively—then my thoughts might veer in the direction of that striking hypothesis advanced by the latest American race researchers, to the effect that for a majority of men the time of death must be regarded as hereditarily determined. They have calculated, in fact, that disease has no decisive influence on the life span of some eighty per cent of mankind; it is heredity, they hold, that contains the factor for this part of individual fate as well. And when I found additional support for this hypothesis in some statistical oddities: that in England, for example, which I had studied, the ideal life span calculated by modern science (equal to the mortality norm, that standard figure checked every five years over a century, in 276 districts) had been established early in the nineteenth century—i.e., long before the so-called victorious advance of modern biology—then it could happen, in considering the ear specialist and his pincers and, more generally, the relationship between disease and man, that I was unable to keep the druids' rune-covered staffs and the sacrifices offered in our forefathers' holy places from intruding upon my reflections.

In any event, here he was standing before me, the biologist, the germ-layer Marxist, the aniline exporter, the man of interest-bearing science, who rose as a lamb and spoke as a dragon. The age of Bacon, the mankind of thought, the cast-iron century, no longer carving gods but smelting devils: four hundred million individuals jampacked on a tiny continent, twenty-five nationalities, thirty languages, seventy-five dialects, international and intranational tensions of extirpative vehemence. Here, a fight to boost wages half a cent an hour; there, the Carlton Club golf tournament in flower-bedecked Cannes, princes in the gutter, tramps as dictators, orgies of vertical trusts, fever of profits: to exploit the continent's limited resources economically, i.e. at a premium.

Dissolution of the classic systems from the Urals to Gibraltar. Ultracapitalism: earthquake in Southern Europe means a high time for builders and interior decorators; iron and steel salesmen are blessed from Mount Athos before go-getting in the Maritza valley. On the front page we weep for the victims, and in back come the black-bordered profit statements. For editorials we have human frailty, and for the business section, geological thrust folds and the economically sound motion of the Earth. And socialism: well-regulated food supply, immortality of the body, salubrious survival—the Hesperidian dream of trade union health insurance.

And on the other side stood the great country with the legend from Philadelphia, the man whose skull was bashed in with a piece of lead pipe because he wore a straw hat on May 14. St. Aloysius of the Delaware, the virginal martyr who would wear a straw hat out of season.—Who had more money in the bank at thirty: Dempsey or Hölderlin?—"Where are the prominent citizens of New Salem?" Lincoln asked when he came to the town. Answer: "New Salem has no prominent citizens; everyone here is a prominent citizen." And there they stood, honest confessors of democratic equality from ice cream to the cut of their pants.

Standard idols, dance-drilled wraiths, staple products. Rites under klieg-lights, Communion with jazz, Gethsemane: the record in ecstasy. Christ—the successful entrepreneur, social lion, advertising genius, and founder of modern business life, who knew how to save the situation at the marriage in Cana with cheap Jordanian rotgut; the born manager, who could invite the rich Nicodemus to dinner even at a time when New Religion was not in demand. For the dollar was agreeable to God, and land-holding as such a moral asset; therefore, Bible lessons to keep the boom going, and the Pentateuch against the soil fixers. The keep-smiling prophet of the New World shaking hands across the Atlantic with the aniline metaphysician of the Old, like code cables concerning oil shares and gasoline exegesis. Knock-out Pullman—the new type whose birthmarks dot the globe: the new suspension bridge from Manhattan to Fort Lee, to be completed in 1932, 3,500 feet long, held up by four cables, each three feet in diameter, a thickness never achieved before; on the Brooklyn Bridge, built 1888 (sic!), the cables are only sixteen inches thick—a difference of twenty! By flight and fire the new type compresses the zeniths; he surmounts time and space—a strange time, a strange space—with conveyor-belt categories and piece-work concepts; he *improves* time and space; the primal visions.

This, my century! Were it my century—ah, it was the eon; it was history, the tribe, Aurignac, the growth in darkness, the unbridled license of the night of creation. Once it was the green luxuriance of the anthracite forest, once the vertebrates' conquering drive into prehistoric seas, once this race, come from the glacier rims of Asia, with shrouded memory, restless, shortening the very periods of the Earth.

Some mass lay in concealment, and something made it realize a compulsion. Age-old urges! The strongholds of diluvial industry in France and Austria, right next to the modern ones at Creusot and the Skoda Works—exquisite skill! The laurel leaf tips of Solutrian culture—the acme of stone work technology! In the warm mid-interglacial period the beauty of Willendorf—primary style impulse, indigenous constructivism. Excavations in the loess of Central Europe have yielded twenty-five thousand artifacts, beside the remains of nine hundred mammoths. The passage of Magdalenian man from stone-hewing to bone work marked the dawn of a new era; the silver lining was the Quarternary hunter with the horn harpoon.

Stimulus and repression. Today's technology, yesterday's mechanics. The first pirogue had greater sociological consequences than the submarine and the airplane; the first arrow was deadlier than poison gas. The people of Antiquity knew W.C.'s as well as elevators, pulleys, clocks, flying machines, automatons; they had a monomania about tunnels, passages, conduits, aqueducts—termites subject to space neuroses, grip compulsions.

Mass in instincts. Brain bubbles into the sink, germ layers into the flower bed, yolk sacs in the thrust of distance. Heritage of exaltation and intoxications, astral conflagration, transoceanic decay.

Crises, mixtures, third century: Baal with the lightning and scourge of the Roman god, Phrygian hoods along the Tiber, Aphrodite on Mount Lebanon—realities in balance, tides in transformation.

Age-old drives of ageless masses in the sound of oceans and in the plunge of light. Life seeks to preserve itself, but life seeks also to perish; urge and denial—games of night. Lost is the individual; down with the ego. Through an indifference of high degree, through a fatigue born of character, a somnolence born of conviction—ah, work: a phantom for the shrunken; greatness: a spectacle for oglers, râles for gold dentures—via science, the commonplace method of veiling facts, and religion, the invective one—dithyrambics of youth, down, down!

I saw the ego, the look in its eyes. I dilated its pupil, looked far into it, looked far out of it; the gaze from such eyes is almost expressionless, more like scenting, scenting danger, an age-old danger. From disasters that were latent, disasters that antedated the word, come dreadful memories of the race, hybrid, beast-shaped, sphinx-pouched features of the primal face. I recalled the dicta of certain profoundly experienced men, that evil would come of their telling all they knew. I thought of the strange adages, that one should give up searching for the ultimate words that need only be spoken to unhinge heaven and earth. I sniffed in masks, I rattled in runes, I dove into demons with sleep-craving brutality, with mythical instincts, in the anteverbal, instinctual threat of prehistoric neura; I began to grasp, I saw the vision: monism in rhythms, mass in intoxications, compulsion and repression, Ananke of the I.

A matchless clarity came over me as, in a way, I saw life conquered. "For this the fleet of a thousand ships?" I asked, like the dialogues of the dead in the late Roman era. In the nether-world, bleaching before the observer, lay the bones of celebrated shades, the jaw of Narcissus and the pelvis of Helen—for this the fleet of a thousand ships, the untold deaths, the ruined cities? For this the heroes, the founders, the sons of gods, Tuisko and Mannus, and the songs men sang to them? None had left more than an outline and a breath. Life was a deadly and unknown law; today as ever, man could do no more than accept his own without tears. Once it was the green luxuriance of the anthracite forest, once the vertebrates' conquering drive into prehistoric seas—recurrence was all.

Recurrence, and this hour of the night. I stood and listened. For a long time I stood breathing the sound. Life sought to preserve itself, but life sought also to perish—long rhythms, long sound. Long was the breath of the night; in play it could gather and scatter. It gave, it streamed, hesitated, drew back. The gods were merely silent. Daphne quivered in the laurel, and by the sea of Amphitrite the hermes slumbered.

And above all: languor and dream. Something, we knew not what, stirred the logs: home fire, early coffins, chairs of old men to and fro. Age-old change, dusk and poppy, to the stairs, downward the purl of remote waters.

(1929)   *Translated by E. B. Ashton*

From The Way of
an Intellectualist

Rönne

In war and peace, at the front and behind it, as an officer and as a doctor, among generals and profiteers, before rubber and jail cells, over beds and coffins, in triumph and decay, I never lost the trance-like feeling that this reality did not exist. A kind of inner concentration began, a stirring of secret spheres; and individuality faded, and a primal stratum emerged, intoxicated, image-laden, Panic. The times reinforced it: the year 1915–16 in Brussels was enormity. There *Rönne* was born, the physician, the flagellant of individual phenomena, the naked vacuum of facts—the man who could bear no reality, nor grasp any; who knew only the rhythmic opening and closing of the ego and the personality, the continual disruption of inner existence; and who, confronted with the experience of the deep, unbounded, mythically ancient strangeness

Benn published *The Way of an Intellectualist* in the spring of 1934, one year after Hitler came to power. The first chapter traced his family tree, to defend his "Aryanism" against suspicions of "racial impurity." The second attempted an explanation and ideological vindication of his previous writings, the poems of two decades and the two main characters of his prose: Rönne, the self-portrait, and Pameelen, the "measurement conductor" whose brain reflects "disintegration of the epoch . . . cortical wilting of worlds, the bourgeois, capitalistic, opportunistic, prophylactic, antiseptic worlds knocked out by the cloudbursts of politics"—yet whose "basic feeling for anthropological redemption by form" inaugurates "the new epoch, the new necessity . . . the world of expression." The third chapter dealt with the concepts of "art" and "intellectualism"; in the fourth Benn addressed "the new youth that has lined up under Hitler's star"; and the fifth ("The Doctrine"; see p. 32 below) summed up his personal creed. The 1934 volume was soon out of print, and in 1950 Benn republished *The Way of an Intellectualist* as Part One of *Double Life*—thus in effect combining his pro-Nazi and anti-Nazi apologias. (E.B.A.)

between man and the world, believed completely in the myth and its images.

"I meant to conquer the city, now a palm leaf caresses me"—thus Rönne sums up his experiences. He could not conquer the city; his situation forbade it. Instead, "he burrowed into moss: at the stem, water-fed, my brow—a hand's breadth, and then it starts. Soon after, a bell rang. The gardeners went to work: then he, too, strode to a can and poured water over the ferns which came out of a sun where much evaporated." In other words, vegetabilia after central destruction.

"Rönne wanted to go to Antwerp, but how, without corrosion? He could not come to lunch. He had to say he could not come to lunch today; he was going to Antwerp. To Antwerp, the listener would be wondering? Contemplation? Reception? Perambulation? That seemed unthinkable to him. It purported enrichment and construction of the soul."

Enrichment and construction of the soul—that was what the old world was doing roundabout, unmoved by the far-reaching collapse of the times that enfeebled Rönne. The old world was still sitting in the officers' mess, eating—as we shall soon see—of a tropical fruit, and waging wars, but he could no longer take part in it. In an age of rockets casually refueling on stars, of Cook's paving the jungle for guided tours, of polar distance shrinking to short-haul rates and dowagers competing in Himalayan excursions, Rönne's travel urge met with an inner resistance.

In the following I have to quote a longer passage from the Rönne stories, though at this moment their implications are somewhat disreputable and bizarre. I must do it to be truthful, and to proceed from Rönne's type to certain historical and epistemological conclusions.

So Rönne wants to go to Antwerp, and "now he saw himself sitting in the train and suddenly recalling how his absence would presently be discussed at the luncheon table—off-hand only, in reply to an incidental question, but still to the effect that he, on his part, was seeking relations with the city, with the Middle Ages and the quays of the Scheldt.

"He felt stunned, breaking out in a sweat. A curvature befell him as he perceived his indefinite, still incalculable, in any case so trivial and meager actions comprehended in the terms of a gentleman's life.

"A rainstorm of inhibitions and weakness burst upon him. For where he was assurance that he would be able to tell, bring back, enliven anything about the trip at all, that he would receive anything in the sense of experience?

"Great asperities—like the railroad, being seated opposite some gentleman, stepping from the station on arrival, purposefully headed for the place of business—all these things could happen in secret only, could only be suffered, deeply and disconsolately, in oneself.

"How had it occurred to him, anyway, to leave in order to fulfill his day? Was he foolhardy, to step out of the form that carried him? Did he defy the collapse and believe in amplification?

"No, he told himself, no. I can swear to it: no. Only in walking out of the shop just now—there was scent of violets again, and talc powder, too—a girl approached with white breasts. Aperture seemed not unthinkable. Flaunting and flowing seemed not unthinkable. A beach moved into the realm of possibilities, washed by the blue breast of the sea. But now, to make my peace, I will go to lunch."

The problem, therefore, which puts Rönne through these agonies is this: what is the origin, the real meaning of the ego? Does it take a trip to Antwerp, medieval studies, a view of the quays of the Scheldt? Does it depend on such impressions, are the potential impressions of the Matsys Fountain and the Plantin Moretus house its necessary components, are there inner, constitutive grounds for such trips—or yet a third motive, perhaps: hybris, intemperance, exaltation? If the go is predestined, it must never leave its form, never transcend its circle of duties, never jeopardize its cast, nor reveal its features; then a trip is dissolution, peril, unbelief within the rigid query after freedom and necessity, and can lead nowhere but to proof of the deepest corrosion. *Is the individual case needed?* These period pieces can have no primary derivation, anyway, and on the other hand, Rönne's experience and disposition did not fit him for the historic approach. All of it swam past each other, merely tiring him with its forces. Something else had to happen, a minglement, and it was this he incessantly strove for—something that was annulment and amalgamation at the same time; but that existed only for moments, in critical plunges, in breakthroughs, and it was always near annihilation. But one was not always capable of it, and so, after this groping thrust into vagueness at an inauspicious hour of the forenoon, we see Rönne recoil, flee from himself, and make sure of normalcy once again. He goes to lunch at the officers' mess:

"His bow in the door acknowledged the individualities. Who was he? Quietly he took a seat. The gentlemen loomed large.

"Herr Friedhoff was telling of the peculiarities of a tropical fruit containing an egg-sized kernel. You ate the flesh with a spoon; it had the consistency of jelly. Some thought its taste was nutty. As for him, he had always found it tasted like eggs. You ate it with pepper and salt. It was a tasty fruit. He had eaten three or four a day and never noticed injurious effects.

"Here Herr Körner found himself faced with the extraordinary. A fruit, with pepper and salt? It struck him as unusual, and he made a point of it.

" 'But if it tastes like egg to him,' countered Herr Mau, stressing the subjective judgment somewhat slightingly, as if he himself could see nothing unbridgeable. Besides, it really wasn't so odd, Herr Offenberg led back to normalcy—how about tomatoes, for instance? And finally, what of Herr Kritzler's uncle, who had eaten melons with mustard at seventy years of age, and that at night, when such things are known to be least digestible?

"All in all: was it in fact an oddity? Was it, so to speak, an occurrence apt to attract widespread attention—whether because its generalizations might have caused alarming consequences, or because as an experience from the special atmosphere of the tropics it was liable to make one think?

"It was at this point that Rönne trembled, found suffocation on his plate, and had trouble eating the meat. But, insisted Herr Körner, had not Herr Friedhoff meant a banana, rather—that soft, mellowish, and elongated fruit?

"A banana, bristled Herr Friedhoff? He, the Congo expert? The Moabangi navigator of long standing? The suggestion virtually made him smile. He soared far above the group. What were their means of comparison? A strawberry or nut, perhaps a chestnut here and there, somewhat more southerly. And he, the official representative in Hulemakong, who came from the Jambo jungles?

"Now or never, ascent or destruction, felt Rönne—and: 'Really never noticed injurious effects?' he groped his way into the whirl, his voice controlled, depicting astonishment and the doubt of the expert. Facing him was the void. Would there be an answer?

"Yet was it not he, after all, who sat on the wooden chair in a chaste aura of knowing about the perils of the tropical fruit—who sat as if pondering and comparing statements and reports of similar experiences, a reticent researcher, a physician of professional and temperamental taciturnity? Thinly, through his eyelids, he looked up from the meat, down the line, slowly aglow. It was not hope yet, only a breathing without distress. And now an affirmation: several gentlemen seemed, indeed, to set store by a reavowal of the fact, to settle doubts that might possibly have arisen. And now it was evident: some of them nodded, chewing.

"Jubilation in him, chants of triumph. An answer rang out, maintaining the claim against doubters, and it was addressed to him. Acceptance followed, evaluation took place; he was eating meat, a well-known dish; remarks were linked to him and he joined gatherings, under a vault of great happiness. For an instant even the thought of arranging to meet in the afternoon flashed through his heart, without tremors.

"Rocklike the men sat. Rönne savored the fullness of triumph. Deeply he felt how each of his table companions granted him the title of a gentleman, one who did not spurn a quick one after the meal and drank it with a light joke that was cheering to the rest, yet firmly refusing all alcoholic excesses, spreading a certain atmosphere of coziness. He was the impression of probity, of artlessly speaking his mind, though always glad to concede a measure of truth to different views as well. He felt his features in order; cool equanimity, if not imperturbability, had triumphed in his face. And that he carried as far as the door he shut behind him."

Here, then, we see a man no longer endowed with a continuous psychology. His existence, in the officers' mess and outside, is indeed one single burning desire for this continuous psychology—the psychology of the "gentleman," who "did not spurn a quick one after the meal and drank it with a light joke"—but for constitutional reasons he cannot find the way back. Or fitfully, at most, conjured out of abysses, in battles of annihilation. The naive vitality which enclosed and carried and pulsed as lifeblood in the psychological process also—in our century until a rather closely determinable time, and thematically to a rather precisely definable extent—will no longer suffice for the further degrees of psychological sublimation in Europe. In Rönne, the dissolution of this natural vitality has assumed forms that look like decay. But is it really decay? What is decaying? Might it not be only a historic overlay, an upper stratum uncritically accepted for centuries, with the other side of the coin the primary one? Intoxication, languor, unwieldiness—might not this be reality? Where does the impression end and the unknowable being begin? Here, we see, we are face to face with the question of anthropological substance, and this is identical with the question of reality. The immense problem of reality and its criteria opens before us. "Sometimes, for an hour, you are; the rest is what happens. Sometimes the two worlds surge[1] into a dream." Which two worlds? The ego and nature. What is the result? At most, a dream. Of course, this principle of Rönne's is a principle of irreality—and when is it operative, when is it "rustling"? "When you are broken." At another time he perceives: "What had been mankind's way thus far? An effort to bring order into something that should have remained play. But after all, it had remained play in the end, for nothing had reality. Did he have reality? No; all he had was every possibility."

Perception is a fine way to perish, and, indeed, from here it goes on to minglement again: "He bedded his neck deeper into the mayweed that smelled of thyrse and Walpurgis. Melting through the noonday, his head pebbled, brooklike. He offered it to the light: irresistibly the strong sun trickled into the brain. There it lay: scarcely a molehill, brittle, the animal scratching inside."

The animal, and the more and more nakedly sublimated thought: is there still a principle common to both? Does the Western world still have such a monistic principle for life and cognition, for history and thought? For movement and the spirit, for stimulation and depth—is there still a union, a contact, a happiness? Yes, answers Rönne, but from far away; there is nothing general; there are strange, all but unbearable regions to be experienced in loneliness: "In itself rumbled a river or, if it was no river, a cast of forms, a game in fevers, pointless, ending around every rim—": he beholds art.

1. Benn misquotes himself. The original sentence in *The Birthday* reads: *"Manchmal die beiden Fluten"*—not *"die beiden Welten,"* as here—*"schlagen hoch zu einem Traum."*

The Doctrine

If all that my generation—and I, as part of it—experienced, all that it expressed in its work and raised to a thesis, is henceforth to be called "formalism," so be it. Again and again I have shown the central significance of the problem of form to Europe, and especially to Germany. But it can also be defined as the very opposite: a hard-earned knowledge of a possible new ritualism. It is an all but religious attempt to shift art from estheticism to anthropology, to proclaim it as an anthropological principle. In terms of sociology, this would mean moving the anthropological principle of form—pure form, formal compulsion—into the center of cults and rites. One might even call it the immaterialization of matter, the obliteration of the object: appearances mean nothing, individual cases mean nothing, sensible objects mean nothing, but expression, the legislative transformation into style, means everything. "But if we were to teach seeing the cycle, and creative mastery of life, would not death be the blue shadow in which felicities stand?" This early doctrine of Rönne's would be the rule that never leaves the substance—be it stone, clay, or words—and yet heeds only creation and its transcendent call. It would be a principle canonizing a power that is inborn only to the loftiest nations of the human species; the power to detach themselves from their contrived and formally wrought product—to dissolve in it, resolve their agonies and urges in it, and then to take their departure, to leave it to itself but so charged with the tension of their kind and so far-reaching, indestructible a meaning that after thousands of years other generations of this kind will still use this product to measure the epochs, will still recognize themselves in it, their mysteries, their eternally veiled nature, and their whole disaster-based existence. Here is shudder and secret once more, before the final decay!

For it is not till today, in my opinion, that the history of man, his jeopardy, his tragedy, begins. Heretofore, the altars of the saints and the wings of the archangels have stood behind him, and his wounds and frailties were laved from chalices and baptismal fonts. Now comes the series of his own great, insoluble dooms. Nietzsche will have been a prelude only, the prelude of the new symbols, the new empires—"white earth from Thule to Avalon"—but also the prelude of the last nihilistic destructions.

Upward, downward, on and on, but where? *Amor fati*—but from which substratum of existence springs this last call? Where does it point, to which oblivion? "Life is a deadly and unknown law; today as ever, man can do no more than accept his own without tears"— a word from *Primal Vision*—but how long will he bear it without tears? On and on, but where? Man's rearward view is dimmed, his forward view non-existent. As a creature he is but half successful, a sketch, a shot at an eagle: the wings, the feathers are already brought down, but the entire figure has not yet fallen—will it ever fall entirely, resting its heart right on the heart of things? So, on and on—nations, races, geological ages—smell of stone and fern and beast: rising from dusk, firm in its kind, and yet in an inconceivable transformation in which this human Quaternary type will also pass away. But while it is here it is marked, strongly marked, imperialistically strongly marked—what is the sign? It is the unreal sign of Rönne, the constructive sign of Pameelen. It teaches: there is no reality; there is the human consciousness ceaselessly forming, reforming, earning, suffering, spiritually stamping worlds from its creative property. In this capacity there are degrees and steps, chiefly preliminary steps. But the uppermost says: there is only the idea, the great, objective idea. It is eternity; it is the world order; it lives by abstraction; it is the formula of art. Through it runs the chain of races and nations; it is the chain. It directs the course—and it will block it, too, before the abyss, over the abyss. If this is intellectualism I will serve it as a trial and a challenge, but its perfection alone lends greatness to the human race. All the corrosion it brings to the individual, all the sacrifices it demands, all the life it takes shall be offered in this time-bound clarity—blindly, that is—for where else should we offer them? There, with the anguish of the Hyperborean: "Dream is the world, and smoke in the eyes of one eternally dissatisfied"—there, in the silence of Tao that cultivates waiting and letting existence work—there, the utmost Oriental and Occidental depth of the great nations: yield thyself.

(1934)   *Translated by E. B. Ashton*

Wolf's Tavern

A certain period of my life was spent in a middling-sized town, almost a city. Bad climate, boring surroundings, all flat, immensely dreary. My profession had never really meant anything to me, here least of all. Just at the point where the cultured, eminent sort of men were feeling the social implications of their profession, whether politically or in the sphere of *Weltanschauung,* and seeing themselves and their work becoming incorporated into a pattern of widely accepted general ideas, my interest in my profession snapped right off. Counting in years, the larger part of my life was over, and it was perfectly clear to me that only considerable charity could call it fruitful. The lapsing of most lives caused no hitch, and neither would mine—at most an incidental, or rather accidental, traffic jam; but all the forces of law and order were ready to forestall that. All crossing of the one-way streets in both directions, the oncoming and the vanishing stream, went on without a hitch.

I had taken an apartment at the back of a house, all the windows overlooking the court. On purpose! For one thing, I can't stand light, can't stand being drenched in strong natural rays; but then, too, in order to hide from both men and women. "Always polite" was my slogan, "but few appearances and never without preparation." I had no telephone either, to make appointments impossible. I went to the usual parties, clinked glasses with the men, ran through the standard gossip with the ladies, and never let the flower girl pass without buying the bunch in season for the lady on my right. I don't think anyone thought of considering me improper.

Of course, there was a lot of calculation and superstructure in all this, yet that was my own business.

I started out in colonial and consular circles. I had spent the main part of my life in the great cities of the world, and a place like this now, with its hundred thousand inhabitants, its three main streets where everyone met, its half-dozen restaurants where everyone met again, its few grass-plots buoyed up with crocuses in spring, geraniums in the fall, struck me as particularly remarkable. My life had never brought me so close to the bourgeois and human core of a community, so close to the historical core—to introduce this expression—to which I then attached particular importance. And so I let all these impressions work on me thoroughly, ready to open my frontiers, to become a new man, to re-examine the fundamental problem of human existence, which—in view of the spiritual situation of the white peoples I had so regularly encountered during my years of travel—had, I must admit, prepared a quite definite answer in my mind.

What gave these peoples the right to lead all others? This was what I wondered. What had they to show in that respect? What spiritual image of man had they evolved, to what depths of being and to what external outlines had they worked out the human idea? Where did their most unearthly, their purest, minds stand? To what coldness of judgment, to what severity of moral decision had their masses attained under their imperial leaders? Recently they talked much of their history. But there was greatness that had no history. Asia had no history. The decline of the Greeks began in the century when Herodotus appeared. They also pointed to their masterhood—master race—all right then, who were these masters?

I never tired of observing things from this point of view. Perhaps I may be more explicit, going off into detail. My evening walk often led me to a little tavern, a place for habitués—the proprietress knowing her customers, chatting with them occasionally—a pleasant woman. There I often sat, behind the mask of my face images and memories, memories of past years, memories of Tahiti's narrow beach, the cabins among the breadfruit trees, the kernels of the nuts so sweet and cool, and the never silent breakers on the reefs; pictures of Broadway, still lit by prairie fires, smouldering sunsets at the end of narrow streets; memories and pictures of worlds old and new, redskins, brown pearl-divers, yellow shadows.

It was far from being romanticism, a hangover from Rousseau, an esthetic lamento, that lay behind these pictures. No, on the contrary, it was the vision of the light-skinned race whose tragedy I bore within myself, whose abysses I had sensed, when I had represented it in all those places. Now my return to it, and to the concept of history it had come to stress so much, had made me consider it in evolutionary terms, codify its course, feel out its past; and many an evening a sort of revue rose into existence about me, a cultural revue of tolerable duration, the first act carrying the falcon on the gauntlet and the last, bird in hand, singing its praises to those in the bush.

A company of white men, historically post-Antiquity, bearing the cerebral imprint of Graeco-Latin humanism, mongrels sprung from the shattered Roman Empire, run-to-seed Merovingians, unleashed Christians, sensual Popes, lust-ridden monks, flaring Moors, attar-of-roses-importing, heron-hunting, luxury-oozing Persians— that's what paces down the untrodden path.

To admit no conviction unless justified by thought—thus the race later described it. No conviction, no art, no religion, no science. Everything must conform to the yardsticks of clear logic: premise, assertion, proof; everything is tested for its emotional content by the logical proposition of contradiction, passed as valid only if the concord between the whole and the parts is seen to be indisputable. The transcendence of an ascetic, self-purifying, eremitical harmony that has left detail behind and stripped itself of confusion and profusion. But also a transcendence by the aid of restrictive hauteur, progressive aridity, self-corseted humanity—and yet transcendent even where this mode of life has not reached its ultimate peak, even in its rudimentary stages and off-shoots. Everywhere patches of élan, self-stimulation, disembodiment: transcendence, extra-transcendence, sectors of upsurge:—sectors of the wheel of Sansara in whirl of infinite possibilities, with interpretations in all the directions of everlastingly inscrutable creation and of dreams. Advance of Occidental sectors, of special combinations, West-Nordic; over against the gentle beach life of the South Seas, it is complicated and conceptually over-ramified; over against the agelessness, the deep-sea swell of China, it is unaristocratic and restless. This was it: this white race with its compulsive pursuit of a downward path of no return, a lost, icy, heat-baked, weather-ravaged *anabasis*[1] not held in the embrace of any *thalassa*.[2]

I was increasingly drawn to these things, to their atmosphere, their roots, their causality, their being. Many an evening I sat there gazing around: it was the same old tavern, yet it seemed to me the room had a heavy list, a suggestion of sinking; its shape and paneling were like the interior of a ship. A torpedo speeding into the depths— yes, that was the impression that thrust itself on me, something gliding away down, a community drowning, its pictures like oil slicks on the surface, stragglers above the chasm. Just as simple as that.

At a neighboring table sat three gentlemen eating mussel ragout, telling stories, exchanging banter with the hostess, a gay party. "I don't mind another year of it so long as it's good," they said, keeping their eating utensils on the move, forkfuls between biting into their rolls, raising their glasses, now and then bending their legs and kicking out. Their arms hung loose in the shoulder-joints; they wore spats. A dog called Krause, due for a bath, an operation indicated in view of the approaching festive season, kept turning up in their talk. Ash lengthened on cigars sucked between remarks passed back and forth—this was how their evening was spent, how uncertainty was distributed, how time took shape.

So these were three of the present-day elect, comrades, bearers of a historic mission, beacon-fires of passion, their faces endowed to express anything that life might throw in their way: relish, hilarious laughter, the finishing-off of competitors, commercial triumphs, and condolences to the widows of business friends.

Personalities! Orgasm at its appointed hour, subsequently incense, also participation in ceremonies and celebrations. Occupational categories! Taking an afternoon train, business trip, taste of stale smoke in the mouth, compartment a bit drafty, scenery flying past, dusk falling—days and lives! Parallel: blonde divorcée (innocent party), husband company director, earning her own keep now, a wife sucked dry.

Specters! Void! Unarticulated billowing! Caesar-like as to the tie;

1. Greek; here: long, strenuous march.
2. *Thalassa*: sea.

red checks, not dots. Own vintage in the rummer: fruit juice, not malt brew. Stimuli, habits, ill-humor—the ace of particularity! Fruitful, inwardly determined impetus—never.

A people's or a race's degeneration always seemed to me to imply a decline in the number of men born with the potentialities and the secure source of inner values that enable them to give legitimate expression to the essential nature of that last, late phase of their own civilization and to carry on, in spite of all obstacles, toward an undefined goal. There was no reasonable doubt as to what that essential nature really was; still, I'll put it here once again in the terms I used then. The essential nature of man lies in the sphere of formal creativeness. Only in that sphere does man become recognizable; only in that sphere do the grounds and backgrounds of his own creation become clear and with them his rank in the hierarchy of animal life. Transforming the plane into depth, organizing and correlating words so as to open up a spiritual world, linking sounds so that they last and sing of the indestructible—*this* is what that sphere does. Peoples whose spiritual message is the housewifely idea of a centrally supplied home-and-town-life are degenerate. Peoples who stand up to the spirit as an autonomous force that attacks, cleaves, decomposes life are racially on a high level. Peoples who see the spirit only in historic victories and successful frontier-crossings are of low race. Peoples who allow the spirit in all its manifestations to rise to the sphere of creativeness are high-bred. So what counts is the sphere of the creative! Of its temporal manifestations we had: individualism, intoxication with forms, tempests of differentiation. On all levels of civilization this has so far appeared only in hints, sporadically, in the great individuals, so it is still a force entirely and deeply veiled. Appearing late, in man only, its concentration for the re-creation of the world was scarcely at its rudimentary stage. On the one hand, life with all its manipulations, the so-called actions, and, on the other, the principle of the new reality. The latter was served by the integer of the great, often physically weak race that lies outside all epochs and all nations. Whenever that race died out in one nation, the torpedo plunged into the depths. Before the impact, however, there came, with oratory, the epoch of the urge towards totality, of parades and collective cults, the epoch of revivals, of turns to the past, the epoch of history. This was how Rohde,[3] in the final pages of his *Psyche,* had described the decline of the Greeks. To me the white nations seemed again in the midst of such an epoch. They had all shunned the decision to adopt a new form of existence, i.e., this attitude to the spirit. For them spirit served life, and they wrote tragedies about the fact that here and there it did not seem to do so. In fact, the spirit was a sort of spoiled reality. Therefore, down with it—and before history, that is, in the next war, they would be victorious all right.

The proprietress got up from the business gents' table and came over to me. "Like something to read?" "No thanks, I don't feel like reading." I was lounging as usual with one arm stretched out along the back of the seat. "Don't talk much, do you?" "Habit!" I relaxed a group of muscles in the shoulder region. "Don't you ever do anything?" I did my job during the day; was I supposed to do some special work on behalf of the universe after hours? "The gentlemen over there meant it in a quite particular sense." I held my own in the world I lived in, so what business was it of theirs? I must say, it was a bit thick. If those gentlemen's views tended toward the universal when they left home—all right, but without me, please. Frankly, I was amazed. The fact was I didn't like walking and I always tried to rest my arm on something. I often refrained from a purchase because at that moment my own shape under my hat-brim struck me as too weird. So perhaps I really did have a morbid streak. Originally I had meant to be a writer, too, but to become a writer you have to be able to read your own handwriting, and that was something I'd never been able to accomplish. For a novel, besides, you must acknowledge the idea of time; but the word was timeless, and I liked putting things into words. So I became a consular official, took jobs abroad, and Tahiti and the Azores slid behind me. Could they read that, by any chance, in my face?

It gave me a start. Supposing they could see deeper? Doing nothing, under favorable meaterial living conditions, was, if I may put it so, in fact my ideal. Doing nothing in a general sense: no office, no definite working hours, no references top-left in the files. No

3. Erwin Rohde (1845–1898), classical philologist, friend of Nietzsche.

roaming about the countryside—I was no dowser or wolf of the steppes, rather one for a quiet hour with worm and rod, waiting for a bite, impressions, dreams—a vast squandering of hours. Goethe's and Hamsun's praise of manual labor on the soil as the ultimate wisdom did not seem especially compelling, since they personally had spent seventy years feeding witches' milk to the entire range of terrestrial and supraterrestrial daemons, at all glands and by all channels, till at the end they felt like nibbling biscuits in their gazebos once again—which struck me as not so much wisdom as fatigue, a fit of yawning. It went with the style of the *Novelle,* that celebrated work of Goethe's old age: a menagerie catches fire, the booths burn down, the tigers break out, the lions are at large—and everything works out beautifully to a happy end. No, that epoch was over, the earth was scorched, flayed by lightning, sore all over. Today the tigers bit.

The hostess moved as if to sit down with me, but I refrained from showing delight at the prospect. Was I disturbed? Busy? Not busy? All these tables and faces suddenly seemed to pose one definite question. These conversations, gestures, exhalations—was it all just by the way? The age that followed on Goethe, my own age, was Manfred's, not Faust's: "I did destroy myself and will myself destroy." Art: no remedy for scabies, but the human manifesto, existence balanced daily on a poisoned arrow, man's capital being disease, his essential nature incurability. "The damage done to the good is the most damaging damage."—"Suffering is the sole cause of consciousness"—nihilism—and: "Nihilism is a sense of happiness"—all the dissolved substances and contents that had been washed through the brains of my generation and kept on washing through them, this delta, these cleavages—and then, if one looked at these heads: immaculately padded tissues; cheekbones, teeth, no irregularity there; posture, expression, grimaces, all upward movements—whose thick skin was it that all these bankruptcies squatted on? Obviously it was all just by the way.

The hostess observed my reluctance, sensed something, turned her attention to other guests, and now our glances passed together, though in different moods, over the various groups and tables in the room. The eminent gray head over there belonged to an aged colonel, the direct descendant of that regimental commander at Malplaquet who took his troops across three deep canals and with soaked ammunition fell upon Villars' exposed, sensitive flank, to be rewarded by Marlborough with a snuff-box—this descendant was now waving his clenched fist as though giving the order to attack. The quiet man over the bottle of Burgundy spent his days insuring lives, demonstrably with success, a thoroughly conclusive man, known to impress the hesitant with Goethe's dictum, which had a place of honor in his firm's prospectus: "What is not done today will be still undone tomorrow." Filling an armchair was a personage from the realm of scientific thought, one known to specialize in derivations: butterflies from caterpillars, colonnaded temples from Indonesian pile-buildings—a specific mode in which a more exalted sphere of life expressed itself. All these were the authentic elect of our age, types whom a later era could not reproach with having unheedingly passed by such new, marvelous, and great events of our time as, for instance, the modern method of transmutations of matter (air and wood into transparent sheets, blocks, fibers), all complete personalities in whom each turn of life, vocation, inner transformation had taken the straight, direct route and always would. Compared with that, what was the sphere in which a life would have been passed by my standards?

Nothing against the order of the world—but merely uttering the word "life" condemns one—there's no getting out of this dilemma, the hostess was obviously telling herself as she took off for the other half of the tavern. Yet if I went on thinking, making straight for my goal, without ado: what these people here called action, activity in which I should be involved, according to the hostess, and miles deep in sociology, if possible—if one deducted all that was merely business, there remained only reflexes, or something like the stuff a shellfish grows to protect its jelly body against its environment. I can see no necessity for it. I can see necessity in all that an age thinks and in the way it links its own thought to that of the past epoch. In Nature itself there is obviously no such thing as necessity; it is only in the dissolution of Nature, that is to say in the mind, which is subject to constraining forces. But action—that is just vagabondage, *plein-air* stuff.

He who rides a tiger cannot dismount. Chinese proverb. Applied to action: what you get is history. Action is capitalism, the armaments industry. Malplaquet—Borodino—Port Arthur—150,000 dead, 200,000 dead, 250,000 dead—no one can now see history

as anything but the justification of mass murder: rapine and glor-
ification—there's the mechanism of power. And what history records is not the nations' folk-memory of themselves, but their funny
papers. If you look at them twenty years later, you recall the fashions
for war-widows, but not a word of what the battles were about.
A shrapnel splinter on the watch-chain draped over the belly of the
good-time boys, the sharks, the profiteers, while they bait a hooker
at a thé-dansant—that's what remains, that is the *aere perennius,*
that outlasts the general staffs, that's the nail that holds history's
flag to the flagpole. All that travail brought forth a stone—that's
history: a legend, a dream! Think of all that is now growing a beard
in some Kyffhäuser[4]: the Manchus and the Hohenstaufens, the Ten-
nos and the Shoguns and the Lancashire woolmongers—the beard
growing without hairtonic through all those table-tops, and the
ravens have croaked themselves hoarse and are sick and tired of it
and have gone flapping off over the hills: history, much too classical
for these down-and-out nations, tacky offspring of the Titans, more
heroin than heroism, froth on their lips from talking platitudes—
counter-jumpers of history!

Anyone who has nothing at all to offer the present day talks history!
Rome, the Rubicon. The jaws of Caesars and the brains of troglodytes, that's their type! Wars, knouts, tyrants, plagues to keep
the masses in check, there you might see a touch of the grand
manner, but history, no, that's nothing for—heroes! À propos,
victories and mis-victories, will and power—what labels for these
broth-cubes! On the table free groceries and under the table looted
Persian carpets: there you have the cold facts of history. What
history destroys is usually temples, and what it loots is always art.
Everyone gets his turn among the firms and the Pharaohs. The
sapphires from Amphitrite's eye-sockets find their way on to the
Madonna's mantle of beaten gold, then on to some imperial Colleoni's sword-knob. Malplaquet—Borodino—Port Arthur—in the
mollifying light of cultural philosophy: states of levitation, that's
all. Yet behind it all there stand, calmly and collectedly, the mis-
sionaries of formal reason, the leisurely collectors and artificers of
decisions.

4. A mythological mountain where the emperor Frederick Barbarossa sits in a
cave, beard forever growing, sending out his ravens for news of the empire.

When I look back on that series of evenings extending through one particular spring of my life, it seems it was then that an odd summarizing tendency developed in me; I saw more clearly a phenomenon that had been a process for centuries but scarcely ever before raised to the level of conscious formulation. It was this: in the white peoples there were two classes of men, the active and the profound, and art was nothing but the making of a method for putting the profound man's experiences into words, and only in it did he come to fulfillment and to utterance. There were—it was necessary to add—two classes capable of vocal expression within the white race, and owing to a weird biological oversight both largely used the same words and ideas, only filling them with two kinds of blood unthinkably alien to each other, mutually hostile, never to be mixed. Just as now male and now female individuals resulted from the same act of procreation, so from the germ, the Creation, the ineffable distance, what sprang was now historical man, now central man, now the active and now the profound man, now life and now the spirit. Sometimes I occupied myself with working out morphological variations on this theme and giving it a point. The superstructure of the higher centers upon the lower was the path of organic articulation; externally that meant the development of the axis, the ever-increasing erectness of the spine, the transmigration of the living essence into the head. Inwardly it meant the ascending hierarchy of nervous function; intellectually it meant consciousness; and for the scale of values and a perspective of the future, it meant a definite and unassailable articulation no longer susceptible to anything except mutations. Both experience and methodically acquired material pointed to one and the same thing: the mind and its anti-naturalistic function. Variations and fugue on a springtide theme! Not that it eased my mind; there was no longer anything that eased my mind, any more than an uncompleted train of thought made me uneasy. It might have bothered me at the next sip of *Spätlese,* but it would have been washed down, submerged, and I would have gone home ready for the hour. I had seen the finishing and re-opening of too many things, and for a long time now I had slept with all doors open, or rather lain there dozing, counting the chimes and the hours.

An odd spring! I remember some of its peculiarities. A slowly yielding winter. A sort of weight lying on everything. It was almost a haze I passed through once on my way to the outskirts of the town, before going to the tavern. Warmth rising darkly everywhere. An usually overcast afternoon. Everything looking down upon the earth with an infinitely mournful, lingering gaze, hardly able to detach itself; almost no difference between leaves and moist ground. Somewhere near where I was walking there was, I gathered, an institution whose inmates gave a sort of extra depth to all this. Lots of cripples on the road, hunchbacks, freaks, also blind men. They crept along everywhere with timid steps, stammering, fumbling with their crutches. The chestnuts were almost in bud. There was this tropical sultriness hanging silently between all shapes, an indissoluble silence linking these figures; all that had risen sank back, all spellbound to what was below—"mingle!" It called me, too, singeing my eyes with salt and fire: give of your bread—diminish the suffering—sacrifice your own flesh against tears and curses—yet if a man bows down, what more can he bear, bowing down before *this?* It is only the highest spheres that count, and the human sphere is not among them. A merciless height, where the undeflectible arrows fly; it is cold, deep blue, only rays prevail here, only one thing prevails: recognize the situation, use your means, you are in duty bound to your method, you can't retreat from what you have created. What you stand for is realms defying interpretation, realms in which there are no victories.

Evening again in the tavern. I sit listening. Listening to the strange life and being emanating from these people's voices. In Tibet it was the wind, in the jungle the insects, here it's the vowels. One was going to the Rhineland—haha, went the rest, he's full of plans, seems out for pleasure. Another had a visitor from America in October—from the USA! rang out from the rest, obviously regarding this as a clarification. Incomprehensible why they sat there so taut with interest, when their talk led simply nowhere at all.

The cloth-covered seats, intimately two and two in each compartment, faced each other with the mistrust of strangers. Fully loaded, they held their occupants as though on hinges, youth with debility, doubts with conclusions, business with love—natural needs meeting, blown together by chance.

How odd it all was! They keep their cities free of mosquitoes, at any rate I never encountered one either in Irkutsk or in Biarritz. Ingeniously, by pneumatic post, they frankly send each other their ideas on certain occasions: the East the machine-gun, the West the tank, and the New World the dew of death, the gas that smells of geraniums. The mind is there to serve life. Cultivation they call it. Later they exchange visits again. In the beginning was lust, later it scarcely had reason to put in an appearance. Women clinging to the jacket of the male, stylized on a titanic scale, demanding and granting; objectively regarded: embracing lapdogs. The jacket-wearers: knobby, no concessions to form—"empty formulae"—realities!—the whistle blows: Ring clear!

This was what had chased me through all the countries that this race inhabited, through all its social stratifications and professions. I surveyed their current cultural values, their so-called theaters, and the lobbies alone condemned the whole epoch. An audience that has to recuperate from the terrors of tragedy by strolling for twenty minutes among counters laden with ham sandwiches and brandy bottles and then goes back to carry on, is ripe for the guillotine. By their metaphors ye shall know them! I eavesdropped on their minor characteristics, on what sufficed to satisfy their minds: a pilot is a Marshal Blücher[5] of the air; a Pomeranian backwoods village with a duck-pond at the back of a stable is a Venice of the North. Then, too, I heard their songs—yes, the linden is their tree all right, sweet and heartfelt and, what's more, you can make tea from its flowers.

What speaks out of me is disintegration, I was often told. No, I answered, as long as I went on answering, what speaks out of me is the spirit of the West, which is admittedly the disintegration of life and Nature, their disintegration and re-integration by means of the law of man, that anthropological principle which separated the waters from the dry land and the prophets from the fools. But that's just it, my opponents said. You're trying to disintegrate Nature— that's the limit! The blood and soil of us all! And is this Nature of yours, I could not help retorting, really natural? Can one make it one's point of departure? I can prove that it is unnatural, a thing of leaps and bounds, indeed the very textbook example of what one means by "contrary to Nature." It begins something and drops it, makes a great stir and then forgets. It is unbridled, it exaggerates, it produces fish in incredible shoals off the Lofotens, or rolling

5. G. v. Blücher (1742–1819), Prussian field marshal, contributed decisively to Napoleon's defeat at Leipzig and Waterloo.

swarms of locusts and cicadas. Or there is peace on earth, everything has the temperature of the stones, one can truly give one's attention to the climate, and then the Aaron's rod shoots up in flower at forty degrees Centigrade, everything is thrown into confusion and the gods insist on warm-blooded animals—is that Nature's doing, or whose is it? Or take geological folding, densification, unimaginable concentration—one of its methods—is that a simple and natural thing to do? Or it takes a fancy to send immense tensions charging across microscopically tiny spaces—is that now the thing to expect? Come to think of it, was the phenomenon of life not nicely looked after in plant form? Why set it in motion and send it out in search of food—is that not a model of uprooting? As for its creature, Man, does it not plunge him headlong into anti-Nature, hurling bacteria to destroy him, diminishing his sense of smell, reducing his sense of hearing, denaturing his eye by means of optical lenses, so that the man of the future is the merest abstraction—where are the workings of natural Nature? No, it is some other face that peers out everywhere, sleeping in the stones, blossoming in the flowers, making its demands in all late forms—a very different face, and the result I arrive at is an alien one.

If I wanted to work out a theory, I should refer you to the way biology is at this very moment busy demonstrating that the inorganic and the organic are two retrospectively associated forms of higher unity, with no transitions or derivations between them, no "evolution" of life "out of" the inorganic now or ever; they are two independent realms, two modes of expression. Today you may say this scientifically—I mean, you won't lose your chair at the university, with attendant benefits, and the specialist journals will publish papers containing this sort of statement. It is not yet the established view, but there are signs that it is coming. Until recently you would have lost your chair at the university. But nobody is allowed to say that a Third Reich claims the same rights to its point of view. The Third Reich "serves" the Second and has spontaneously wangled its way up from it. Millennia are based on this theory. But it is not a theory, it is a procedural code that can be used for acts of power. In graphic terms, its results for the tavern are: steel chairs, Reich Number One, laden with Reich Number Two; the load enjoys mussel ragout and talks as vowel-bearers of the category "Life"; if they burp on bicarbonate, it is done scientifically, revealing Reich Number Three. Signed: Historical World. Point of departure. Departure not by any means in the tragic sense, quite the contrary: historical man is supposed to act, and the man of action is what history wants; let them act and trade and pile things up till they rupture themselves—let them fulfill themselves, manifest themselves—only one more hour to nightfall—then glow-a-low, high-low, hell-hello-low!

If one casts a glance at the leaders of the nations, all of them and in all their respective forms of government, one must imagine them standing in time on the brink of one or the other of the great movements of mankind, with the power to suppress it. What would they do? About Christianity, they would ask if the budget could stand it. About Buddhism, how it would affect the phonograph record and flag-making industries. About Mahomet, would it not hurt the banana crop? About art, would it not undermine the demand for new housing? About every religion, would it not hold up potato exports? About abstraction, summarizing thought, might it not dent the little man's watering-can? Multiplication of protoplasm and raw materials are their standards, everything else is agitation and calls for suppression—and that goes even for Plato. But always, at all times, every one of them has claimed to be the creative fulfillment of cosmic reason. Obviously there are contradictions involved—glow-a-low, high-low, hell-hello-low!

If now the tables themselves were to try persuading each other that it was consoling and elevating to each—giving it a deeper significance, in fact giving it all the significance it has—for others to live just this way in the future and for ever new figures to be born into the same environment, crawl around the same tables, go on living for centuries in the same flats, a so-called posterity that cannot be or become anything but the recurrent embodiment of the same nullity: publicly trying to persuade each other of this, proclaiming this as doctrine, strikes me as a spiritual perversity compared with which the worst monstrosities of scorched earth, fakirs' tricks, religious belly-dancing, Indian bowel-and-liver-exercises are like the pure breath of umbelliferous blooms.

In the tavern I beheld a dream. A very quiet animal-keeper led white-skinned human creatures around in a circle until they became discolored. Then he pried open their jaws and yelled: "Spirit or life! There's no more realizing the spirit in life."—"Who's of the spirit?"

one gasped.—"This one talking!" was the answer.—No, we do not want to go that far; there is some truth in it, but it provokes justifiable opposition. Shut the jaws—there, there's the world looking natural again! Then one of them called out through teeth once more safely clenched: "Haven't you any mercy, any human feelings? Don't you know everyone wants to be better and more beautiful?" The answer came: "Mercy is not mine to give. Crave mercy from those who have brought you where you are, crave mercy from yourselves, you who let yourselves be led, crave it from your own baseness and greed. Time and again words have been uttered, warning you against life. Time and again the Other Thing came and set up its images before you—in human form, yes, even in human form! Set up before you the images of that force to which it would be too little to ascribe a religious or moral nature; it is the universal challenging, uplifting force, the entelechy—admittedly the very force that comprises heaven and hell within its infinity and yet gazes so visibly upon all man's damming and regulating characteristics and casts so strange a light on all heaven's slowly accumulating and always so hard-won achievements.—Did you ever worship it? Did you keep watch over it? All you wanted was to live your life, your white, fulfilled life, realized in Derby glitter and yachting spray— no, there's no more mercy. Now comes nightfall."

Everyone sees that the truth looming up among the vats here in this tavern is an extra-human truth. It is, besides, in a peculiar position, for it should most passionately combat its own generalization, should condemn its own projection into time, its own testing for realization, as the most decisive blunder. Realization is a concept that this truth excludes, one that it deliberately eludes; wherever it catches a glimpse of it, it lowers its gaze. Is it then a truth at all? Is it not perhaps an untruth for all; in other words, a prematurely dispatched message written in a code intended only for a certain few?

For a certain few? That is to say, for initiates of esotericism, for decadents, cliques, destructionists, divisionists, anti-social types, lone wolves, intellectualists, marked men? Let us consider this question in the twilight of truth among our vats. If one surveys the white nations in the course of the last five hundred years and looks for a yardstick to assess their great minds, the only one to be found is the degree of ineradicable nihilism they bore within them and spasmodically hid under the fragments of their works. It is quite obvious—all the great minds among the white nations have felt only one inner task, namely the creative camouflaging of their nihilism. This fundamental tendency, interwoven with the most varied trends of the ages—in Dürer with the religious, in Tolstoy with the moral, in Kant with the epistemological, in Goethe with the anthropological, in Balzac with the capitalistic—was the basic element in all their works. With the utmost gingerliness it is brought up again and again. On every page, in every chapter, in every stroke of the pencil or brush they approach it with ambiguous questioning, with turns of the most exquisitely groping, equivocal character. Not for an instant are they unaware of the essential nature of their own inner creative substance. It is the abyss, the void, the unsolvable, the cold, the inhuman element. Nietzsche's place in their ranks is for a long time that of an idealistic Antinoüs. Even his Zarathustra—what a child of Nature, what evolutionary optimism, what shallow utopianism about the spirit and its realization! Only in the last stage, with *Ecce Homo* and the lyrical fragments, did he let that other datum rise into his consciousness, and that, one may suppose, brought about his collapse: that brown night when he stood on the bridge staring down into the abyss, beholding the abyss—late—too late for his organism and his role as a prophet. On that bridge, in that night, a twilit form soared up on bat's wings, the earth gaped open, one age wrested its symbols from the other, and there came about that antithesis of life and spirit which we bore within us so long and now see again beyond the confines of Earth.

What is it that we see beyond the confines of Earth? Taking a closer look for a moment at the last hundred years, the century around Nietzsche, the laboratories and the prisons from Siberia to Morocco, we see the spirit from Dostoievsky to Céline in an attitude of sheer despair, its screams more terrible, more agonized, more evil than ever were the screams of men condemned to die. These screams are of a moral nature, definite in meaning, they are substantial and always "against" something, at war "with" something, struggling "for" something, trying to include "everything" and to remain honest, to improve, to complete, to purify, to deify. They are Lutherian screams in a Faustian skirmish. Mythopoeic puberty and prometheid biology extend right into their orbit. Only today, before so much absurdity and torment, we dimly sense that life is not meant to gain possession of knowledge, and man, at any rate the higher-developed race, is not meant to struggle for an explanation of the material world. It all looks more like an experimental step taken by that remote distance which yielded the formula for some monstrous alkaloid but withheld the substance itself in all its purity. And which still preserves it unchanged, in all its purity, not intending any such struggle or any further surrender in terms of temporal knowledge. The experiment was meant to indicate delimitation, abstractive elimination, formulae directed against Nature. The aim was not to intensify life biologically and to perfect it racially by means of stimuli to knowledge, but to set the formative, formula-wielding mind against life. Hence it is not the Faustian-physiological, but the anti-naturalistic function of the mind, its expressive function, that we see holding sway over the earth today.

This is the point of departure. We have to trouble history and the times for this assertion. We are no longer concerned with breeding for a future we can neither await nor utilize, but with our own bearing in an eschatological present that has become an abstract experience only. Thus reads the coded message. Here the certain few come to a halt: before the remote signs that are drawing steadily nearer, the invisible protagonists of the impending transformation.

This is said by a life-long, case-hardened expert in realities, one well acquainted with the body, with war and with death, skilled in several occupations, all of them carved out of the abdominal fat of capitalism and each one refined to ultimate craftsmanly finesse by the personal necessity of turning them into a living. It is said by one who always lived under the pressure of specific tasks, deliveries, contracts, market conditions, without room for romanticism or time for illusions. One who lived in the social style of his century, at times in tails and at times in dress uniform, traveling by the Blue Train and by caravan in the company of a Rurik and a Rochefoucauld (only recently on a ferry-boat he found himself sitting next to the last Romanov princess). One who loved an Austrian girl and a Czech one, a Rumanian, a Belgian, a Dane, a woman from Cape Town, a halfbreed from the South Seas, Russian girls on shores, fjords, salt lakes, in many landscapes and from many tribes, in Ritz Hotel suites and in tents. Let's call it an average life, with work and toil and the sort of understanding that a man's own time allows him—which says: No propaganda can turn excrement into lilies-of-the-valley. The white peoples are on the way out, no matter whether or not the theories about their doom are now accepted. Decomposition is palpable, a return to earlier conditions impossible, the substance spent; this is where the Second Law of Thermodynamics applies. The new power is there, holding the cigarette-lighter to the fuse. Whether by moon plunge or atom-smashing, by entropy or incendiarism, by whatever method it prefers, it is the transformation, the eternal element, the spirit, the antagonist of dreary rationality and mere consumption—in short: the end of the natural view of the world.

So let tem try regenerating things by economics and biology and vegetarianism—all these are specters of annihilation. The race is more intuitive: it will no longer adapt itself, it has grown inert, it lies immobile round its core, and this core is the spirit—that is to say, nihilism.

He who cannot bear this thought stands among the worms that breed in the sand, and in the moisture that the earth has given them for their own. He who still boasts of hope, gazing into his children's eyes, tries to hide the lightning with his hands but cannot escape the night that blasts the nations from their dwelling places. This is the law: Nothing is, if anything ever was; nothing will be. The fairest and profoundest of all gods is passing us by, the only one who bore the mystery of man: the greater the knowledge, the more infinite the grief.

There is nothing that can be turned into reality. The spirit hovers in silence over the waters. A road has come to an end; here is the sunset of a cosmic day. Perhaps it bore within it possibilities other than this gloaming, but now the hour is upon us—ecce homo—this is how man ends.

Such were my thoughts in that spring. I knew there would be other springs, and perhaps I myself would see another, whole weeks of beauty, in the multiplicity of unfolding leaves and petals, and roses would bloom for this man and for that, but one thing I knew: history had lost its power over man. His inner core had once more begun to glow, had written a word on his garment and a name upon his hip.

They will keep coming, but he will melt them down. They are approaching with nails, with knives to stab him in the back, and all he raises is a twig of hyssop and a cup of hemlock. A vast, millennial battlefield, and the victory is his. Only no action! Know this and be silent. Asia is deeper, but hide that! Face things in the spirit; it will be carried on, it helps to shape existence. Open your eyes only to the night; by day clink glasses with the men, run through the standard gossip with the ladies, and never let the flower girl pass without buying her posies. Live and observe to the end. Think always: transformation! We too have signs! One must be much, to cease expressing anything. Be silent; pass away.

(Written 1937, published 1949)   *Translated by Ernst Kaiser and*
Eithne Wilkins

Block II, Room 66

This was the designation of the quarters assigned to me for many months. The barracks lay on high, fortresslike above the town. "Montsalvat," said a first lieutenant who evidently had heard operas; and, indeed, the place was inaccessible to loafers at least: 137 steps had to be climbed after making one's way from Bahnhofstrasse to the foot of the hill.

Nothing dreamier than barracks! Room 66 faces the drill ground: before it grow three small rowan trees, their berries without purple, the leaves as though stained with brown tears. It is late August; the swallows still fly, but already are massed for the great passage. A battalion band rehearses in a corner, the sun sparkling on trumpets and percussives as they play, "Die Himmel rühmen," and "Ich schiess den Hirsch im wilden Forst." It is the fifth year of war, and here is a completely secluded world, a kind of béguinage. The shouts of command are external; inwardly all things are muffled and still.

An eastern town topped by this high plateau, and that in turn topped by our Montsalvat with its bright yellow buildings and vast drill ground, a kind of desert fort. The immediate vicinity also full of oddities. Unpaved streets running half on low ground, half on hillsides; isolated houses without road connection—inconceivable how the occupants get in: fences as in Lithuania, low, mossy, damp. A gypsy wagon fixed up as a dwelling. At dusk a man comes carrying a cat on his left shoulder; the cat wears a string round its neck, stands askew, wants down; the man laughs. Low drifting clouds, black and purple light, scarcely a bright spot, eternal threat of rain, many poplars. At the wall of a house three blue roses grow lyre-shaped, horticulturally unmotivated. Mornings, the settlement is bathed in a peculiarly soft, aurora-like light. Here, too, universal unreality, a sense of two-dimensionality, a stage-prop world.

Around the drill shed the garrison blocks: dreams. Not the dreams of fame and victories, but dreams of loneliness, of transience, of shadows. Reality is far removed. Over the entrance block, the so-called hall of honor, stands a general's name in large letters: "General von X Barracks." A general of World War I. For three days, each time I passed, I would ask the arms-presenting sentry: for whom were the barracks named? "Who was General von X?" Never an answer. General von X was unknown, unremembered. In oblivion his standard, his auto pennant, the swarm of staff officers in his retinue. It has no effect over two decades. Strongly you feel the mortar, the ephemerality, the false values, the distortion.

Flowing through the blocks are waves of conscripts. There are two kinds: the sixteen-year-olds, underfed, slight, miserable Labor Service types, scared, submissive, assiduous, and the old codgers of fifty to sixty, from Berlin. On the first day these are still gentlemen, wear mufti, buy papers, walk in strides that say, We're corporation lawyers, business representatives, insurance brokers, have pretty wives and central heating: this temporary situation can't affect us, it's rather funny, in fact. . . . On the second day they are in uniform, and their name is mud. Now they must flit through the halls when a non-com barks, jump in the barracks yard, lug boxes, press on steel helmets. Training is short, a matter of two or three weeks; interesting that they take target practice from the second day on—formerly this came after four or six weeks only. Then, one night, they line up with full pack, rolled-up mantle and pup tent, gas mask, machine-pistol, rifle—almost a hundred pounds of weight—and off they go to be shipped out, into darkness. This departure in the dark is weird. An unseen band leads off, playing marches, gay tunes, trailed by the soundless company that heads for permanent oblivion. The procedure is swift, a mere crack in the black silence, then the plateau lies in the dark, earthless, skyless night again. New ones come in the morning. They also leave. It gets colder outdoors, during drill. Now they are ordered to rub hands and slap their knees with their fists to stimulate circulation, keep life awake—militaristic biology. The blocks stand, the waves roll. Successive waves of men, new waves of blood due to trickle into the Eastern steppe after a few shots and manipulations in the direction of so-called enemies.

The whole would be unintelligible if the general were not so impressively behind it, standing fascinatingly in his purple and gold, firing and commanding to fire; there is as yet no direct threat to his retirement pay.

At noon the officers meet at table. Since the start of the war there has been no distinction in fare between officers and men. A colonel, like a grenadier, gets two loaves of kommissbrot a week, with margarine and artificial honey on paper strips to take out; lunch is a deep dish of cabbage soup or a pile of boiled potatoes that must be peeled on the table (covered with oilcloth, if available, otherwise with "organized" bedcloth)—you put the peeled potatoes to one side and wait for the soup or the gravy. One day the colonel commanding my unit appears—unshaven. There are no more blades, nor any honing implements. Someone knows a place in Berlin that will "organize" things in that line. An Austrian ally contributes the story that in the Austro-Hungarian monarchy only the Windisch-grätz Dragoons had the right to go clean-shaven—in memory of Kolin, the battle that was decided by the arrival of the new, young beardless recruits. A stick of shaving soap must last four months. Enlisted men are forbidden to shave, to save matériel. In America they shave lying down—typically lazy plutocratic rabble.

The conversations are those of nice, harmless people without an inkling of what threatens them and the fatherland. Badoglio[1] is a traitor, the King of Italy a rickets-shrunken crook. On the other hand, a burial mound in Holstein has yielded a Teutonic ceremonial cap testifying to the highly developed cap-making art of our ancestors, 3,500 years ago. The Greeks, too, were Aryans. Prince Eugene of Savoy outlived his fame; what he finally did in France was nothing to brag about. Wearers of the newfangled short dagger are demimonde—cavalry still wears the long saber—cavalry! Now it's a bicycle squadron. . . .

All these, no matter how sharp in demeanor, think fundamentally only about bringing the wife a dish of mushrooms when they go on furlough, about the boy's marks in school, and how not to land in the street again as in 1918, in case—this is the term heard at times, the term they permit themselves—in case of "a wash-out." Almost all are officers of the old army, around fifty, World War

1. Pietro Badoglio (1871–1956), Italian field marshal, helped to remove Mussolini in 1943 and later signed armistice with the Allies.

veterans. In the interim they have been cigarette or paper salesmen, farm supervisors, riding instructors, all with a hard row to hoe. Now they are majors. Not one speaks a foreign language or has seen a foreign country, except in wartime. Only the Imperial-and-Royal ally, ever alert and suspicious of being looked down on, has a somewhat broader outlook, probably because of Old Austria's Adriatic and Balkan ties. . . . Even though there was no great spiritual world to be discovered, I tried attentively to penetrate my environment. Who did not constantly turn it over in his mind, the single question how it had been and still was possible for Germany to stick unswervingly to this so-called government, this half dozen loudmouths who for ten years now had been periodically reeling off the same twaddle in the same halls; before the same howling audiences? Those six buffoons who thought they alone knew better than the centuries before them and the rational rest of the world? Gamblers setting out to break the bank in Monte Carlo with a shady system, con-men dumb enough to think their fellow players would not notice their marked cards—saloon-fighting clowns, chair-leg heroes! This was not the Hohenstaufen dream of uniting North and South, not the idea behind the eastward drive of the Teutonic Knights, who were colonizers at least—it was sheer dross in concept and form, primary rain magic celebrating nocturnal torch fumes before requisitioned caskets of Henry the Lion.

This, plainly, was the government; and now we have the fifth war year, somber with defeats and miscalculations, evacuated continents, torpedoed battleships, millions of dead, bombed-out giant cities, and still the masses go on hearing and believing their leaders' twaddle. There can be no mistake about it: outside the bombed cities, at least, they firmly believe in new weapons, mysterious engines of vengeance, imminent, dead certain counterblows. High and low, general and soldier on KP make a mystical totality of fools, a pre-logical collective of gullibles—something doubtlessly very Germanic and centrally explicable only in this ethnologic sense. Of peripheral ethnologic explanations two come to mind. First, war today is not felt so much by people in smaller towns and in the country itself: they have to eat, can "organize" what is lacking, have not been bombed, are supplied by Goebbels with all the emotion required for stable and house—and the weather always plays a larger role in the country than any train of thought. Second, family casualties are far easier to get over than the nation would have it. The dead die quickly: the more die, the sooner they are forgotten. Between fathers and sons there is probably as much basic antipathy as its opposite; the tension of hatred links them as strongly as the bond of love. Fallen sons can help materially, bring tax relief, make age important. Teaching this to the young would be most educational; then they would know what to think later, when the immortality of heroes and the gratitude of the survivors are served up again.

The following particulars were noteworthy: two ranks carry the army in the fifth year of war, the lieutenants and the field marshals—the rest is detail. The lieutenants, products of the Hitler Youth, have received an education whose essence was the systematic uprooting of any mental and moral content of life from books and actions, and the substitution of Ostrogoth princes, daggers, and haymows to spend the night in after a forced march. They have been insulated from parents who still may be cultured, from educators trained in the old sense, from clergymen and humanist circles—in short, from culture carriers of any kind—and that in peacetime; thus well equipped, they consciously, purposefully, and deliberately set out on their Aryan mission of destroying the continent. Just one word about the field marshals: it is not well known that they get their marshal's pay for life, tax-free, plus a permanent staff officer as aide-de-camp, and a country estate or a fair-sized Grunewald[2] property on their retirement from active service. As the marshal-maker under our government of laws is also the marshal-breaker, and as in his latter capacity he vigorously wields the clubs of withdrawing titles, medals, pension claims, and holding the next-of-kin responsible, the marshals, as good family men, stand virtually exonerated—as demons they will have impressed nobody, anyway.

In looking at this war, and at the peace that preceded it, one thing must not be ignored: the vast existential emptiness of today's German man, stripped of whatever fills the inner space in other countries—decent national contents, public interest, criticism, social life, colonial impressions, genuine traditions. Here was nothing but a vacuum of historic twaddle, crushed education, bumptious political forgeries by the regime, and cheap sports. But to wear an

2. Fashionable district in Berlin.

eye-catching uniform, to get reports, bend over maps, trot with retinue through enlisted men's quarters and across squares, to announce dispositions, make inspections, talk bombast ("I command only once"—the subject was latrine-cleaning): all this creates a space-filling impression of individual expansion and supra-personal effect, in short, the complex which the average man requires. Art is forbidden, the press exterminated, personal opinion answered with a bullet in the neck—to gauge the space-filling by human and moral standards, as in civilized countries, was no longer possible on the premises of the Third Reich. What prevailed here was space-shamming; pontoon-bridge crossings, blasts about to go off, telescopic gunsights made the individualist feel like an immediate cosmic disaster. . . .

Autumn around the blocks was dangerously dry, as throughout the Reich. The fields are mice-eaten, the potato crop is catastrophic, the beets contain too little sugar. The loss of the eastern areas curtails the food supply by two months' bread, one month's fats, one month's meat. Rations are cut. There are no more high boots, for want of leather; there are no more artificial limbs for the handicapped; the materials are at an end. There are no more shoelaces and no more dentures, no gauze bandages and no specimen glasses. There is a shortage of doctors. Entire divisions take the field without a surgeon; of the civilian population, 25,000 may depend on one woman doctor, and she without gasoline. But the Führer awards chevrons, sets the width of ribbons on military funeral wreaths, forbids the soldiers to marry foreign girls, even Scandinavians: "the noblest Nordic woman" remains "racial driftwood" by the Great German yardstick. Putrefaction in every pore, but the propaganda runs at top speed. We look at magazines: Nera and Sehra, the "elves of Mostar," are so glad to be allowed at last to work in the great Organization Todt; Goebbels blinks his white teeth at the wounded; Goering comes as Father Christmas—the fairy tale entwines us.

One day in November I had to go to Berlin, on duty. It was the time when travel ranked with the most arduous sports. Regular rail service was a thing of the past. At 2 a.m. a marvelous train pulled into my station: eight sleeping cars, four practically empty first- and second-class cars, at the rear end a car with a flak crew. I got on. An SS man promptly hauled me back. I did not understand.

He reported that this was the train from the Führer's headquarters, only for gentlemen of the top staffs. I realized that my brief case might well have held a hand grenade. I boarded the next train, i.e. I squeezed myself into a third-class toilet—I in a colonel's uniform, between East laborers. The toilet stood open. Women and children had to use it, the door was not to be closed, shifting was impossible, but no one minded. I had to change trains. In the next, I stood in a second-class compartment while three young louts in party uniform, stout fellows, sprawled on the cushions. White-haired women, women with children stood in the aisle with me. The master race produced a bottle of brandy and a few packs of cigars (the "people's community" got one cigar a day, at the time, and no brandy) and spent the three hours to Berlin fortifying itself for the party tasks to come. On the same day all the papers carried an article to the effect that the party's percentage of Knight's Cross winners and casualties was far higher than that of the rest of the people, and that home duty for party members did not exist. There was a sentence: "The contrary optical picture that occasionally presents itself is definitely misleading." Evidently my three fellow travelers were part of this optical picture.

Block II lets one understand the misty Niflheim of Germanic mythology, the eternal fog and fumes and the need for bearskins of those "splendid old Germans," as the radio just described them. From here, Taine would geophysically deduce the primary national estrangement from clarity and form—and, one might say, from honesty. In December, 1943, when the Russians had driven us back a thousand miles and punched dozens of holes into our front, a lieutenant colonel, small as a humming bird and gentle as a rabbit, says at lunch, "Main thing, the s.o.b.'s don't break through!" Break through, roll up, clean up, mobile tactics—how potent these words are, positively for bluff, and negatively for self-deception! Stalingrad: a tragic accident; the rout of the U-boats: a chance technical discovery of the British; Montgomery chasing Rommel 2500 miles from El Alamein to Naples: treason of the Badoglio clique.—At the same time, a party boss has business with our command. He eats with us, and my colonel, a cavalryman of the old school, a Knight of St. John who wears his monocle on steeplechases and to bed, exchanges it for black, horn-rimmed glasses, lest he offend the big shot's sense of the people's community and jeopardize his own future. ("Fearless and faithful"—"*Semper talis,*" it said on the helmets of the old Prussian Guards. . . .)

Meanwhile, Christmas approaches. There is a special issue of four ounces of mettwurst and 25 per cent *Ersatz* fish-powder on the weekly meat ration. Moreover, anyone willing to give up an ounce of margarine and four ounces of sugar may order a stollen. I put my name on the list. Christmas songs are forbidden, winter solstice reflections in line of duty desired, with emphasis on the renewal of light from the womb of All-Mother Nature—commanding officers are to proceed accordingly. For the present, no renewal is noticeable. I stand by the window of Room 66; the drill ground spreads in a gray light, a gray from the wings of seagulls that dove into all oceans. The feast has come. In the morning there was a big raid on Berlin; you wonder if the apartment stands, and what is left of the few acquaintances still living there. Then it is evening, and the rations are brought up. I ask the orderly about his asthma; he is hard of hearing; communication is difficult. I look farther over the ground and beyond it, at the lowlands, the steppe, the East—everything so near, everything so present, all these horrible hosts of generations that failed to obtain clarity about themselves. And then it descends, the Holy Night of the year 1943.

Soon after Christmas orders came to evacuate the blocks, to make room for troops flooding back from the East. We move, I go along. Actively, passively—the louse in the fur, the wolf in sheep's clothing, the goat as cultivator of sprouts and shoots: do they move, go along? What a bloated concept: action! To be under duress and obliged to draw subsidies—it may be action; but to want to unify action and thought—what a redneck notion! Imagine a modern physicist trying to express his calculations, his professional work, in his life, to harmonize them with his life, to "realize" them—or Bachofen, his matriarchal theories; or Böcklin, his "Isle of the Dead"— how comical! If chance, the events of his time, compel a man to live in the historic world, among sharpshooters and profiteers, trappers and rabbit thieves, should that cause him to step out of himself and forcefully to voice opinions?

Is there an idea of mankind? There may have been times when one existed in the universal consciousness. But today opinions are constitutional, like fits of migraine—a hereditary ailment. One might have the opinions of a prophet and still would not need to raise a green flag and take to the high hills with snake and eagle. That men are not changed, not improved, not reformed by prophetic opinions has been shown by the failure of the most recent Dionysus; the "blond beast" has raved itself out. Opinions—just to stimulate the peristalsis of the historic world, as a lubricant—what man of mark today would make a public appearance for that reason? Historic world—brazenly grown and devoured off-hand; the potbellies sit in a box with their paramours and parasites, and violins play winged music for the killers, but in the darkness nameless victims trickle their life-blood away, and the strangled are hidden. No, there is nothing to step out and nothing to fight here, neither with a small slingshot nor with a big trumpet. Let them run their thresher over the corn!

That which lives is something other than that which thinks—we must accept this basic fact of our existence. It may have been different once upon a time; it may be that a sidereal union will dawn in some unimaginable future—today the race lives in this form. What thought in me was moving in a realm of its own; what lived of me was considerate, well-bred, and sincerely comradely in my allotted environment. That which thought was guileless, cross-questioned no one, insinuated nothing to anyone, did not come to light at all; it was relaxed, and could be, it was so sure of being right and possessing the truth against all the facts of life within the barracks we inhabited together. "He that believeth shall not hasten," says Isaiah. Of course, one might say that this belief must be made known—that one who thinks, who sees things as I have just stated them, must act, oppose, make a revolution, or let himself be shot. I do not share this view. These matters are not susceptible of general proof; there are existential reasons only. For me these reasons lie in my personal disbelief in the significance of the historic world. I have not managed to be more than an experimental type that turns certain contents and complexes into closed formal structures, a type that can see the unity of life and spirit only in their common secondary results: in a statue, a verse, a structure worth leaving behind—I touch life and finish a poem. Whatever else affects life is dubious and indefinite. We no longer feel a religious link as a fact, to say nothing of the so-called national link; as a fact we only feel their incorporation in some expressive esthetic work. Biologic tension ends in art. Art, however, is no motivating force in history; it cancels time and history, rather, to work on the gene, on the internal inheritance, on substance—a long inner road. The entertaining and political aspects of a few specialties such as the novel are deceptive; the essence of art is infinite reserve. Its core is crushing, but its periphery is narrow; it touches little, but that with fire. Existential reasons are not causal but constitutional, obliging no one, valid only for those in whom they prove to be facts; they may be mutational variants, attempts that thrive or vanish again, or, as I said, experiments. They are not transferable, nor can we test them; they seek substantiation in the irrepressible world of expression that does not fail to encompass even these blocks—in which, in fact, these blocks seemed to create a special need for reviewing its own foundations.

The blocks will firmly reject this relationship. Such talk, the blocks will reply, comes from thought, from the cold, barren thought that threatens warm, natural life, from a roving intellect antagonistic to the patriotic impulse, to the idea of the Reich, to harvest festivals and Snow White and the Seven Dwarfs. Didn't we see today in the paper for the pretentious a photo, "Creative art at the front," with the caption, "Fleet commander gives morale officer his critique of picture, 'At the foe!' "—so? Yes, the fleet commander! An admiral, to be sure—and the gale lashes the wave, and the lighter or the freighter and the minelayer or the destroyer rolls or steams, and there's no lack of foam, either—at the foe, at the friend—this whole groveling historic victory craze—yes: compared with this, the thought represented by me is relentlessness—without asking where it may lead, this is my cruise at the foe, at the friend; this is my primary humanity, all else is crime!

True, it has already occurred to thought itself that Something came into the world to redeem the absolute, something called love, and that the Gentle one was sent to make thought bow down voluntarily—but, as I said: love, not obtuseness. Whenever there is interplay and counterplay of love and thought, there will be the higher world for which man also struggles in his striving for expression. Yet this is the terrestrial age of thought: thought works out the measure of things, the expression, the features, the mouth—and that ends its mission on earth. True, love is said to be even the criminals' due, but not, I suppose, at all hours. It was Rodya's due, when he took Sonia and suffered—Rodion Raskolnikov who first dared all, dared to spit in the faces of all, dared to seize all power, dared even to kill—it was his due when Sonia said, "Go at once, this very minute, stand at the crossroads, bow down, first kiss the earth which you have defiled and then bow down to all the world and say to all men aloud, 'I am a murderer!' Will you go? Will you go?"—And this one went.

(Concluded for publication in 1950)

And then came the end in the East. If you called the garrison command on January 27, 1945, to ask, "What about the stuff we've taken so much trouble to bring here from Berlin—what do we do with it when the Russians come?" you were told by the adjutant, an SS captain: "Anyone asking that is going to be stood against a wall! The Russians won't get through! Maybe you'll get a look at some tank patrol in the distance; but the town will be held—and anyone who thinks of sending his wife back to Berlin will be shot, too." At five o'clock the following night there was alarm, artillery fire, and we ran home in a blizzard at 10 above zero, on foot, carrying a briefcase, over icy highways clogged up with the endless rows of refugees in covered wagons from which dead children fell. In Küstrin we were loaded on an open cattle car that took twelve hours under airplane strafing to bring us the twenty-five miles to Bahnhof Zoo in Berlin. Thus the end came all along the East, town by town. In the apartment were strangers; the rooms were bare; we covered ourselves with my uniform cloak and newspapers, to wake up when the sirens screamed. Thus it faded out—the block life in Room 66.

In these barracks I wrote *Novel of the Phenotype* and many parts of *World of Expression,* including "Pallas," and of *Static Poems,* e.g., "September" and others.

(Written 1944, published 1950)   *Translated by E. B. Ashton*

The Glass-Blower

A scorching summer and a city dying of thirst. Burnt lawns, trees suffocating in dust. Among the ruins, languishing bodies, sweating salt from their pores without hope of replenishment, decrepit, gasping for shadows—between spells of unconsciousness, cardiovascular disturbances, faltering blood circulation.

On the boulevards, a desert life—lively bordellos and uniforms. The brass band of the eighth Amurian regiment—armistice garrison Lo-sha-go—blasting the air with its long trombones. The bars filling up: the dregs of Hawaii and Siberian spot-blood. White vodka, gray whisky, Ayala and Widow Cliquot from unwashed crystal glasses. Gentlemen and gospodins step-dancing on the red glass floor, flood-lit from below, dancing with Helen-the-Nose, Robber-Sonya, Eye-Alexandra (she has a glass eye). The populace greedily staring through the windows: culture's on the march again, less murder, more music and sound. The inner life of the vanquished is taken care of as well: a transatlantic bishop comes to visit and murmurs: My brothers; a humanist shows up and speaks in dulcet tones: Western civilization; a tenor lifts his voice: Oh glorious Art—the reconstruction of Europe is under way.

It's thought, the brain, that has Europe in its keeping, but the continent trembles, thought has its cracks and fissures. A famous writer from one of the Mediterranean countries writes to his adoring Egyptian fans: "the few shall save the world." The few—save it from what and to what end? No doubt whatever created the world must have been first-rate, super, top class; you can bet it's still writhing in its unspeakable sphere, serene, closed off, stilling its thirst with its own substance, eliminating itself, maintaining an unimaginable balance. But there's something in us that won't go along with this, that gets annoyed, that turns itself inside out, asks questions, engages in discussion with those of like mind; in short, betrays the absence of that serenity that is the hallmark of things that repose in themselves, the things made of glass.

A striving for perfection that leads to suffering; intuitions, surmisings, never a certainty. If one could put up with hunger, with thirst, with the fact that one's hands aren't germ free after washing, that one's moods don't end harmoniously, that dreams sink away without becoming realities, that love suffers change and change is endless to the point of oblivion; if this were taught, this second thermodynamic law of existence, this apology of decay, these universals of the soul—if we bowed our heads instead of senselessly holding them up—would such a teaching lead us out of ruin? Is that what the above-mentioned writer meant when he spoke of the world being saved by the few?

These were my impressions and thoughts as I stepped into my establishment one morning in July. The clients were already waiting. The gentlemen wanted a stylish look, no more bunches of hair peeking over the collar in back; the ladies, beauty: a gray strand over the forehead, get rid of skin pigmentations (part and parcel of the general dislike of freckles, incomprehensible to me)—in short, I had to take care of business, but inwardly I continued my train of thought.

Giving instructions concerning the application of poultices with hot cloths, proffering advice on the treatment of a split fingernail, evaluating combs, singing the praises of birch balsam, and inwardly thinking about destroyed and destructive things—I had developed this paradoxy to the point of virtuosity. On this day, while I modeled a head of long hair with brillantine—concocted of benzoic acid, purified lard, and gardenias—I pursued my visions. Li-Hung-Chang had huge rotten fangs which he bared each time he emitted his uncanny laugh, a tall man with boisterous, jovial manners—how was that for a point of departure, set in the Far East. Isvolsky was supposed to have been short; his feet were always wedged in patent leather shoes; his suits came from Savile Row and had a white stripe on the vest; he shakes your hand but turns his head elsewhere, always exuding a slight odor of Violet de Parme. Then Caruso: the first act is over; Gatti-Casazza, the Metropolitan's business manager, visits him, kisses him on both cheeks with great seriousness and dignity, every evening. Caruso reaches for the vial full of salt water in his pocket; dressing room attendants and servants to his right and left, one of them offers him a glass of whisky, another immediately hands him a glass of bubbling water, after which he consumes a quarter of an apple. Always stage fright! The cold cream for removing makeup must not contain any glycerine and is produced exclusively for him by a druggist he himself trained. That, more or less, was the age, and this leads me to the European question: *Is thought compulsive?* A tenor is an industry: estate managers, chefs de cuisine, throat specialists, agencies—in the case of an intellectual genius one finds a few sausage peels on the plate in the morning, and the room needs airing—is it believable that anyone would voluntarily subject himself to this?

Admittedly: panopticon, pictures, fragments, colored by my questions! But thought in its search for the interconnections strikes me as much more imperfect. If one looks across Europe, one sees masses of people thinking, in back and in front, on the top and on the bottom, on land and on water and on traveling ships, thought proceeding from primitivity the way monkeys climb trees, and thought proceeding from art like trapeze artists balancing balls, and there's thinking in the four world languages and the twenty-two Balkan dialects, with the result that no one knows what sort of activity this is and what it's there for. If one looks into things laterally, as I do, one sees quite a lot of color, at any rate; for example, at this moment the many sloops outside Yucatan with whose help the Spanish elemental hypertension bled so profusely it had to drop several European jewels from its crown, among them my fatherland—in short, some lost swishing sounds of palms by the Caribbean Sea, the twanging of a few bowstrings, and various coolie castes elsewhere, all these occur in my system. The caiman too, dripping with guano because the white heron stood on its scales on the lookout for fish, and red parrots. Lava and gaily shimmering rivers. Furthermore flora and fauna, lucullic and prophylactic: when the giant locust devastates the sugarcane fields and the vine louse endangers the Mosel wines, when para-rubber is water-impermeable and the waterproof coat is created—these are the sculptors of my hours. The gentleman would like to have more hair on his head, which I am treating with benzochlorid acid. I rub more forcefully, praise the substance doubly, claim to have noticed a bit of new hair coming in, a slight fuzz, a willing epidermis, joyfully opened pores. We discuss the matter, he as an optimistic idealist, I as an expert. "Has the future already passed?"—we both recalled this headline in yesterday's newspaper. They had dug out a Negro skull and found it bore the signs of today's hypermodern man: a stunted set of teeth, more brittle than today, missing wisdom teeth, a high forehead (connected with hair loss)—"less simian than any contemporary skull," fifteen thousand years old, strewn along the coast of southern Africa. "Premature birth of the European," "succumbed to a rough environment," "what a surprise for the archaeologists," "hyperdevelopment of the Caucasian type," also an enlarged brain volume—presumably, therefore, an intellectual life, mental elaborations of sensory impressions, poetry—steers instead of roses, conch cadenzas in place of radio—the mystery grew.

I take the liberty, in this context, of mentioning a gentleman who regularly honored my establishment with his presence. A truly distinguished figure, though I never learned his profession—perhaps he had been a diplomat or an artist who was holding himself back at this time. A remark on social life: the times were such that rapprochements in conversation took place even between separate classes and professional groupings; need, the great leveler, had made everyone equal. The future preoccupied us in equal measure; we were facing new worries, were threatened by new wars. An elegant man, then, always *tiré à quatre épingles,* he'd been around, a grand-seigneural globetrotter who had regularly rushed from Deauville to Biarritz every first of August, and had driven those famous coaches with the silver gas pedals from London to Ascot for seven years wearing a long, light gray tuxedo and a light gray hat with a black band, and had also been active on the grounds and behind the dogs. I shall cite one of our conversations:

"When I come to you through what used to be streets and see those malicious, pinched, and yet empty faces on the way, these ugly faces, I always think: Considering we are related, it's sad, but from a historical point of view, how logical and how true! A people that wants to make world politics but can't keep to the terms of a treaty, wants to colonize but hasn't mastered any languages, wants to play the middleman but is engaged on a Faustian quest—no

distance, no rhetoric—when they see an elegant man they call him
a fop—and wherever you look they're applying themselves en masse,
their opinions come with fat behinds—they don't know how to fit
into any association, they'd stand out in any club—for three decades
they may have had money, but that's really not enough for truly
well-tended lawns—did you read what Bülow[1] wrote about the
interiors of Friedrichsruh:[2] not one beautiful painting, no sizeable
library, no ornamented ceilings, no Gobelins or oriental rugs. Homer's sun never smiled on this house, and the splendor of the Italian
Renaissance, which had cast a reflection on at least a few northern
German castles like Tegel[3] and the Goethe-House, was lost here.
And, I should add, everything's bare and destitute like the landscape
around Fehrbellin. Individualists in the provincial sense, dissatisfied
with everything, bad losers—walking through the streets nowadays
you see dust rising everywhere, but it's not the light white dust of
the Mediterranean countries that covers your Chrysler with snow,
it's not the bright happy ash of crumbling Hermes figures and tired
Aphrodites wafted again over roses and oleanders."

"A world of compulsion, this whole political world of today, a
world under the sway of the divining rod from the Antarctic to the
Erzgebirge: Uranium, pitchblende, isotope 235! Far- and deep-
reaching neurosis! *Zoon politikon*—a Greek blunder, a Balkan idea!
Whoever makes a plea for the political world is surely being ca-
pricious. If you were to consider how many individual fates were
affected and destroyed because a uniform failed to arrive in time
for a great king to perform a visit—or because a boat showed up
an hour late, having suffered some damage on the way, thereby
disgruntling the emperor at the very start of the conversation—if
you took this into consideration, you would think twice about the
merits of this kind of caprice. If you had any idea what series of
accidents contribute to an empire's maintaining its policy, its perhaps rationally conceived farsightedness, in a halfway stable condition for just three generations through all the embassy palaces,
enterprises, regattas, revues, plebiscites; if you knew what series of
lucky coincidences of unimaginable variables are needed to make

1. Bernhard Fürst v. Bülow (1849–1929), as Chancellor (1900–1909) one of the
successors of Bismarck.
2. Estate of Bismarck near Hamburg.
3. Villa of Wilhelm v. Humboldt (1767–1835) in Berlin.

this possible, you would think more than twice about it. And if then you were to give serious thought to the question of just what is the content of this political world—namely, progress, for instance from the wheel to the guillotine, this humane progress that so greatly facilitated the first European genocide of a social class in the French Revolution—or the importation of African slaves into tropical America by a Jesuit padre who wanted to save the indigenous Indios—but how this slave trade stood godfather to the whole of Western civilization by means of the so-called Assiento-rights which Madrid sold to Genuese, Frenchmen, Englishmen for thirty years— from the dark bellies of these ships flowed gold, flowed treasures, flowed Piccadilly and the Ville lumière—flowed the potato—and then the bombastic abolition of this slavery, the handwringing over the niggers, and today the North Borneo Company spews contract- coolies and Kanakas from the same kind of ship-belly into the lead mines and rubber plantations of Insulinde, creating the foundations for Albert Hall concerts and the happy splendor of summer resi- dences—a blunder! And when I retrospectively add that within the political world, the blowpipe is superior to the Colt, since it doesn't betray the killer, and the dugout canoe does not have to contend with submarines, at most with crocodile snouts—and when I finally prognostically ask you to let the inner face of white colonization appear before your mental eye: first the whip across the dappled blood and petroleum on the mosquito puddles, then tar and steam- rollers for the highway from Balboa to Colon, and in the third generation the colored gentleman playing his baseball in the Wash- ington Club, dividing the world into 'remarkable' and 'shocking,' and taking part in the 'fishing, swimming, shooting, and hunting' of the unitarian mayonnaise from Palm Beach to Havana—do you follow me?"

I followed him; indeed I was fascinated. In the same way, little Pfordte of the Hotel Atlantic in Hamburg, a former waiter, was frequently included in the conversations of his most important guests, and old Pinnow had not just gone down to the cellar to fetch burgundy and Lachrimae Christi on good and on bad days; there were human ties connecting him with the great soloist in the woods of Saxonia.[4] That's how it was with this gentleman: I took his

4. Reference to Bismarck.

remarks as a sign of recognition for my satisfactory service. He continued:

"Please do not think, sir, that I do not have a feeling for the great hours of history. It's 11:30 on 2 September 1899; Kitchener's putting his field-glasses back in their case with a calm gesture; the battle of Omdurman has been won; thirty thousand Dervishes dead or wounded; the Mahdi vanquished: for forty years the Sirdar prepared for this hour, and England with him; Gordon is avenged—very well, I understand that. Much the same thing in Königgrätz when Moltke waves his silk cloth and the empire is born—all right, it didn't last long, but so what: fine! But in the meantime, modern physics and the old religion, existentialism and paleontology have directed our attention to transmundane perspectives and found a language for infinite spaces, distances, eternities, and fatalities as well, and now we're supposed to cling to these one or two continents, attach our whole existence to these fleeting and quickly outdated floors of the earth, entrust the few hours of our existence to a government apparatus, allow a state to order us to do a good job—how contradictory all that is!

"Don't think you could confirm or dispute my views, sir. Rest assured that for me the *consensus omnium* is little more than a cabbage butterfly of the sort that flutters about any peasant's garden. If you should wish to hear the maxims of my life, they would be the following: Number one: Take stock of the situation. Number two: Reckon with your defects and rely on your resources, not your slogans. Number three: Instead of perfecting your personality, perfect every one of your works. Blow the world as glass, as a breath from a pipe-tube: the stroke with which you complete everything: the vases, the urns, the lekythoi—this stroke is yours and is decisive. Number four: Fate only interferes with mediocrities, those above them conduct their lives by themselves. Number five: If someone accuses you of estheticism or formalism, observe him with interest: he is the caveman, his words express the sense of beauty inherent in his clubs and loincloths. Number six: Take an occasional dose of bromine; it cushions the brainstem and regulates the affects. Number seven: Once more take stock of the situation."

He concluded:

"Part of this situation, if you allow yourself to be affected by it, is that you find yourself surrounded by a human type that hasn't found its expression and cannot find it—because of the state-organized destruction of everything essential. If a dramatist wants to see his play performed, he has to create conflicts, but there is only one modern conflict: the one between freedom and the state, and so the author has no choice except to draw on rabbit hutches or stolen milk canisters or hotel apartments for his enterprise. If in a modern novel you read patronymics like Burckhardt or Hallstrom, it makes you sick because they're all nothing but Mullers and Schulzes and whatever happens to them is as general as can be. Intra-individual conflict is extinct, and so is any form of centrifugal expression. By pasting a beard on his face, the actor may afford himself the opportunity to transfer his existential monotony to a so-called character; so he raises his right arm and then the left; that takes care of expression; and if he shakes both extremities it signifies screams and creaturely writhings, but he's really just plundering corpses and showing off. Contemporary man has one trait: he is centripetal—presumably a way of protecting the core; he holds his hand in front of the candle, he lives in a veiled light.

Man is in a completely different place from his syntax; he is far ahead of it. Modern man does not take account of the past or the future. The sentence he's writing at the moment must contain everything, perhaps the paragraph, and in the painter's case it may be the picture; but everything reaching over and beyond that is a product of incapacity and counts on the indulgence of others. The artist is the only one who comes to terms with things and is in a position to judge them. All the other types just go on wetting the problems, wetting them from one generation to the next, for centuries, until they stagnate and rot, until (speaking from an evolutionary point of view) brains are transformed and nature takes over—in short, an enterprise unworthy of human striving. Therefore I say: the stroke against the tube, the stroke that solves everything—therefore I say: the glassblower."

Thus spoke Herr von Ascot. My rendition may have been a bit rambling. But if two volumes can be devoted to the history of the formerly thornless olive tree, published by the Heidelberg Academy of Science, and several works on the dark-brown eye pigmentation of the flour moth Ephestia, as well as an encyclopedia concerning extracts of blowfly pupae, one may be permitted to quietly take note of such calmly expounded views. I have always lived in such a way as to make myself a large brain by reading, by taking notes, and by means of various mnemonic aids, and it was into this vessel I now conveyed the gentleman I've described. How scorchingly hot those days were! But I had known different days too, gentle summers, the flower beds unimaginably colorful; it made you quiet and the eternities passed by, everything gathering into silence and dream, and you could see what was separate. Similarly now, as I mentally went over the above remarks with their perhaps occasional contradictions.

For one could actually already see into many a distance. Everything was already very close together; there were times when all the sails were right next to each other: those of Salamis and those of the Mayflower and those of the regattas of Cannes. The rose went on its own sweet path, and filled but a single gaze with all its umbels: from Asia through the gardens of Midas, yard-high on the marble floors through Cleopatra's feasts, and on went the rose, losing in odor and sweetness, and became the Black Rose in Finland and the Rose of the Dead elsewhere and elsewhere again the oil-rose—and now the whole path filled but a single gaze.

The gaze back! But the forward gaze also knew what the hour had struck; it saw the riddles of the path, but couldn't unveil anything. Even in the wasteland of this destroyed city, the scorching waterless heat, the thoughts without companions, the monologues that weren't even new—even faced with all this, which really should, in a manner of speaking, have obliged the forward gaze to come up with more sophisticated results—it always discerned only this: that either everything was nothing or everything was something. This latter proposition, however, it could never embrace, due to its constitution, its mood, its optical instrument of registration, quite aside from the fact that the condition of this latter mechanism amounted to a complete moral dereliction within the individual system, a promiscuity, a formal leveling that was aboriginally and teleologically identical with the void.

The intellectual fluid had assumed a catastrophic quality; it was one of those essences that were called "inner" ones in recent centuries, but which were now used up, empty, collapsed—a few furs of skinned cats were still disintegrating in some corner. And the "outer," which sent certain signs in advance and perhaps came closer at some time, did not have any depth yet, probably didn't have any at all; it had other dimensions which no one had explored yet.

The hopelessness of this fluid which saturated the continent with thought had long been recognized; nevertheless, the countries were going full blast to get it back in shape. It was in this sense that I asked, earlier: Is thought compulsive? And now I ask further: Is there a seriousness in things? Are there features engraved in them, rules and regulations, letters of marque and seizure—no, they are an alien world, insulated, indifferent, with cold shoulders even. How, then, does one meaningfully manipulate them into a structural unity, apply mental operations upon them, complementations, discriminations, juggle them conceptually? Why does one have to be in agreement, establish proof and confirmation? Or does anyone seriously believe that any sort of identity could be experienced by this method? What are the features of one who claims to find his necessity in this?

They are the features of a local celebrity, and the most obvious thing about him is that far from needing an identity, he categorically evades any substantial answer. For him, to be asked for an answer is a degradation in rank. This kind of thinking has no intention of answering the question of what life or heredity or the nature of matter are; it's thought pursued as an end in itself, it mirrors questions, but as an eye it is blind. It gratifies itself and lets everyone watch, and whoever watches, knows exactly that something utterly abnormal is being performed here, but there's no more strength anywhere to stop it, for that would require the presence of a will to bring about a new corporeal reality with more sublime intellectual requirements and a genuine ritual of identification, but the race is too exhausted for that.

For this reason, I often thought of emigrating and settling on a continent where a different kind of thinking prevailed. My notes indicated Lhasa (its conquest by the English in 1904, incidentally, was one of their more farsighted political excursions). There sits the Tobden-Lama on seven yellow silk cushions, the King of the Word, The Ocean of Wisdom. The continent is dominated by prayer mills with and without bells, prayer cylinders revolving around an axial rod, prayer wheels up to five meters in diameter in houses especially built for this purpose, wind- and water-driven prayer machines. Conch trumpets, long trumpets that have to be borne by four men, kettle drums, clarinettes, more than a quarter of the world striving to reach this place, Chinese, Mongolians, Buriats, Indians, Turkmenians, from Lake Baikal, from the Caucasus, from the Volga, from Siberia. All the caravan roads converge here. *Om mani padme hum:* oh, jewel in the lotus, amen—everyone prostrate in the dust. Here the world of things is external, they don't weigh as much, no one is trying to establish any so-called connections between them; the people collect horse dung or yak dung, and fallen fruit, not for the sake of structural unity but for fuel. However: Take stock of the situation! However, I said to myself right away, the Lamas' orchestras make an extremely shrill music—even for someone who comes from a land as tolerant of music as mine, this would be unbearable; listening to drums beating day and night, and to monks singing at their work or in lock-step, on the pasture, in the bazaars, kettle-drum symphonies, church-father syncopations; it's supposed to bring incalculable benefit, but for me it would be too much. Their cosmetic culture, too—for example, never washing one's face with water, only greasing one's face with butter—is something I could never support, given the nature of my establishment, which is dedicated to modern hygiene and subject to the jurisdiction of the board of health. "Jewel in the Lotus"—an advertising slogan for one of my balsamic products, but concrete relations with the Karakoram: impossible! Thus I found myself confronted with two quite opposite forms of thought, and I was neither willing nor able to commit myself to either.

In my search across the continents I had also cast a glance on the religions, which had caused Nietzsche so much suffering. How passé all that was! Flora and Fauna exchanged places here too. There were religions without the concept of God, without any of those conceptions of divinity around which Europe had wound its way upward in centuries of such stubborn controversy, while among them it was Buddhism, the greatest of all, which knew neither God nor immortality nor an individual soul—those experiences that, in our climes, provided the foundation for the inner lives of our predecessors; so this, too, had been a regional mood with monologues, dialogues, sacrifices, benefices, looking back upon which, today, fills one with melancholy like the memory of a life lived on the stage. If this was the most sacred of all that was given to man, why was this, too, so changeful, contradictory, so needful of theses and antitheses, born of stone in one instance and of a virgin in another; how had doubt even become possible, faced with a creature like this, from what background did he emerge—given this state of affairs, it was only too understandable if today little weight was accorded to that which once clove to religious faith. And finally, disenchantment came even to that idea which was so frequently cited with such emotion, and which was to be decked out today with historical tasks of supposedly primary importance—*Humanity:* there have been high cultures, close to our own, without any humanity: the Egyptian, the Hellenic, the Mayan and Yucatan cultures, the latter with music of the most sublime sadness, the music of a matured, overripe people conscious of its decline, music of pure gold; in short, whether my glance fell on mirror-thinking or yak dung or scholastic controversies and historical tasks, all it could see was cat furs everywhere, and if at the outset I said euphemistically that the continent was shaking, it was surely something more than a tectonic quake whose genuine symbols were these ruins that surround us—presumably the Royal Air Force never dropped its bombs.

I am convinced that the above facts are well known to mature individuals among the educated circles; they will find them banal, but I had to experience my overviews gradually. This cost me some supplementation of a bodily kind, which I shall mention. I remember an instance from my youth. I was standing by the harbor of Santos. On my left the Hotel Guaruja, whose gambling casinos had been closed down for several months—the *jeu* was taking place in one of the nearby villas. The beach was empty, the tide was out, some cars were chasing about on the sand, which had dried immediately—it was that firm—and on the right a German steamship was leaving the quay, traveled upstream a bit, and entered the open sea, and beyond was Europe; I shuddered.

The steamship had polo horses on board, they would be galloping and trotting in Surrey or nowadays perhaps in Frohnau, and I saw the playing fields, the exquisite committees on the ponies and on the grass, one was as beautiful as Adonis, another superhuman like Holofernes, a third indifferent like Diogenes, nabobs from cities built around wells, and others from concrete skyscraper cities, and then the women, a subject I'm versed in, I decorate them, carnation-scented perfume, clouds of incense extracts, summer hats: straw and a rose of black tulle—this casual something whose artless candor means so much to us. Parasols gaudy as parrots, saccos of wonderful vanilla-ice-cream-colored balloon silk—they were flown in on an airplane. But behind these polo fields my gaze met with similar scenes, an evening by the Nile, where the club of the masters of "incomparable living" convenes for a festival, the Egyptian woman had just dropped the pearl in the wine and seven dromedaries laden with melons were made to lie down. Then the Provence, the courts with the troubadours, the feasts where violets were tossed—then a Grecian scene: beautiful naked Sileni, barrels with red wine, fruit-bearing hands, lips full of grapes, everything in motion, Venus laid down the sea shell, and a shepherdess raises a flute. And as the images passed by in succession, I saw over my continent a commotion of lurching figures, a continent utterly saturated with falling and bending, with sinking down, the individual appearances divesting themselves of their forms within me, no doubt a regressive tendency: to turn into water, seek out the lowest level which everyone avoids—a completely anti-European tendency, close to the Tao.

A strong panic force was active within me, urging me to establish immediate union with the world of things, to leave behind the stigmata of the centuries, rouse to rebirth the buried, infanticidally drowned unity of being, and consign the occidental phantoms of space and time to oblivion. Here on the beach of Santos, in the company of a European! I had read that Plato originated the idea of so-called anamnesis, according to which everything within us is remembrance, that our life was not what we saw and did, but what was within us and which we were destined to give rise to in thoughts and images and lend it expression. Also a Greek idea, but completely opposed to the above-mentioned Balkan idea! A doctrine of primordial experience, this doctrine under the plane trees before which he lay with Phaidon, these white trees, heralds of the well where one could unharness and water the animals and moisten one's own lip to the choiring of cicadas. I often experienced such states of anamnesis, even long after leaving Santos and the surrounding fever-holes; in fact, I was occasionally able to induce them, and they became the light-effects of my existence and of its inner surveys.

"You must have nothing to do"—that was the regular response of clients and acquaintances with whom I cautiously broached these subjects. Of course I had nothing to do; what was there for me to do, the business to pay the rent and black-market dealings—but what to do, faced with this overpowering humanity, within which my idea stood in relation to their historical idea as 1 to 20 million—what to do—but when I suddenly see the sails above all the seas and waters, white and brown and many-hued, the sails of Salamis, of the Mayflower and possibly some from Lake Titicaca, from prehistoric times to the meetings at Cowes: was that nothing—that, I distinctly felt, was what I had to do.

One has to be honest no matter what the risk; incidentally, what dangers do these continents have to offer, bourgeois dangers; death is too far outside the human sphere to be degraded to the level of danger—so, one must be honest, and therefore I admitted to myself that the only fragments of soul I was completely certain of were this disintegration which annulled the hour and staked everything on one card and played that card, soberly at first and then with passionate abandon, heedless of gain and loss. And from there I found a new connection to Herr von A., to his glassblower, and to a statement he often added to something he had said, which I often caught but whose painful meaning I began to discern only after some time. It went as follows: "All this is valid only in the context of my words"—only for his own few words did their meaning have any validity! The situation wasn't such that one could speak for others, or to others, the sentences barely reached across a room; it was for oneself that one brought forth forms and images.

Out there the world in its intellectual disintegration, in here the ego with its historical failure. And then the doctrine of the plane trees and the glassblower's high esthetic: the incandescent stream and then the blow against the pipe, a breath—and then the brittle walls in a web of nothing but shadow and light. "Is not everything but clay in which we playfully search for gods"—someone else's voice calling, one of the great ones of the moment, upon whom it was worth one's while to look back, and whose work permitted us to believe that all destinies do not end. You step back into the shadows, but some part of you will remain. And though what remains of you be merely vases and glasses released by your breath, not bas-reliefs and flights of sculpted figures, though your works be of lesser worth, may you too endure in the land into which you are drawn by your dreams and where you exist in order to silently bring to completion the tasks that were given to you.

(Written 1947, published 1949)   *Translated by Joel Agee*

Letter from Berlin, July 1948

(To the editor of a South-German monthly)

Berlin, Summer 1948

... In answer to your suggestion that I send a contribution to the *Merkur,* I should like to make the following remarks: I am in the peculiar position of having been banned and excluded from literature since 1936, even today remaining on the list of undesirable authors. Thus I cannot bring myself to come before the public after so long with some contribution that might, perhaps, fit into the framework of a periodical with a set policy and accord with the taste of an editor licensed[1] within certain intellectual limits. I would have to insist on myself deciding exactly the nature and scope of the contribution, and make a point of its representing my new ideas. ...

For in the past years I have written several new books that have widened my own experience, but which would not meet with approval in the German literary and cultural arena. ... Lest this give you mistaken ideas, I add that my *Fragebogen*[2] is satisfactory; as countless inquiries and investigations into my professional record have shown, I did not belong either to the Party or to any of its subsidiary organizations, I am not affected by the law—which makes it all the more grave that certain circles argue against my readmission to literature.

I do not know who belongs to these circles, and I have not taken any step towards getting in touch with them. The wings of fame

1. This refers to the Military Government licensing of publishers in occupied Germany.
2. Questionnaire used in denazification proceedings after 1945.

are not white, as Balzac says; but if, like myself for the last fifteen years, one has been publicly referred to as a swine by the Nazis, a halfwit by the Communists, an intellectual prostitute by the democrats, a renegade by the emigrants, and a pathological nihilist by the religious, one is not particularly keen on pushing one's way out in front of that public again—all the less if one does not feel any inner bonds with it. For my own part, I have, as a matter of fact, not failed to keep abreast of the literary productions of the last three years, and my impression is this: here in the West, for the last four decades, the same set of brains has been discussing the same set of problems with the same set of arguments, resorting to the same set of causal and conditional clauses and arriving at the same set of either conclusions, which they call synthesis, or inconclusions, which they call a crisis—the whole, by now, seems pretty well worked to death, like a hackneyed libretto; it seems petrified and scholastic, a stereotype of stage-props and dust. A nation, or a West, hoping for a new lease on life—and there are signs pointing to the possibility of such a new lease on life—cannot be regenerated by these means.

A people is regenerated by an emanation of spontaneous elements, not by conservative care and chinstraps applied to historicizing and descriptive elements. Among us, however, the latter fill the public space. And as the background to this process I see something that, if I put it into words, you will regard as catastrophic. The fact is that in my view the West is doomed not at all by the totalitarian systems or the crimes of the SS, not even by its material impoverishment or the Gottwalds[3] and Molotovs,[4] but by the abject surrender of its intelligentsia to political concepts. The *zoon politikon*, that Greek blunder, that Balkan notion—*that* is the germ of our impending doom. The primary importance of these political concepts has long ceased to be doubted by this brand of club-and-congress intelligentsia; its efforts now are limited to tail-wagging and making itself as acceptable as possible. This applies not only to Germany—which even in this respect is in a particularly difficult, almost excusable position—but equally to all other European in-

3. Klement Gottwald (1896–1953), led Communist coup d'etat in Czechoslovakia in 1948.
4. Vyacheslav Molotov (1890–1986), until 1952 Soviet Secretary of Foreign Affairs; first delegate to the UN in 1945.

telligentsias; only from England one occasionally hears a different tune.

Let us now cast a brief glance at these political concepts, and what they contain by way of degenerative and regenerative substance. Democracy, for instance—as a principle of government the best, but in practical application absurd! Expression is not achieved by majority vote, but, on the contrary, by disregarding the election returns; it is wrought by the act of violence in isolation. Or humanitarianism, an idea that the public invests with a positively numinous character—of course, one should be humane, but there have been great civilizations, among them some very close to us, which did not put this idea into practice at all: Egypt, Greece, Yucatan; its secondary character within the framework of productivity, its anti-regenerative trend, is obvious. All that is primary arises explosively: the leveling-off and the final polishing come about later—this is one of the few indisputable findings of modern genetics. The mutations of the entelechy are discontinuous, not historical. This is a universal law. But among us, wherever in the sphere of the mind a sign appears of anything primary, any volcanic element, the public intervenes with abortion and destruction of the germ-cell; the above-mentioned set appears with its club debaters, its round-table chairmen and members, its stump orators, issuing manifestoes, collecting signatures in the names of past and future, of history, of provision for grandchildren, of mother and child. The social philosophers, the interpreters of cultural values, the phenomenologists of crisis flock together, denouncing, eliminating, exterminating—and of course the editors-in-chief in their big press limousines, the professional patchers-up of perineal ruptures, which now, as usually, unfortunately occur before parturition—and all this in defense of democracy and humanitarianism. So why all this claptrap about the West and its rejuvenation and crisis, when all they want renewed is what has long been there—useful within its limits, but as a regenerative principle in terminal or crucial hours portending only atrophy and slackened forms?

The situation is deplorable, for there are new elements in existence and the West would like to take a bold new plunge. For me there is no doubt that a cerebral mutation is going on, held down by all that is called public, guided by the state-controlled extermination of all entity. And here the tragedy begins. The public is right, it is historically right. For the elements indicate an entity that has destructive new features, always new and frightening features of the depigmented Quaternary—man is something different from what the past centuries believed, from what they assumed, and in his new intellectual constructions he will allot the Western idea of history the same place as Voodoo or the black magic of the shamans.

It is not my job to bring my own tragic ideas forward against this public. I bear my thoughts alone; according to their law, one who oversteps his own inner frontier in search of universality will in this hour seem uncalled for, un-existential, and peripheral. The objections to these thoughts I also bear alone. Estheticism, isolationism, esotericism—"the migration of the intellectual cranes over the heads of the people"—indeed, I am a specialized ornithologist for this sort of migration, this migration that harms no one, which everyone can look up to, gaze after, and yield his dreams to. So they turn against that bestial monism which insists that everything must fit together, that everything must be there for everyone without inner effort, without setbacks, without the experience of failure, without the sort of resignation that determines one's bearing. And then they aim at a process that seems to me to be drawing near: the coming century will exert a compulsion on the world of men, will confront it with a decision one can neither dodge nor emigrate from—it will permit no more than two types, two constitutions, two forms of reaction: the active and ambitious and those waiting in silence for the transformation, the historical type and the profound type, criminals and monks—and I plead for the black cowls.

And so ends my letter, for the length and nature of which I apologize. You gave me a friendly wave of a glove, and I have replied with something like a bull whip. But let me repeat: I do not generalize, I do not extend my own existence beyond my constitution. I simply want you to gather from these lines that my fear of not being published again cannot be great. My nihilism is universal, it carries—it knows of the unfathomable transformation.

And so farewell, and greetings from this blockaded city without electric power, from the very part of the city which, in consequence of that Greek blunder and the resulting historical world, is on the brink of famine. Written in a room of many shadows, where there is light for two hours out of twenty-four; for a dark, rainy summer, incidentally, robs the city of its last chance of brief happiness, and the spring lays autumn over these ruins. But it is the city whose brilliance I loved, whose misery I now endure as that of the place where I belong, the city in which I lived to see the Second, the Third, and now the Fourth Reich, and from which nothing will ever make me emigrate. Indeed one might prophesy a future for it now: tensions are developing in its matter-of-factness, changes of pace and interferences are developing in its lucidity, something ambiguous is starting up, an ambivalence such as centaurs or amphibia are born from. Finally, let us thank General Clay,[5] whose Skymasters will, I hope, convey this letter to you.

(1949)   *Translated by Ernst Kaiser and Eithne Wilkins*

5. Lucius D. Clay (1897–1977), deputy to Eisenhower in the Military Government of Germany since 1945, and as such responsible for the "Berlin Airlift."

Part Two

ESSAYS

The Problem of Genius

The modern science of pathography—that is the name given to the psychiatric study of the lives of famous men, collected in the works of Kretschmer and Lange-Eichbaum[1]—employs evidence furnished by genetics and individual statistics, which, if examined in the light of a certain sociological hypothesis, leads to the development of one of the most remarkable ideas. It has to do with the problem of genius—with its central problem; it concerns one of the most passionately disputed subjects known to mankind, of primary interest for the past two thousand years—ever since Socrates declared that madness was not necessarily an evil but the source of the greatest benefits that had befallen Greece, and ever since Plato taught that the song of the merely reasonable man is ineffectual compared to that of a man enraptured. The issue is: genius and madness.

Let us not begin our investigation by defining who is a genius and who is merely gifted and talented—that would be fruitless. Let us take as our point of departure the fact that the spirit of our time has designated a fairly precisely delimited group of names as geniuses, perhaps 100 or 150, most of them dead, most of them men, few of them scientists, some of them generals, most of them artists, poets, philosophers, and various combinations of these. The framework encompassing them is huge; it reaches from Plato to Baudelaire, from Weininger to Goethe, from Menzel to Palestrina. Most of them left behind documents of an artistic or literary nature; one

1. Ernst Kretschmer (1888–1964), psychopathologist, author of *Körperbau und Charakter* (1921); Wilhelm Lange-Eichbaum (1875–1950), author of *Genie, Irrsinn und Ruhm*.

of them dyed his hair green, another cut off his left ear as payment for a bordello; some were military leaders who burst through the gates of all nations, noblemen, poorhouse dwellers, hermaphrodites; some were still boys.

Who were they, where did they come from, who were their families, what do we know of their biology? First of all, they were not made of common clay; their history shows that they were more likely to die in the gutter than to be born in it. For genetic science has shown old, highly cultivated, talented families to be among the most frequent preconditions for the appearance of genius. Not just in those famous and exceptional families that produced the greatest talents for four or five generations—the Bachs in Germany, the Couperins in France, the Bernoullis in Switzerland, the Strausses in Austria—genetic science finds that generally, intellectual talent is inherited along with physical qualities. It is therefore possible for genius to be bred, as it were, within certain limits, but we must immediately add that it cannot be inherited. In order to examine these matters more closely, Galton, a cousin of Darwin, conducted extensive genealogical studies and calculated that a person from a highly talented family is 100 times more likely than the average human being to have a great man among his relatives. In America, Woods examined the family relationships of thirty-five hundred well-known Yankees, and while any average American citizen had one chance in 500 of being closely related to one of these famous figures, the statistical probability of these important men being related to each other was one in five. This peculiar fact could also be expressed as follows: these significant Americans are 100 times more related to each other than they are to other Americans. We find a quite similar situation in German intelligence-breeding. For example, the close blood relationship between a majority of Swabian poets and thinkers has been proven. The Burckhardt-Badili's family tree shows the common ancestral roots of Schelling, Hölderlin, Uhland, and Mörike, and further family connections extend from these four to Hauff, Kerner, Hegel, and Mozart. Goethe's relationship to Lucas Cranach is well known and has been firmly established by genealogical studies.

In Germany, certain professional groups are more strongly involved in the breeding of talent and genius than others. A demonstrably high incidence of great musicians and painters can be found in the genealogical tables of families in art-related professions. This is true of the following famous musicians, in whose genealogical milieu we find cantors, music teachers, organists, conductors, members of orchestras: d'Albert, Beethoven, Boccherini, Brahms, Bruckner, Cherubini, Hummel, Löwe, Lully, Mozart, Offenbach, Rameau, Reger, Schubert, Richard Strauss, Vivaldi, Stamitz. The list of famous painters with parents or ancestors who worked as engravers, lithographers, jewelers, decorative painters, includes Böcklin, Cranach, Dürer, Holbein, Menzel, Piloty, Raffael, L. Richter, Hans Thoma. A second group that is of exceptional importance for the breeding of genius in Germany are old families of scientists and churchmen. In them, the selection of talented individuals was guided for centuries by a humanistic viewpoint with an emphasis on the development of the gifts of language and logical abstraction. This orientation of talent proved to be so one-sidedly and sharply defined that one can almost describe it as a self-contained hereditary mass which provided the principal genetic foundation for the specifically German type, the combination of poet and thinker or scientist. Schelling and Nietzsche, Lessing, Herder, Schiller, and Hölderlin belong in this group.

It seems that the more disparate the genetic material of the two parents, the greater the likelihood of providing a basis for the formation of genius: people of alien racial stock, Slavic and German blood, in the cases of Nietzsche, Leibniz, R. Wagner; or a marked difference of character and constitution, such as an extreme schizothyme and cyclothyme type—in short, anything aiming at unmixability, incompatibility, bastardization, unresolved tension. The same tendency was surmised by Reibmayr, and modern genealogical studies have confirmed his view: genius is most frequently produced in areas and landscapes known for their blood and race mixing. If we mark on a map of Europe the birthplaces of the most important geniuses as well as the sites of the most important and lasting cultural monuments, the overwhelming significance of the Nordic-Alpine blood- and race-mixing zone will become powerfully evident. This Nordic-Alpine zone comprises the greater part of France, further, Flanders, Holland, the middle and southern part of the German-speaking areas including the Rhineland and Thuringia, and finally upper and central Italy. This is the ancestral zone of modern European culture and the central source of its geniuses. The races, then, play the part of an expanded parentage, and the genetic tension begins when alien or not easily combined materials from widely disparate zones come together with an urge to mix. A term has even been coined to describe this relationship: *genetic enmity*.

Naturally, we must also mention that again and again we find cases where genius looms out from the mass of the people, a lucky hit in an unsuspected place, without any preparatory breeding, for example, without there being any evidence of an especially high talent or vocational predisposition in the family (Kant, Fichte, Hebbel, Handel). The law of probability accounts for such occasional chance combinations of hidden talent drawn from a pool of millions of people. But according to the science of genetics, these accidents would not suffice to cover a nation's demand for leadership.

This gives rise to a question that is particularly important for our investigation: At what point, under what conditions does genius manifest itself within a family? The answer is scientifically obvious: when the family begins to degenerate. When after generations of accomplishment a descent begins—bankruptcy, suicide, criminality—the hour of genius has struck as well. This degeneracy of the genius-producing family announces itself either in the genius's own generation or in the generation preceding his. It occurs with particularly surprising frequency and severity in the case of the very greatest geniuses—we need only consider the families of Goethe, Byron, Beethoven, Bach, Michelangelo, Feuerbach. But let us dispense with the formulations "genius" and "madness," since insanity is a psychiatric-diagnostic concept, and let us instead speak of genius and degeneracy, while noting that degeneracy is neither clinical idiocy and delirium nor a cultural and nervous contradistinction to the rustic majority type. Let us say that degeneracy is a combination of a physical minus variant and a psychic occurrence which makes a life of the majority type of the species impossible and puts the continued existence of the individual in question, if it does not annul it altogether. But let us immediately add that psychopaths as such are minus-people as regards the orientation of their intellectual and social achievement, that the vast majority of psychotics are waste material incapable of high achievement; for example, that, for the group we are discussing, something else, something we shall leave undefined, must be added in order to arrive at the type that concerns us here. Thus, to sum up the question of genius and degeneration, we arrive at a first position: yes, genius is a particular form of degeneracy that involves a release of productivity. Proof: the position of genius in the generational sequence, its occurrence at a point in time where the psychopathic-degenerative process clearly and generally begins to make its appearance in the phenotypes.

Let us now turn to the biographic material, which is not journalistic gossip but strictly scientific source material. Lange-Eichbaum's and Kretschmer's conclusions are complemented by those of Binder, a Württemberg psychiatrist who began by rejecting the whole idea of genius and madness but nevertheless had no difficulty finding hundreds of geniuses afflicted with a common psychosis. Then there are the findings of Birnbaum,[2] who collected psychopathological material about 150 geniuses in his book *Documents*. And if we consider that the subtlest and most intimate things frequently go unregistered, for example, a great deal that falls in the general area of the eccentric, the socially peculiar, the crankily domestic, the secretly corporeal and mood-induced conditions; that, furthermore, there is a great deal of material that is irretrievable in the cases of people who have died—considering all this, we may estimate the implications of the following statistics.

The following suffered from outright clinical *schizophrenia:* Tasso, Newton, Lenz, Hölderlin, Swedenborg, Panizza, van Gogh, Gogol, Strindberg; while Kleist and Claude Lorrain were *latently schizophrenic.* Gutzkow, Rousseau, and Pascal were *paranoid.* The following suffered with *melancholia:* Thorwaldsen, Weber, Schubert, Chopin, Liszt, Rossini, Moliere, Lichtenberg; with *fantasies of being poisoned:* Mozart; with obsessive *thoughts of suicide:* Raimund. Platen, Flaubert, Otto Ludwig, and Moliere were subject to *attacks of hysteria.* The following died of *paralysis:* Makart, Manet, Maupassant, Lenau, Donizetti, Schumann, Nietzsche, Jules Goncourt, Baudelaire, Smetana. Kant, Gottfried Keller, Stendhal, Linné, Böcklin, and Faraday died of *arteriosclerotic dementia.* Kleist, van Gogh, Raimund, Weininger, and Garschin committed *suicide.* Forty geniuses were *homoerotically* inclined. Kant, Spinoza, Newton, and Menzel (whose testament included the famous statement: "there is a complete lack of self-made glue between me and the outer world") were cases of lifelong *asexuality.* The following were *drinkers* (and

2. Karl Birnbaum (1878–1934), wrote on criminal psychopathology.

what is meant by drinking here is not a middle-class standard of liquid intake, as in the case of Goethe, who drank one to two bottles of wine a day throughout his life, but drinking with the declared intention of getting drunk); of *opium:* Shelley, Heine, De Quincey (five thousand drops a day), Coleridge, Poe; of *absinthe:* Musset, Wilde; of *ether:* Maupassant (in addition to alcohol and opium), Jean Lorrain; of *hashish:* Baudelaire, Gautier; of *alcohol:* Alexander (who killed his best friend and mentor while drunk and who died of the effects of extreme excesses), Socrates, Seneca, Alcibiades, Cato, Septimius Severus (died in a state of drunkenness), Caesar, Mohammed II, the Great (died in delirium tremens), Steen, Rembrandt, Carracci, Barbatello Poccetti, Li T'ai-Po ("the great drunkard poet," died in alcoholic stupor), Burns, Gluck (wine, liquor, died of alcohol poisoning), the poet Schubart, Schubert (drank since he was fifteen), Nerval, Tasso, Handel, Dussek, G. Keller, Hoffmann, Poe, Musset, Verlaine, Lamb, Murger, Grabbe, Lenz, Jean Paul, Reuter (dipsomaniac), Scheffel, Reger, Beethoven (died of alcohol-induced cirrhosis of the liver). Almost all of them were unmarried, almost all were childless; happy marriages can be found only among half-a-dozen musicians and in the cases of Schiller and Herder. Many had physical malformations: Mozart had crippled atavistic ears; Scarron was a legless cripple; Toulouse-Lautrec was paralyzed in childhood; Verlaine had jug-handle ears; this one had a hydrocephalus, that one a prognathous criminal upper jaw, another a bestially receding forehead, and a fourth produced idiot children. The productive, wherever one touches it, is a mass suffused with stigmas, with intoxications, half-sleep, paroxysms: a to and fro of sexual variants, anomalies, fetishisms, impotences. Is there any such thing as a healthy genius?

There are instances of *antinomy compensated* by the most enormous intellectual power, of a *primary disharmony* that has to be overcome again and again by *intellectual* achievements: Goethe is a case in point, Schiller a similar one, also Leibniz. And yet even Goethe was, as Mobius has demonstrated, an extremely sensitive, highly irritable and emotional psychopath; in fact, he additionally suffered—and this has been proven beyond doubt—from a very slight form of cyclothemia with depressions that put a complete stop to his productivity, followed by periods of hypomania and exaggerated youthfulness. Lombroso, too, who was always looking for the *génies intègres* and counted Voltaire among them, stands corrected by contemporary findings that show Voltaire on closer examination to also have been a dangerous, irritable, and hypochondriacal psychopath. The following must also be taken into consideration: there are apparently healthy individuals whose closest relatives show classical signs of psychopathology: Hegel, for instance, was healthy, but his sister was mentally ill; Hauff's and Kerner's mothers were sisters, but the third sister was mentally ill, while the grandmother was a somnambulist; Balzac was apparently healthy, but one day his father lay down in bed without any motive and didn't get up for another twenty years: surely these are cases of latent lability; these men were apparently spared the symptoms of an already incipient genetic degeneration. But I should mention a remark of Kretschmer's to the effect that a strong dose of health and philistinism is a necessary part of the greatest genius, a part that is expressed in the enjoyment of eating and drinking, in a solidly responsible comportment, in good citizenship, in officious dignity—qualities and attitudes that lend a great genius those qualities of industry, constancy, and quiet self-containment that raise his effectiveness far above the loud and ephemeral attempts of the merely attitudinal genius. This strikes me as an excellent observation. No doubt but that the geologically extensive terrain of genius, especially epic genius, contains immobile bourgeois strata against which the demonic clashes and breaks in particularly impressive formations, and at whose borders the flowers of evil grow with particular assurance and conviction. But this does not in any way alter our thesis, for which we have now found a second position on the basis of material drawn from individual statistics: genius and degeneracy—indeed, the psychopathic element is an indispensable factor in the psychological complex which we call genius.

So: genius is sickness, genius is degeneracy; the evidence, it seems to me, is convincing. But now the question arises whether the whole problem doesn't require another twist: How does the analysis of genius and madness look when one transposes it from the biological to the sociological domain? Here we meet with an idea which pervades modern research into the question of genius, an idea which at first has something disappointing and sobering about it, but which has proven its fruitfulness and methodological persuasiveness in the most recent ground-breaking results of genius-studies; a thought which essentially opens up an even more abysmal perspective than that of the genius who directly and personally storms the heavens and succeeds in entering them, too. The idea is the following: genius is not born, it develops. Biological disposition, achievement, even success is not enough. To become a genius, something else must be added, and that is the acceptance by the group, by the people, by the spirit of the times—usually the spirit of a later time. Genius has to be experienced. One should therefore not speak of genius but of the *formation* of genius. It is a sociological process to an extreme, but one that has nothing to do with a vague metaphysical maturation of history toward the reception of individuals and ideas. It is a phenomenon of collectivistic trans-formation: at its beginning stands the historical figure and at its end, the genius. Of course they belong together, of course they have various correspondences and points of identity, but genetically they are far apart. Let us take a concrete case: Rembrandt. During his lifetime he was a respected painter, though nothing exceptional; in the second half of his life he was considered mannered and was no longer receiving commissions; finally, as is well known, he died in a poorhouse, alcoholic, after all his possessions had been impounded. After that his name was forgotten. In the 1880s he was considered a middle-range talent. Then the book by the Rembrandt-German[3] appeared, and now he became the world-historical personality and genius. A typical case of genius-formation, as seen by sociology, and it is very probable that there are other Rembrandts for whom this process did not take place. Why here, why not elsewhere? Or Walther von der Vogelweide: he was not only forgotten but was completely and absolutely unknown, his name was nonexistent until Uhland wrote the famous biography of Walther von der Vogelweide in 1822, and suddenly and abruptly he had become the greatest lyric poet of the Middle Ages. Most probably there are several such minstrels, but why he? There was, to begin with, an obvious external occasion in each case: the Rembrandt-German in one, Uhland in the other. This by itself was not enough, though. However, there was an opportunity for the above-mentioned transformational process to begin: the painter becomes visible to an era. His life is investigated: one discovers a descent from a summit, a miserable derelict old age. The

---

3. Reference to J. Langbehn, author of *Rembrandt als Erzieher* (1890).

poorhouse is a highly suggestive image, the bloated face, the dull eyes; and now the myth begins. The group sets about elaborating a theme that has been popular since the age of legends: the creator fighting for money with tooth and nail, the aged visionary for whose burial no one wants to pay, and there develops that emotional relation to the subject of one's attention which modern psychology, taking a lesson from the science of religion, calls *numinous*, a mixture of holiness and dread; and from there the election and formation of genius approaches and reaches that height which we behold today. Note that all this has nothing to do with fashion, finagling, advertisement, economics; these could provide an impetus, could play a part, but by and large the process takes place in very deep regions, close to religiosity and to the archaic rumblings of the earliest strata. Walther von der Vogelweide, on the other hand, is the vagrant and homeless wanderer, driven away from his fiefdom, which he holds in loving and faithful memory—a frequent motif in the formation of genius, for we recognize it again in Rimbaud, Verlaine, François Villon, Li T'ai-Po, the German balladeers; the chords it strikes are "fugitive and vagabond," and it bears the mark of Cain on its brow.

This is not in the least a rationalistic explanation, an antiheroic relativization, an American-style smart-aleck reduction; it's not an explanation at all but an examination of fame, its path and its dissolution in the collective. For it has turned out that fame and eventually the formation of genius are never immediately connected to achievement, *but always to something accidental,* to an outer and inner fatality. The initial situations are quite prototypical. Here is Burckhardt's description of the outward kind: "Even Erwin von Steinbach[4] or Michelangelo would not be considered the greatest architects of art history if one of them hadn't accidentally been commissioned to build the tallest of all towers and the other to build the main temple of a world religion. Phidias is not the most famous of all sculptors because he was the greatest but because he was commissioned to produce the statuary for the representative buildings of a very rich age." To rise to the top, then, one must build the highest tower or be allied with the greatest power. It is not the work as such that brings its creator fame—not even in

---

4. Thought to be the main architect of the cathedral of Strasbourg.

Michelangelo's case! But it is precisely Michelangelo, one of the most psychopathic figures in the history of art, sexually deviant and afflicted by extremely severe depressive-schizoid tendencies, who immediately directs us to the much more important inner points of departure: sickness, suicide, early death, drug addiction, criminality, abnormality, and, particularly obvious and massive in his case, psychosis. Let us now look at our statistics backwards, and suddenly the relationship of genius and madness is illuminated: though the genius carrier is degenerate, this is not sufficient for the formation of genius, which is accomplished by the collective in response to the demonic and mysterious appeal of the symptoms of degeneration.

Consider, what a peculiar position on the part of the collective! What a strange cycle it rejoins: moving into the realms of early strata with the primitive demand for the sacrificed god! Consider the colors it takes on: hues of legends and myths with their multitude of sick and misshapen gods: Odin has one eye; Thyr had one hand; Loki is lame; Höder is blind; Vidar is mute; Gunther and Wieland are lame. Consider how it adopts the muse's treatment of Homer: she took his eyes and gave him the gift of sweet song in return; he was to live in the dark, then, and know the ways of shadows. And in this sociological and genetic context, fame and genius, which are perhaps very nearly absurd from an individual, historical, and normative standpoint, acquire the character of a collective symbolism of the degenerate, of a religious aphoristics of degeneration.

Let us take cognizance of what this means! Let us consider among what worlds and what values this century took its course. They were all biological values: optimal health, optimal capacity for life and achievement, qualities favorable to the preservation of the species, reproduction not as a demand in the interests of the nation but out of a genuinely biological *furor* for everything carnal, organic, pullulant, proliferous, as a so-called triumph of supposed life; they were all values pertaining to breeding, classified according to their rank as aphrodisiacs, a lust-centered yohimbin morality, always driven by the notion of a more highly developed species. And now our examination of genius suddenly confronts us with preconditions that are opposed to these values. We are confronted with abnormality and degeneration, and it is from these that humanity receives the great suggestive impulses of art. We see a downward trend, lethal variants, and these produce a mixture of fascination and decay. Right before our eyes we see a counter-complex splitting off from the ideality of the sociological and medical norm, the only case within the scientific-hygienic-technical world where a separate counter-value develops and collects the whole gamut from enjoyment to submission, from admiration to horror. What we are witnessing is the concept of the BIONEGATIVE (Lange-Eichbaum), and we see it not only in its personal form exemplified by the naturalistic figure of the "carrier" of the quality called genius, but, much more remarkably, we see him honored, supported, and courted by the social group, by the cultural community, which is seeking something quite different from Harvey's circulation, namely, this circulation of psychopathy and minus variants—producing, in short, at its own expense, not just health but a modern mythology of intoxication and decay, and calling it genius.

*Let us recapitulate: the creative, vulcanic brains—let us call them genial—*some of them rise; some are seized by the hour; some become geniuses; many remain down under as if they had never occurred. An image forces itself upon us: here the vagabonds, the alcoholics, the poorhouse dwellers, the jug-eared, the coughers, the sick horde, and there Westminster Abbey, the pantheon and Valhalla, where their busts are kept. The pantheon constructed, the bust sculpted, not out of gratitude for their achievements (who should thank them, anyway, since what they gave was nothing but products of their own compulsions and predilections?), nor out of admiration for their fortitude (for who knows what fortitude is and how fortitude does), but rather out of a collective need for degeneration and decay, all the more emphatic in view of the enjoyment procured for the normal by the Bacchae who dance in their chains in celebration of that priceless and irredeemable victim who fell in the whirl of his own intoxication.

Tension and decay of tension—and side by side with these, the bourgeois ideologies. Monologue of creation: slabs of ice tossing their last life at each other and wounds that show their scabs in chorus—and the yohimbin society watches in a concordance of pleasure. Nobody's fault, not even tragic; just let no one say that these circles became one, that they generated each other or were logically interdependent, that genius receives a posthumous justification in the sense of a historic quality, as is claimed by the hypo-manic value-mongers of hero-apologetics: Carlyle, Emerson, the students of Ranke. Rousseau is *supposed* to have paved the way for the French Revolution, *Uncle Tom's Cabin* is *supposed* to have sparked the Civil War against the southern slave-holding states—supposed to, in the historical hindsight of journalistic biopositive mood-enhancement! Let us rather keep to what is right in front of our eyes: Did Nietzsche move or retard anything? This infinite genius, this vulcanic mountain range against the rise of mediocrity—was he effective? Not in the least! If not for his madness he might have remained unknown or been long forgotten. All these great tensions of bitterness and sorrow, these destinies of hallucination and defect, these catastrophes of fatality and freedom—useless flowers, powerless flames, and behind them the impenetrable with its bound-less No.

(1930)	*Translated by Joel Agee*

Can Poets Change the World?
Radio Dialogue

A.: In numerous essays on the role of the poet you took more or less the following position: that the poet does not influence his time, that he does not and cannot affect the course of history, because by his nature he stands outside history. Isn't this a rather absolute position?

B.: Would you have preferred it if I had said the poet should be interested in parliament, in municipal policy, in property sales, in the industrial malaise or the rise of a fifth estate?

A.: But there are a number of well-known writers who do not share your attitude of rejection and operate on the assumption that we are at a historical turning point, that a new type of humanity is evolving and that it is possible to describe a path into a completely transformed and improved future.

B.: Of course it is possible to describe a better future. There have always been utopian storytellers, Jules Verne, for example, or Swift. As for the historical turning point, I have repeatedly focused my investigations on the fact that the times are always changing, that a new human type is always evolving and that formulas like "the dawn of humanity"[1] have by now turned into concepts of an almost mythical solidity and regularity.

A.: So you consider it a mistake for a poet to participate in any discussion of social and historical issues?

B.: I consider it a pastime. I see one group of writers advocating the legalization of abortion, another trying to get rid of the death penalty. This is the type of writer who has assumed a visible position

1. Reference to *Menschheitsdämmerung* (1919), the first programmatic anthology of expressionist poetry, edited by Kurt Pinthus.

in public life ever since the Enlightenment. His agitations are of the local, his aspirations of the free-thinking kind, in which one can hear the unmistakeable echo of Voltaire's famous defense of Calas and Zola's *J'accuse*.

A.: And you do not include this literary tendency within the confines of poetry?

B.: Experience shows that it rarely finds its way into those confines. Writers whose work is aimed at empirical arrangements of civilization join the ranks of those who experience the world realistically and think of it as materially constructed and feel its effects in a three-dimensional manner; they join the technicians and warriors, the arms and legs that shift boundaries and cover the earth with wires; they move into the realm of superficial and accidental changes, while the poet possesses a fundamentally different kind of experience and strives for syntheses that are different from the practically effective and so-called progressive kind.

A.: You said: the technician and the warrior. Are they the only ones who change the world, in your opinion?

B.: They change what is susceptible to change. Yes, I do believe that the concept of the scientist, to which the other two are subordinate, is the essential and principal counterpart of the poet; the scientist who lives by a logic that is supposed to have universal validity but is actually merely lucrative; who has won recognition for a concept of truth which largely conforms with popular notions of verifiability, accessibility to general experience, and applicability; and who propagates an ethic which ensures the primacy of the mediocre. I understand that a people that has not learned anything other than to name science and art in one breath can't do otherwise than to greedily absorb that Enlightenment wisdom which always places these two words side by side, especially in a century in which science really had a vitality that presented itself as creative. But I understand even more: take a trip on a Sunday 100 kilometers north of Berlin to the realm of the Great Elector,[2] Fehrbellin,[3] and to Frederick's locations: a barren, arid landscape; it's beyond description, little villages, the living image of poverty and deprivation, veritable breeding sites for the causal drive; and you will realize

2. Friedrich Wilhelm (1640–1688), grandfather of Frederick the Great.
3. Site of the battle that drove the Swedes from Prussia in 1675.

why the creator of *Penthesilea*⁴ always had to remain an embarrassing and arrogant figure among a people that had been educated by the examples of the farming townsman and chief magistrate to make practical utility the foundation of its colorless emotions.

A.: What you mean to say, then, is that *Penthesilea* is a great work of poetry but that it hasn't had the slightest effect, either politically or socially or educationally.

B.: That is exactly what I mean to say. I mean furthermore that the next great German literary work after *Penthesilea,* Heinrich Mann's *The Small Town,* has had just as little influence, even stylistically. There is no other way to put it: works of art are phenomenal, historically ineffectual, without consequence in reality. Therein lies their greatness.

A.: Surely this is a completely nihilistic conception of poetry?

B.: If social progress is positive, absolutely. Let all the works of art which history has bequeathed you pass by in a pageant. Nefertiti and the Dorian temple, *Anna Karenina* or the song of Nausikaa in the *Odyssey*—there's nothing in these works that points beyond the work itself, nothing requiring any explanation, nothing that seeks to affect anything outside. It is this procession of silent shapes and images sunk into self-contemplation—if you want to call that nihilistic, it's the special nihilism of art.

A.: You see this procession of silent shapes—I will show you a different procession. Thirty-six thousand people with open tuberculosis living in Berlin who can't get into a sanatorium; forty thousand women who die every year in Germany of the consequences of an illegal abortion, as a direct result of the paragraph you cited. Consider the unspeakable and heart-rending struggle for education that is waged by the majority of our fellow Germans. Consider the unemployed, young men, thirty years old, who find neither work nor salary in the city, but find night-lodgers and rats in their homes instead. Consider the following document: A family of eleven; the father drinks; the mother is expecting her tenth child; the fourteen-year-old daughter buys cow's blood at the butcher's for ten pfennige and pours it over her breast hoping that this simulated hemorrhage will help her get out of her overcrowded apartment and into a TB

4. Heinrich v. Kleist.

sanatorium. This is misery, these are tears, innocent suffering, bastardizations of happiness—and the poet just watches?

B.: I don't hesitate for a moment: the poet watches. Not the author of civilization-literature and of an evening's intellectual pretexts for shifting the stage-props, the one who sits next to the minister at the banquet with a carnation in his swallow-tail coat and five wine glasses behind his plate: he signs declarations against the evils of our time. But the other one watches; he knows that the innocent misery of the world will never be removed by welfare measures, never be overcome by material improvements. Hygienic wish-intoxications of short-legged rationalists: with my pension in my heart and a heat-lamp in my house. A creation without horror, jungles without bites, nights without mares that ride their victims—no, the poet watches in the conviction, which is not to be denied in the face of any death, that he alone possesses the substance that can banish horror and reconcile the victims: sink, he cries out to them, sink, but I could also say: rise.

A.: Remarkable substance! But on the other hand—

B.: On the other hand! You believe that everyone who thinks and writes in our time must do so in the interests of the working class, has to be a Communist, lend his strength to the rise of the proletariat. Why? On what basis do you make this claim? There have always been social movements. The poor have always wanted to get to the top and the rich have always refused to step down. A horrible world, a capitalistic world, ever since Egypt monopolized the incense trade and Babylonian bankers began the money business, taking 20 percent interest on debts. Advanced capitalism of the ancients, in Asia, in the Mediterranean. Traders in the color purple forming trusts, shipping merchants forming trusts. Import-export, speculations in corn, insurance combines, insurance frauds, factories run along Tayloristic lines: this one cuts leather, that one sews coats; rent gougers, housing swindlers, warmongers with exemptions from military service for the shareholders—a horrible world, a capitalistic world. And always the counter-movements: hordes of helots in the Kyrenian tanneries, slave rebellions in the Roman era, the poor wanting to get to the top and the rich refusing to step down—a horrible world, but after three millennia of such goings-on one may be permitted to incline to the thought that all this is neither good nor bad but of a purely phenomenal nature.

The question, then, is whether it is rational or heroic or radical to pretend to the poor portion of humanity that it could be better off as a whole. The "brilliant tomfoolery of hope" with which, according to Burckhardt,[5] the nations have been misled, is it not fooling us here? That "wangling of the mass" of which Lassalle[6] spoke, is it not being attempted here? Life as an orange suspended in a tree, and whoever has a tall enough ladder can pick it and hold it in his hand all round and golden and self-contained—can this still be called knowledge? I read recently—and I am not speaking here about poverty or the unjust distribution of goods, but about a propaganda complex of the political movement—I read a work by an English national economist who says that the workers in England live in a more comfortable and worldly style than the great landowners and princes of previous centuries. He demonstrates this in detail by showing that houses used to be dark and narrow and cold; that all livestock had to be slaughtered on St. Martin's Day because it couldn't be fed through the winter; that there were countless diseases against which there was no defense. So, today the workers live the way the rich did three centuries ago, and today and in three centuries the same relationship will exist, and so forth and so on, upward and beyond and with *sursum corda*[7] and *per aspera ad astra*[8] and with dawns of humanity to boot—all of this is no longer available for individual experience; it's just a functional process of the fact of human society; it's extrahuman; so how can I be duty bound to embrace a process whose ideological makeup I perceive as one that flies in the face of reason and whose human origin began its course and took its direction far before me and far away from me and of its own accord?

No, the thought occurs to me whether it wouldn't be far more radical—because more revolutionary and far more demanding of a strong man's hardness and fitness—to teach the human race: this is how you are and you will never be otherwise: this is how you live, how you have lived, and how you will always live. He who has money gets healthy; he who has power swears the right oath; he who wields might determines what's right. That is history! *Ecce*

5. Jakob Burckhardt (1818–1897), Swiss historian of art and culture.
6. Ferdinand Lassalle (1825–1864), friend of Marx and founder of the German Socialist Party.
7. "Lift up your hearts," exhortation in the Latin Mass.
8. "Through hardship to the stars."

historia! Here's today, take its body, eat and die. This teaching strikes me as far more radical, philosophically deeper, of far greater psychological consequence than the political parties' prophesies of happiness. Indeed, it strikes me as positively fitting, after the last ten years and after everything we've been hearing about Russia, that we look all this in the eye for once: the typicality of the proletarian process; the immanence of revolutionary shock; the mere rearrangement of a power situation with an unchanged imperialistic and capitalistic tendency. But this of course requires more courage than straining to hear the dying echos of the French Revolution, draping oneself in the late colors of Darwinism, burdening the future and summoning up dreams which one expects others to realize. For the gentlemen we were discussing earlier don't go any further than writing hymns and articles. Sticking out one's neck at the moment of truth is left to the man on the street, the comrades in the labor force, the proles; the others are there to spur them on from their apartments or health spas.

A.: Let me ask you directly: Are you fundamentally in agreement with the current economic system?

B.: Let me answer you directly: I consider work a law forced upon us by creation, and I consider exploitation a function of life itself.

A.: Very cosmic indeed!

B.: But after all, I'm leaving you your technicians and warriors, your science, economic theories and literature—all the free-floating braying and bleating of civilization. And the only thing I ask for the poet is the freedom to shut himself off from a contemporaneous mass, half of which consists of disinherited small pensioners and petulant advocates of the revaluation of the mark, while the other half's made up of a bunch of Hertha- and Poseidon-swimmers: he wants to go his own way.

A.: Artistry.

B.: No, morality. Impenetrable murk of civilization faddism, ethos conceived as mere regulation of social bonds. The artist has no ethos, he's a marauder, a freeloader, an esthete. He pulls his stuff out of his sleeve; he's a fool, a bare-footer's drama yesterday, a Promethean pamphlet tomorrow. Ah, to whom can one make this clear: there was a man who wrote: for seven years I fought alone in the city and in the country, for seven years I strove for a page of prose, a verse, the way Jacob strove after Rachel! To whom shall one point out this essay by Heinrich Mann. It is about Flaubert. It describes how Flaubert, after writing so much art, wanted to write something else, something humane and good, something lovable, the cares of everyday life, the happiness of all. But it was out of the question, technically impossible. There was no way to capture it in the novelistic way of cognition; he had to go on in his style, in the yoke of his sentences, over and over into that proverbial bed which mutilates head and limbs: art. I often think, too, how enormously a man as delicate as Nietzsche must have suffered when he wrote that sentence: he who falls, give him a push as well—this hard, this brutal statement. But he had no choice, he had to board the ship. The noonday sun slept in space and time, and only one eye regarded him: infinity.[9] There was no other morality for him than the truth of his style and of his understanding, because for the poet all ethical categories converge in the category of individual fulfillment.

A.: That's truly horrible. But isn't it true that artists, from immemorial times until today, have served humanity by imitating and poetically portraying disquieting phenomena and thereby robbing them of their frightening and terrible aspects?

B.: That is precisely what I was indicating before when I spoke of substance. The poet, born by fate into the ambiguity of existence, having burst into the abyss of individuality amidst Acheronian shudders by ordering and clarifying it in images, raises it above the brutal realism of nature, above the blind and untamed desire of the causal drive, above the vulgar timidity of the lower degrees of cognition, and creates an order that is essentially lawful. This, to my mind, is the position and the task of the poet with regard to the world. You believe he should change it? But how should he change it? Make it more beautiful—but according to whose taste? Better—but according to whose morality? Deeper—but according to the measure of which insights? Where should he take the gaze with which to encompass it, the knowledge with which to lead it, the greatness with which to do justice to its goals—and who should he depend on—on her who "lives in many children," as Goethe says, "but the mother, where is she?"

9. Paraphrase of two lines from Nietzsche's poem *Nach neuen Meeren.*

A.: So he takes his measure only from within himself, pursues no goals, and serves no political trend?

B.: He follows his individual monomania, which, when it is comprehensive, produces the most extreme image of the ultimate greatness attainable by man. This greatness does not want to alter and affect anything; this greatness wants to be. Always objected to by the stupidity of rationalism, always confirmed by the geniuses of humanity itself. Of a humanity which, insofar as I can survey its destiny, has never followed convictions, but only appearances, never teachings, but only images, and whose change is proceeding from so far away that it is impossible to follow it with our eyes.

A.: So the poet writes monologues?

B.: Autonomies! What is at work here, to use a phrase of Schiller's, is the boundless roving of freedom tethered to necessity. But this necessity is transcendent, not empirical, not material, not opportunistic, not progressive: it is Ananke,[10] it is the song of the Fatal Sister: from the gorge of the depths, a just judgment. It is the secret of thinking and of the mind altogether. It strikes only a few, and poets and thinkers are in their final form identical before it. Just as that sculpture of Rodin's, *The Thinker,* standing above the entrance to the underworld, was originally called *The Poet.* The inscription at the base of the pedestal applies to both: The Titan Absorbed in a Painful Dream. Just as Nietzsche's unsurpassable image in his essay, "Philosophy in the Tragic Age of the Greeks," applies to both: "There is no custom from which they could draw sustenance or comfort"; one giant, he writes, calls out to another through the bleak intervals of the ages, and the lofty conversation of minds continues undisturbed by the frolicsome clamor of dwarfery creeping away beneath them.

(1930)   *Translated by Joel Agee*

---

10. Compulsion, coercion.

After Nihilism

In the following essays and speeches (which don't systematically deal with a common theme, because they are the response to the most various occasions and the outgrowth of all sorts of moods) two concepts nevertheless assume a foreground position, due to the constant and rather specifically directed thrust of the author's philosophical preference. The two concepts are progressive cerebration and nihilism, and they are juxtaposed, in several places, with the concept of constructive intelligence, an expression for those forces and efforts that seek to counteract the lethargizing influence of the former. Do we still have the strength, asks the author, to oppose the scientific-deterministic world view with a self that is grounded in creative freedom. Do we still have a strength drawn from the power of traditional Western thought, not from economic chiliasms and political mythologems, to break through the materialistic-mechanical form-world and to design the images of deeper worlds out of an ideality that posits itself as such, and in a measure that sets its own limits? A constructive intelligence, then, as an emphatic and conscious principle of far-reaching liberation from materialisms of every stripe—psychological, evolutionist, physical, not to mention the sociological variety—constructive intelligence as the essentially anthropological style, as the essential hominid substance which, through its mythopoetical unfolding, its eternal metaphorical irradiation, would fulfill human destiny in the unreality of light, in the phantasmic nature of all things, and pour itself out among the stars, their space and their infinity in a kind of far-flung play, commingling the genii in one's own breast with vast swarms of creative spirits in their heavens and their hells.

As for the two initial concepts, they are inseparable, connected both by content and chronology, both of them having risen into the European consciousness in the last century, the first one very recently indeed. This concept of progressive cerebration originated from a combination of anthropology and the study of the brain and was established by von Economo[1] in Vienna. According to this idea, humanity has experienced a clearly perceptible, irresistible increase of intellectualization, has, in short, become more brainy. In my essay, "The Structure of Personality," I thoroughly described the biological-organic foundation of this notion and placed it in perspective. Some characteristic details of its corresponding psychology, which could be defined as a frigidization of the ego—the direction being from affect to concept ("Cognition as Affect")—are given in the Academy speech.[2]

As for nihilism, it is a fairly well-known phenomenon, and I have contributed some observations concerning its genesis in "Goethe and Natural Science." In this essay, I demonstrate that the seventeenth and eighteenth centuries appear to have been an age when the German nation's creative life occurred in a closed spiritual space which remained undisrupted even by the internal struggles of generations and ideologies, because there was *one* faith, *one* feeling that remained untouched throughout all the changes; and that the end of this age coincided approximately with Goethe's death. The faith or feeling that prevailed at the beginning of this epoch was called God, and the feeling or faith prevailing at the end was called Nature. But a conception of nature that had been formed under the influence of Leibniz and Spinoza. Nature: a pantheistic universe, already atomized, or rather divided into monads, since the concept of the atom did not exist before Dalton's chemical investigations of 1805; but the topmost monad was still called God. In Goethe, we still frequently find this expression, but even more frequently the impersonally universalistic expression "Nature," which is really his characteristic expression: a Nature that is still experienced in a purely irrational manner, is lyrically greeted in stanzas to the moon; Nature again in her ancient veiled maternal form; explanations are not to be stripped off her body, he says; she is everything, I entrust myself to her, let her do with me as she will, I shall praise her in

1. Konstantin v. Economo (1876–1931), neurologist.
2. Benn's speech upon his election to the Prussian Academy of Arts, 5 April 1932.

all her works—and these lines from the hymn to Nature published in the journal of the Tiefurter Gesellschaft in 1782 are in a sense Western civilization's farewell to a world which for two thousand years, for example, since the mythological age of Greece, had been felt to be permeated with spirit, its trees and creatures given to man but ensouled by the presence of gods.

The dissolution of this feeling began around the time of Goethe's death. A world view developed that lacked any relationship to a beyond, any obligation to an extrahuman existence. Man became the crown of creation and the ape his favorite beast, providing him with his phylogenetic confirmation, a glory to which he had attained by the excellence of his metabolism. Two dates are of special importance in this development, for they provide the chronological basis of the new age and the supposed solidity of its truth. The first date is 23 July 1847, the date of the meeting of the Physical Society of Berlin in which Helmholtz supplied the mechanical proof of Robert Mayer's thesis of the conservation of energy and computed it as a general law of nature. That day marks the beginning of the idea of the world's complete comprehensibility, of its comprehensibility as a mechanism, and it is just as epochally significant as an earlier date that lives among us with post- and ante-. Consider that until that day the world could not be comprehended, only experienced; that it was not approached and computed with physics and mathematics but was felt and experienced as a gift of creation, as the expression of a supraterrestrial order. To make it very clear, Goethe said: "Man finds himself quite satisfactorily part of the world by his experience, there's no need to surpass it conceptually." Now began the conceptual surpassing, the beginning of modern physics.

The second date is 1859, when Darwin's theory was published. A time of racial boom, inextricable conglomerations of enormous population growth, Wall Street intervening in the money market, a frenzy of colonizations, continent-wide intensifications of instinct and luxury, ascension of groups fit and ready for usurious expansion, economic strangle holds, imperial proclamations and debacles, and now this theory of the animal race's attainment of fitness and of the reward accruing in struggle and victory to the strong. These two dates gave Europe a new impetus; they provided the source material for a new human type, the materialistically organized commodity type, the montage character, optimistic and shallow-layered, cynically emancipated from any conception of human fatality—minimal pain for the individual and maximal comfort for all, wasn't that the gist of Comte's philosophical welcome to the new age?

The age began with the doctrine of man's essential goodness. Ricarda Huch[3] gave an incomparable description, in her book *Old and New Gods,* of the depth and radically transformative powers of the spirit that are expressed in this conception. It provided the formula for the rearrangement of the innermost spheres. From the glowing darkness of the many churches, wrote Ricarda Huch, there came a trembling, heavy with tears, a drumming and trumpeting; the striving of the human heart is toward evil from childhood on. The steady consonance of this tragic chord, the awareness of being in need of salvation, gave medieval life its depth and boundlessness. Penetrated by the sense of his own limitation, man turned in prayer to a perfection that he could imagine without having witnessed or experienced, an eternal realm beyond the desolation of the earth. And this contrast between a hither and a yon (which, of opposite nature like fire and water, nevertheless interpenetrate) charged the atmosphere with electrical tension, produced deeds like thunderbolts, and illumined the heart with flashes of realization. But now came the new song, Man is good, and its jaunty tune displaced the stern chorale of the past.

So far Ricarda Huch. Man, then, is good; that is, insofar as he appears to be bad, the environment is at fault or heredity or society. All people are good; that means all people are equal, equally valuable, with an equal voice equally worth listening to in all matters. Just let's not get too far away from the average type; let's not have any greatness, anything out of the ordinary. Man is good, but not heroic; don't make the mistake of conferring responsibility on him; he should be useful, expedient, idyllic—devaluation of everything tragical, devaluation of everything fateful, devaluation of everything irrational; only what's plausible is granted validity, only what's banal. Man is good. This does not mean that Man should *become* good, that he should struggle to attain to a goodness, to an inner rank, to a state of being good. No, Man is not supposed to struggle at all, since he's good to begin with. The Party will fight for him,

3. German essayist, historian, novelist, 1864–1947.

society, the mass, but he should live and enjoy, and if he kills someone he should be consoled, for it is not the murderer but the murdered who is at fault.

Man is good, his nature is rational, and all his sufferings are hygienic and socially controllable—this on the one hand and creation itself on the other. Both were supposed to be accessible to science. From both these ideas came the dissolution of all the old bonds, the destruction of the substance, the leveling of all values; from them came the inner situation that produced that atmosphere in which we all live, from which we all drank to the bitter dregs: nihilism.

This concept took shape in Germany in 1885 and 1886, the years when *The Will to Power* had been partly conceived and partly written, the first part of which bears the subtitle: "European Nihilism." But this book already contains a critique of this concept and designs for overcoming it. If we wish to trace its earlier history, if we wish to determine where and when this fateful concept first appeared as a word and as a spiritual experience, we must, as is well known, turn to Russia. The hour of its birth was in March 1862, the month when Ivan Turgenyev's novel *Fathers and Sons* was published. That's as far back as anyone, even Russian historians, can trace it. But the hero of this novel, named Basarov, is already a full-fledged nihilist, and Turgenyev introduces him by that name. This name then became popular with great rapidity. In his afterword to the novel, the author tells how the word was already in everyone's mouth when he returned to Petersburg two months later, in May. It was the time of the great incendiaries, the burning of the Apraxin court, and people cried out to him: "Look at your nihilists, they're setting Petersburg on fire." It is of great interest, in this context, that this Basarov's nihilism wasn't an absolute form of nihilism at all, wasn't negativism pure and simple, but a fanatical faith in progress, a radical positivism with regard to natural science and sociology. He is, for the first time in European literature, the mechanist confident of victory, the plucky materialist, whose somewhat dubious grandsons we can still see engaged in lively activity among us. Let us listen to these familiar strains from the 1860s: a decent chemist, we hear, is worth twenty times more than the best poet. I prefer a piece of cheese to all of Pushkin. Don't you have any regard for art? Sure, the art of making money and curing hemorrhoids! Any shoemaker is a greater man than Goethe and Shakespeare. George Sand is a backward woman, she knew nothing about embryology. In addition to these truths, the low-life bar introduces its milieu as the *dernier cri* of life and art. So, here and then that style was developed which we can trace all the way to certain operas and opera treatments: the cult of the athlete, the hymn to normalcy, the childish social criticism: get rid of the courts, get rid of education, forbid the ancient languages as lacking in genius. The instinctual sphere is favored instead: people should be dirty, we should swap wives and let others support them, we should drink because drinking is cheaper than eating, and besides it makes you smell afterwards. Yes, even Dadaism, whose recent appearance in Zurich and Berlin was found so interesting by our times, can be found in a novel of the 1860s, *What Is to Be Done,* by Cherni-shevsky: art, we read there, means moving two pianos into a draw-ing room, seating a lady in front of each instrument, letting a half chorus form around each, and having every participant sing or play a different song simultaneously and very loudly. This was called the melody of revolution and the orgy of liberty. So we can see that the intellectual effects of the materialistic philosophy of history begin in the sixties and are therefore at least eighty years old, so that strictly speaking it is *they* that are old and reactionary. Strictly speaking, and here we are pushing ahead into the future, all ma-terialism is reactionary, whether as a philosophy of history or as a political faith: namely, backward-looking, backward-acting, for we are already faced with a completely different kind of man and a completely different goal. A goal before which man as a being purely dedicated to drives and pleasures already represents a quite cre-puscular theory. Engineering the soul, spare parts for a so-called collective or normative humanity, that's no more nor less than stale rococo. All these attacks against the higher man we've had to listen to for the past eighty years, and that includes Shaw's farces, it is all downright old-fashioned by now, flat and intellectually poverty stricken. There is only the higher, that is to say, the tragically struggling man; he is history's only subject; only he is anthropol-ogically in possession of all his senses, which is more than can be said for the instinctual complexes. So it will have to be the Superman after all who overcomes nihilism, though it won't be the type Nietzsche described in a pure nineteenth-century spirit. He describes him as a new, biologically more valuable, racially improved, vitalistically stronger, eugenically perfected type, justified by a greater capacity for survival and preservation of the species; he sees him as *biologically positive*—that was Darwinism. Since then we have studied the *bionegative* values, which are rather more harmful and dangerous to the race but are a part of the mind's differentiation: art, genius, the disintegrative motifs of religion, degeneration; in short, all the attributes of creativity. So today, we do not posit the mind as partaking of biological health, nor do we include it in the rising curve of positivism, nor, for that matter, do we see it in tragic, eternally languishing conflict with life; rather, we posit *the mind as superordinate to life,* constructively superior to it; as a formative and formal principle: intensification and concentration—that seems to be its law. This entirely transcendent attitude may result in an overcoming, namely, an artistic exploitation of nihilism; it could teach us to look at it dialectically, that is to say, provocatively. To let all the lost values remain lost; to let all the expired motifs of the deistic epoch remain finished and gone; to put all the force of nihilistic feeling, all the tragedy of nihilistic experience at the disposal of the mind's formal and constructive powers; to generate and cultivate a morality and a metaphysics of form that would be completely new for Germany. There are more than a few indications that we are on the verge of a decisive anthropological turning point. A banal way to put it: displacement from inside to outside, a surging forth of our last specific substance in formative activity, translation of powers into structure. Modern technology and modern architecture point in this direction: space is no longer philosophic-conceptual, as it was in the Kantian epoch, but dynamic-expressive; spatial feeling is no longer in-drawn in lyrical lonesomeness, but projected, extruded, metallically realized. There are numerous signs, such as expressionism, surrealism, psychoanalysis, that suggest we are advancing *biologically* toward a reawakening of myth, and *cortically* toward a build-up by means of discharge mechanisms and pure expression. Our resistances against the purely epical, against any influx of external matter, against rationalizations, psychological glue-jobs, causality, milieu development, contrasted with our urge for direct contact, for cutting, for arrangement, for pure behavior, suggest the same. The last specific substance wants *expression,* leaps over all ideological interpositions, and assumes naked and immediate control of technology at the same time that civilization in its inward content turns back to myth—that appears to be the final stage. Primordial, eternal man, the primal monist, catches fire in the glow of his ultimate image, an image under the golden helmet: how many rays still fall through the runes, how much radiance still on the shadows' edge, how multifarious: tied to frenzies and eugenics, to the tension of departure toward the finale, with the elemental synthesis of creation in memory and the progrediently cerebralized analysis of his historical mission in the brain, throwing aside Europe's normalized masses, brushing past Yucatan's white crumbled rock and the Easter Islands' transcendent colossi, he ponders his ancestors, aboriginal man, proselenic man, ponders his incalculably ancient but unrelentingly murderous, antidualistic, antianalytic struggle and rouses himself once again to a final formula: constructive intelligence.

"An antimetaphysical world view, fine—but in that case, let it be artistic." This sentence from *The Will to Power* would then acquire a truly final meaning. It would acquire for the German, as an indication of a last escape from his lost values, his addictions, his riotings, his wild enigmas, a quality of tremendous seriousness: the goal, the faith, the overcoming would then be called: the law of form. It would acquire for him the character of an obligation to his people, to struggle, to fight the fight of his life, in an effort to work his way close to those things that are really in essence unconquerable, the possession of which accrued to older and more fortunate peoples from their endowments, their limits, their skies and their seas when they were still young: a sense of space, proportion, magic of realization, adherence to a style. Does this imply esthetic values in Germany, artistry in a country so given over to dreams and obfuscation? Yes, the cultivated absoluteness of form, whose degrees of linear purity and stylistic immaculateness must by all means be equal to the degrees of perfection in content achieved by earlier cultural epochs, including the degrees marked by the cup of hemlock and the cross. Indeed, only out of the ultimate tensions of the formal, only from the utmost intensification of the spirit of construction, pushed to the limits of immateriality, could a new *ethical* reality take shape—*after* Nihilism!

(1932)   *Translated by Joel Agee*

Art and the Third Reich

1. General Situation

Life is beyond doubt inextricably bound up with necessity, and it does not release man, the attempted deserter, from the chain; but the chain need not clank at every one of his steps, need not drag its whole weight on every breath. Such a moment, when the chain temporarily loosened, came at the end of the last century, when, for instance, the English Queen's Diamond Jubilee in 1897 gave the whole rest of the world a chance to see the immense riches of the Empire. The white race's two continents were both enjoying a high degree of prosperity: new oil fields, depth-drilling in Pennsylvania, forest conservation, winter-hardened wheat—all this had brought it about. Those who organized and enjoyed this prosperity had for years been in the habit of meeting for the Season in London, the Grande Semaine in Paris, the salmon-fishing in Canada, or in the fall in the valley of the Oos. Some events overlapped in the calendar: on the first of September the bathing season began at Biarritz, lasting till exactly the thirtieth of that month, followed by the after-cure at Pau in the gigantic hotels on the Boulevard des Pyrénées with its incomparable view over the panorama of the Monts-Maudits, or in the shadow of the sixteen rows of plane trees bordering the avenues at Perpignan. In England the thing was to go North on August 12th, to shoot grouse in Scotland, and to return South on September 1st, for partridge-shooting. In Germany those were the great days of Baden-Baden, which came alive in Turgeniev's *Smoke* and a remarkably large number of other Russian books. There were certain families from the old nations, and the intruders from the new ones. The Ritz concern had a special card-index to deal with them. Such items as, "Herr X sleeps without a bolster. . . . Madame Y takes no butter on her toast. . . . Lord G. must have black cherry-jam every day," were telegraphed back and forth between London, Lucerne, and Palermo.

The modern nomad was born. About 1500, painting conquered landscape, the day in the country and the long journey. The voyages around the world had begun, and with them came the sense of distance and vast spaces. The religious and eschatological hue of man's sense of infinity was overlaid by the geographical and descriptive. Now, about 1900, the luxurious note was added, and what had sprung from necessity was turned into a source of sensory experience and enjoyment. How much history there is in the Blue Trains and the Golden Arrows! Those luncheon-baskets, a specialty of Drew's at Piccadilly Circus, with their little spirit-stoves, those flasks for distilled water and boxes for meat and butter, were now transformed into the dining-car; the luggage-racks, where for several decades the children had been put to sleep, into Pullman cars and *wagons-lits*. The hotels far surpassed the town halls and cathedrals in significance, taking on their century's identity as the town halls and cathedrals had betokened theirs. At the laying of the foundation-stone for Claridge's in the Champs Elysées, Lady Grey performed the symbolic ceremony with a silver trowel. When the Ritz was furnished, the artistic legacy of Mansard and his masons—which the Place Vendôme still exemplified, uniquely undisturbed from the 18th century down to the present day—was faithfully preserved in months of inventive toil by a staff of architects, interior decorators, artisans, art historians, and other experts. The differences between *petit-point* and tapestry, between porcelain and *faience*, between the styles of the Sung and Tang dynasties had to be no less precisely observed than the subtle distinctions between the Italian and the Spanish Renaissance. It took careful research to discover and select the right shop for silver, for glass, for carpets, brocades, and silks, for table linen, sheets, and pillowcases. In Rome there was a first-rate place for Venetian lace and embroidery, and as for lighting, the novelty was indirect light, casting no shadow. How many tones were compared until it was settled at last: a muted apricot in alabaster bowls, the beams cast up onto the warmly tinted ceilings. A Van Dyck portrait in the Louvre, in which luminous brown tones contrasted with a matt turquoise, served as the model for harmonizing the color scheme of blinds, carpets, and wallpapers. Escoffier, the chef, did not permit gas in the kitchen: "A faultless pie can be baked only with the old, tested fuels." Coal and wood were vastly superior to gas, in the opinion of Escoffier, who was Sarah Bernhardt's sole guest at a birthday party she gave at the Carlton in London—Escoffier, who named his creations after Coquelin and Melba.

It was the age of the great dinners, meals of fourteen courses, with the sequence of wines following a tradition that went back four hundred years to the pheasant banquets of Burgundian days, of the fleur-de-lis princes. A banker who had successfully brought off an important transaction handed the paladins of the Ritz a check for 10,000 francs for a meal with a dozen friends. It was in winter, and fresh young peas, asparagus, and fruit were hard to obtain; but it was done. The Jeroboam de Château Lafitte 1870 and the Château Yquem 1869 were brought from Bordeaux by a special messenger, who had to make the night-long journey with the priceless casket on his knees lest the sensitive old wine should suffer any jolting. Among the 180,000 bottles the house had in its own cellars, of which 500 different varieties could be ordered from the wine list every evening, there was nothing fit to go with the *bécassine* and the truffles *en papillottes*.

The restaurant trade becomes out-and-out aristocratic and industrialized. The inaugurators and main pillars of the "Ritz idea" are Colonel Pfuffer of Altishofen in Lucerne, Baron Pierre de Gunzburg in Paris, Lord Lathom in London, the last board chairman of the Savoy Company. Marnier Lapostolle, an industrialist in St. Cloud, concocted a cordial whose march of triumph, under the name of *Le Grand Marnier,* doubled its inventor's fortune. Apollinaris was to start on its career with a celebration at the new spring, the Johannisbrunn. Among the guests were the Prince of Wales, who happened to be in Homburg, Russian grand dukes and Prussian princes, twenty in all. A special freight-train had to transport foodstuffs, plates, cups, glasses, potted plants, armchairs, ice, and a kitchen-stove from Frankfurt am Main to the remote valley of the Ahr. The twenty covers cost 5,000 Swiss francs, but the Derby victory of his horse, Persimmon, combined with the presence of attractive women, put the prince in one of his most charming moods. Socially and, as the concern foresaw, commercially, it was a great success.

The second third of the last century had witnessed the rise of the great gambling casinos—forever linked with the names of the Blanc brothers from Bordeaux—above all in Homburg and in Monaco. *Grand joueurs* like Garzia, Lucien Napoleon, Bugeja, and Mustapha Fazil Pasha lost or won half a million in a few hours: dangerous people, the terror of the management that had to keep in constant telegraphic communication with three big banks while they stayed. *Trente-et-quarante* was the game for high stakes; they played with a cool million in cash piled before them on the table. But also playing were Adelina Patti, by marriage Marquise de Caux, Madame Lucca, Madame Grassi, and Jules Verne. Rubinstein scarcely stopped to bow to his audience after the last notes had faded away at his concerts, so eager was he to get back to the tables. Paganini gambled away two millions. Dostoievsky at roulette—probably the most famous and most incomprehensible of gamblers, a gambler to the point of degradation, a real addict. The Rothschilds, Bismarck's son, Gortschakoff, Gladstone, gambled at Homburg. Then, for political reasons, Homburg had to close down, and the last game was announced: "Messieurs, à la dernière forever."

On July 1, 1869, an edict was issued, declaring that henceforth the district of Saint-Devote on the cape of Monaco, Les Speluges, was to be known as "Le Quartier de Monte Carlo." A quay was built, the harbor of Condamine enlarged, the Hôtel de Paris smothered in flowers. The railway and the road from Nice were completed, the Casino was built. As early as 1869 all taxes were abolished in the territory, and made up by the gamblers. In 1874 the fourth roulette table had to be set up. When Saxon-les-Bains in Switzerland was closed, too, the only casino left in all Southern Europe was this one at "the Dives," Les Speluges, on the Côte d'Azur. Secure in its monopoly, it could now afford to admit only gamblers holding tickets made out in their names, to permit only play with *refait*, to present building-plots to newspapermen, and to hand considerable sums and a railway ticket to suicide suspects. The environs were organized: golf matches at Cannes, horse-racing at Nice, pigeon shooting. One Blanc was dead, the other, François, was the main shareholder; out of his private fortune he lent the city of Paris five millions to restore the Opéra, for which the Ministry of Transport gave him faster trains to the Mediterranean. One of his daughters married a Prince Radziwill, the other a Bonaparte, and her daughter a son of the King of Greece. Blanc's godfathers back in Bordeaux had been a stocking-weaver and a shoemaker. He left his family eighty-eight millions, made in Homburg and Monte Carlo and soon to be squandered on racing stables, yachts, castles, hot-houses for orchids, and *bijouterie*. What is remarkable is how little the persons of this circle and their institutions were moved by the events of the time. It is known that the last Czar did not break off his game of tennis when he received the news of the fall of Port Arthur. The day after Sadowa[1] there was an open-air masquerade in the Prater,[2] with a Venetian *corso;* beer-gardens and wine-gardens were filled to overflowing, and in the Volksgarten, where Strauss was conducting, all seats were sold out. The Casino of Monaco kept open during the war of 1870–71, and its profits were only two millions less than in the preceding year of peace; it still paid out a dividend of five per cent. In Homburg the profits were lower, but exceeded half a million even during the year of war.

One can look at world history from inside and from outside, as a sufferer or as an observer. Art is expression, and since its last stylistic transformation, it is more so than ever. It needs means of expression, it goes in search of them, there is not much can be expressed by potato-peelings—not so much, anyway, as a whole life tries to express. More can be expressed by gold helmets, peacocks, pomegranates; more can be associated with roses, balconies, and rapiers; princes can be made to say what coopers cannot, and the Queen of the Amazons what a factory-girl cannot; people who have had the experience of Antiquity, who have spent years observing forms and styles, people who travel, whose nerves are sensitive and who have a weakness for gambling, may well be more complex and more fractional than savages, and with their modes of expression they will do more justice to their era than the partisans of Blood and Soil, who are still close to totemism. The more austere the artist is, the deeper is his longing for finesse and light. His

---

1. Decisive defeat of the Austrians at Königgratz in the Austro-Prussian War of 1866.
2. Amusement park in Vienna.

participation in an era of squandering and sensual enjoyment is existentially moral; Balzac could write only within the daemoniacal orbit of high finance; Caruso's voice became perfect only when he sang before the Diamond Horseshoe at the Metropolitan. Thus we see the artist play his part in the epochs we are concerned with, and the public, in its turn, took note of the things that art produced, including their peculiarities and their inner meaning.

2. Art in Europe

Those were the decades of Duse as Camille, of Bernhardt as l'Aiglon, of Lily Langtry as Rosalind, and large sections of the nations shared in that. Remember, there is the press, criticism, essayism. Capitalism can afford a public; it does not compel valuable components of the nation to emigrate, its *Lebensraum* has not been limited to torture and extermination. When Zola entered the dining room of the Grand Hotel in Rome and a puritanical Englishwoman jumped up indignantly at being expected to lunch in the same room with the author of *Nana,* there was a public to notice it, full of alertness and warmth and that fluid which goes to create the flair of an era— undoubtedly trivial things, too, at times, but how deep a background it built for achievement and rank to stand out against! How much brilliance it cast round Kainz,[3] for instance, not because he hobnobbed with a king, but because by giving a word the right emphasis he could make people feel the powers of the deep, could make men and women, lemurs and masks, grow pale merely by the way he descended a flight of steps or slung his arm round a pillar! There was one nation in which literature had long been a public power that even the government had to reckon with: the French. Now they had created a new rank, that of *grand écrivain,* successor to the great *savants universels* of the 17th, 18th, and 19th centuries, and socially the successor to the *gentilhomme*—a blend of journalism, social criticism, and autochthonous art: *grandseigneurs,* marshals of literature: Balzac, the Goncourts, Anatole France; in England, Kipling. A new form of modern creativeness. In Germany the type was largely rejected, the musical-metaphysical factor re-

3. Joseph Kainz (1858–1910), actor in Berlin and Vienna.

maining the core of the "unreal" German endeavors. In Norway, by contrast, Björnson came close to becoming king.

An age in motion: inflation of themes, chaos of stylistic attitudes. In architecture: glass and iron displacing wood and brick, concrete displacing stone. The age-old problem of rivers was solved by the suspension-bridge; hospitals abandoned the palatial style for that of the barracks. Public gardens, Boy Scouts, dancing schools.

The Third Estate at the zenith of its power: the bourgeoisie advancing into rank and title, into commanding positions in army and navy. The great cities: the proletariat lives in them, too, but did not build them. Modern constitutional law, the mathematical sciences, biology, positivism—all this is bourgeois; so is the counter-movement: modern irrationalism, perspectivism, existentialist philosophy. The white bourgeois colonizes, sends the sahib to take charge of the yellow, brown, and black riff-raff. European art turns in the opposite direction, regenerating itself in the tropics: Gauguin on Tahiti, Nolde in Rabaul, Dauthendey in Java, Pierre Loti in Japan, Matisse in Morocco. Asia is opened up mythologically and linguistically: Wilhelm devotes himself to China, Lafcadio Hearn to Japan, Zimmer to India.

A spiritual intensity pervades Europe; from this small continent a spiritual high tension makes the unspeakable, the undreamed-of, take shape. It is hard to say which is more remarkable, the way the public follows and takes an interest, or the harshness, the dedication to truth—brutal, if necessary—on the part of its creators, those great intellects which bear the responsibility for the race's destiny. Immensely serious, tragically profound words about that work: "To say Poetry is to say Suffering" (Balzac); "To say Work is to say Sacrifice" (Valéry); "It is better to ruin a work and make it useless for the world than not to go to the limit at every point" (Thomas Mann); "Oft did I weary wrestling with Thee"—the line that a galley-slave had carved in his oar, now carved by Kipling in the table he worked at in India; "Nothing is more sacred than the work in progress" (d'Annunzio); "I would rather be silent than express myself feebly" (Van Gogh).

Cracks in the positivist picture of the world: influx of crises and menaces. Postulation of the concept of the bio-negative (intoxication, the psychotic, art). Doubts about the meaning of words: for instance dissolving and destructive; and for a substitute: creative

and stimulating. Analysis of schizophrenia: in the oldest evolutionary centers of the brain, there survive memories of the collective
primal phases of life, which may manifest themselves in psychoses
and dreams (ethnophrenia), primal phases! Pre-lunar man comes
upon the scene, and with him the ages of geological cataclysm,
world crises, doom by fire, moon disintegration, globe-girdling tides;
secrets from the beginning of the Quaternary: enigmatic similarities
between the gods, the world-wide legend of the Flood, the kinship
between linguistic groups in the Old and the New Worlds—problems of cultures, prehistorical cultures, pre-Atlantean links; the
complex of problems posed by Negro sculpture, by the cave draw-
ings of Rhodesia, the stone images on Easter Island, the great deserted cities in the primeval forest near Saigon.

Deciphering of the Assyrian clay cylinders: new excavations at
Babylon, Ur, Samara: the first coherent presentation of Egyptian
sculpture—an analysis of composition methods in the reliefs leads
to the surprising perception that they correspond exactly to the
theories of Cubism: "the art of drawing consists in establishing
relations between curves and straight lines." Promiscuity of images
and systems. Forming and re-forming. Europe is on the way to new
glory, the shining examples from the past being the grandeur of the
fifteenth and the fulfillment of the eighteenth century. Germany
hesitates, for here intellectual talents are few and far between, yet
an élite answers across the borders, stirred by the truth of an ethos
now revealed, manifest for the first time in this insistence on clarity,
craftsmanly delicacy, brightness, audacity, and brilliance—the
"Olympus of Appearances"; within Germany it means discarding
the Faustian urge in favor of work with defined limits.

Ever new throngs of ideas come charging in, the problems become
inflated, remote distances draw nearer, displaying their miseries and
their splendors, worlds lost and forgotten loom into view, among
them some that are cloaked in twilight, equivocal, deranged. The
amount of real intellectual discovery during these fifty years is une-
qualled, and, all in all, it really expands the pattern. Rembrandt,
Grünewald, El Greco, long neglected, were rediscovered, the strange
and disquieting phenomenon of Van Gogh was given a place in the
world of the intellect; the riddle of Marées' Arcadian dream was
solved, the unrecognized Hölderlin was conquered for that circle
to which his bio-negative *problematik* was intelligible ("If I die in

shame, if my soul is not avenged on the brazen . . .") Bertram's[4] book appeared, and, in an unending sequence of analytical works transforming themselves in their own dialectics, Nietzsche was placed among the very greatest of Germans. Conrad's fascinating novels were translated. Hamsun became "the greatest among the living." The North had long established its supremacy with Ibsen, Björnson, and Strindberg; by producing *Niels Lyhne*[5] the small provincial town of Thisted in Jutland had helped to form the taste of at least one of our generations. The New World came—Walt Whitman's lyrical monism had a great influence—and conquered; everyone knows the situation today; Europe's last great literary form, the novel, has largely passed under American control.

Diaghilev appears, the real founder of the modern stage. Composing music for his ballet are Stravinsky, his own discovery, Debussy, Milhaud, Respighi. His dancers are Pavlova, Karsavina, Nijinsky. His stage designers are Picasso, Matisse, Utrillo, Braque. Moving through Europe, he revolutionizes everything. The intellectual novelty of his ideas is the concentration and toughening of all the arts. This is how Cocteau put it: "A work of art must satisfy all nine Muses."

Slavonic and Romance elements combined here in a distinct trend: *against* mere feeling, against everything inarticulate, romantic, amorphous, against all empty planes, against mere allusions in punctuation; and *for* everything perfected, clarified, tempered by hard work; *for* precision in the use of materials, organization, strict intellectual penetration. What it comes to is a turning against inner life, mere good will, pedagogic or racial side issues, in favor of the form-assuming, and thus form-compelling, expression.

Everyone knows how this new style suddenly appeared simultaneously in all the lands of the white race. Today its implication is clear: producing art means purging the inarticulate, nationalistic inner life, dissolving the last residue of Post-Classicism, completing the secularization of medieval man. That is to say: anti-familiar, anti-idealistic, anti-authoritarian. The only authoritarian factor left is the will to express, the craving for form, the inner restlessness that will not leave off until the form has been worked out in its proper proportions. This will take absolute ruthlessness toward the

4. Ernst Bertram, *Nietzsche* (1918).
5. *Niels Lyhne,* novel by the Danish writer Jens Peter Jacobsen (1847–1885).

beloved, time-tested, sacred things. But what we might then see is the epiphany of a new image casting its radiance over the anxieties of life, a new image of man's fate, which is so hopelessly, disconsolately laden.

These were not "artists of talent" winking at each other; there was no conspiracy between Montmartre, Bohemian Chelsea, the ghetto, and the barnyard; it was a secular surging of life, racially and biologically founded, a change of style brought about by a mutational *ananke*. Scheler[6] somewhere speaks of "feelings that everyone nowadays is aware of having in himself but which it once took men like poets to wrest from the appalling muteness of our inner life." Such wresters come to the fore now. After all, the whole nineteenth century can today be interpreted as an upheaval within the gene, which saw this new mutation ahead. Things had lost their old relevance, not only in morals but in physics; they even broke out of the mechanical world view that had been held inviolable since Kepler. When this happened the public realized that something had been going on secretly for a long time. For centuries all the great men of the white race had felt only the one inner task of concealing their own nihilism. This nihilism had drawn sustenance from a variety of spheres: with Dürer from the religious, with Tolstoy from the moral, with Kant from the epistemological, with Goethe from the universally human, with Balzac from the social— but it had been the basic element in the work of every one of them. With immense caution it is touched again and again; with equivocal questions, with groping, ambiguous turns, they approach it on every page, in every chapter, in every character. Not for a moment are they in doubt about the essential nature of their inner creative substance: it is the abysmal, the void, the cold, the inhuman. The one who remained naive the longest was Nietzsche. Even in *Zarathustra*, what meaningful disciplined élan! It is only in the last phase, with *Ecce Homo* and the lyrical fragments, that he admits it to his consciousness: "Thou shouldst have sung, oh, my soul!"— not: believed, cultivated, thought in historical and pedagogical terms, been so positive—: and now comes the breakdown. Singing—that means forming sentences, finding expressions, being an artist, doing cold, solitary work, turning to no one, apostrophizing no congre-

6. Max Scheler (1874–1928), German philosopher.

gation, but before every abyss simply testing the echoing quality of the rock-faces, their resonance, their tone, their coloratura effects. This was a decisive finale. After all: artistics! It could no longer be concealed from the public that here was a deep degeneration of substance. On the other hand, this lent great weight to the new art: what was here undertaken in artistic terms was the transference of things into a new reality, a new, authentic relevance, a biological realism proved by the laws of proportion, to be experienced as the expression of a new spiritual way of coming to terms with existence, exciting in the creative tension of its pursuit of a style derived from awareness of inner destiny. Art as a means of producing reality: this was the productive principle of the new art.

Undeniably: this art was capitalistic, a ballet demanded costumes, a tour had to be financed. Pavlova could not dance unless she was lodged in rooms filled with white lilac, both winter and summer, whether in India or in the Hague. Duse suffered much, everything around her had to be hushed, far away from her, with the curtains drawn. For some of his paintings Matisse received sums in six figures. Some went to bathe at Lussin-piccolo even at the height of the season; composing a new opera paid for a new car. The high-tension, condensations, oscillations of intensified life were part of this order of things, but so were the sufferings, the hagridden dread of losing the inner voice, the vocation, the visions overbrimming with imagery. Exhibitionism and breakdown alike were filled with truth, they were sovereign. The intellectual nonsense about the es-thetic sense of the common people had not yet been trotted out to idealize the microcephalic; Bronze-Age barter was not yet pro-claimed an economic dream full of possibilities for the future; people could travel, spend their money, take on the imprint of many skies, be transformed in many cities.

There were also some perfectly successful representations of the social milieu: Van Gogh's "Potato-Eaters," Hauptmann's *The Weavers*, Meunier's sculptures of miners, Käthe Kollwitz's draw-ings; and, for the rural milieu: Millet's "Sower," Leibl's "Forester." But compassion and an intimate sense of one's own country were not all the emotional content and formal motif, no more than "The Return from Hades," or a woman bathing or a jug filled with asphodels. The human and humane was only one of the currents flowing toward the distant shore. And what peopled that shore was goddesses or orange-pickers or horses, girls from Haiti, postmen, railway-crossings, also flute-players and army officers—but all craving for the life of shadows. A very selective, exclusive start. A vocation. A great peculiarity. It meant elevating everything decisive into the language of unintelligibility, yielding to things that deserved to convince no one. Yet art should not be said to have been esoteric in the sense of being exclusive; everyone could come in and hear, open doors and see, draw closer, join, or go away. The tragic distances between man and man are felt a thousand times more as a result of other phenomena: the cruel accumulation of power, justice corrupted by politics, unbalanced passions, senseless wars. This is, perhaps, the place to point out that we had successful novels that were German in the good sense, best sellers such as *Ekkehard, Debit and Credit, Effi Briest, Jörn Uhl, Das Wunschkind*.[7] There was nothing remotely like a bar to German production in any foreign or racially alien works. It is one of the countless political lies to assert that only now was there any guarantee that the true-blue German would get true-blue German books. Rather, what made certain groups loathe the modern style was its exciting, experimental, controversial quality—in short, the intellectual quality of what was going on, and what their own meager talents could not cope with. Besides, there was the hatred of seeing the public reached by anything at all, other than their own political and nationalistic belly-aching. Thus the intellect in itself became "un-German," and at its particularly abominable worst: "European." The rest of Europe thought that a general paganization of form might perhaps reconsecrate the race whose gods had died; it did not expect this from fairy tales and dialect and Wotanisms.

It was this concept of "Europe" that in 1932 gave birth to the notion of a Mediterranean Academy, the Académie Méditerranéenne which was to have its seat in Monaco. All the riparians of that "narrow sea," the directly and indirectly Mediterranean countries, were asked to join. D'Annunzio, Marshal Pétain, Pirandello, Milhaud took the lead. The Royal Italian Academy, the Gami-el-Azhar University in Cairo, and the Sorbonne were among the co-

---

7. *Ekkehard* by Viktor v. Scheffel (1826–1886); *Debit and Credit (Soll und Haben)* by Gustav Freytag (1816–1895); *Effie Briest* by Theodor Fontane (1819–1898); *Jörn Uhl* by Gustav Frenssen (1863–1945); *Das Wunschkind* by Ina Seidel (1885–1974).

operating institutions. All that the pagan and then the monotheistic generations had produced in esthetic and conceptual values was here to be clarified anew, for the enrichment and edification of today's world. All that had created and formed us, too, up in the North: the enigma of the Etruscans, the lucid centuries of Antiquity, the inexhaustibility of the Moors, the splendor of Venice, the marble tremors of Florence. Who would deny that we, too, were formed by the Renaissance and the Reformation—whether in devotion or in battle—that the monks, the knights, the troubadours, that Salamanca, Bologna, Montpellier, that botanically roses, lilies, wine, and biographically Genoa and Portofino and the Tristan palace on the Grand Canal, down to this hour of our life—that by all this breathless creativity Rome and the Mediterranean left so indelible an imprint upon us that we, too, belonged to it? But the invitations sent to Germany fell into the hands of the Gestapo. Art was closed down. "Messieurs, à la dernière forever!"

3. Art and the Third Reich

It is only against this background situation that one clearly sees what was special about the "German awakening." A nation broadly speaking without any definite taste, as a whole untouched by the moral and esthetic refinement of neighboring civilized countries, philosophically embroiled in confused idealistic abstractions, prosaic, inarticulate, and dull, a practical nation with—as its evolution demonstrates—only a biological way to spirituality: i.e., by Romanization or universalization; such a nation elevates an antisemitic movement that demagogically conjures up before its eyes the meanest of its ideals: low-income housing developments, with subsidized, tax-favored sex life, home-made rape-oil in the kitchen, self-hatched scrambled eggs, home-grown barley, homespun socks, local flannel, and, for art and the inner life, S.A. songs bellowed in radio style. A nation's mirror of itself. Parallel bars in the garden, and St. John's fires on the hills—there's your pure-bred Teuton. A rifle range and the pewter mug filled with ale, that was his element. And now they gaze questioningly at the civilized nations and wait with childlike naiveté for their amazement and admiration.

A remarkable process! Inside a Europe of high brilliance and joint intellectual endeavors there evolves an inner-German Versailles, a Germanic collective based on a society of criminals, and whenever there is a chance they belabor the Muses. They are not content with the big cars, the hunting lodges where the bison roar,[8] the stolen island in the Wannsee[9]—Europe has to marvel at their culture! Haven't we talents among us with the resonance of tin cans and the pathos of waterlogged corpses, and painters whom we need only show the direction: say, His Nibs at the end of a shoot, the gun still smoking, one foot on the felled sixteen-point stag, the morning mists rising from the ground, furnishing a touch of the primeval woodland murmurs? And the block warden[10] goes in for colored saucers—they will make Europe sit up! But above all one must exterminate: all that is Eastern, or Southern, or Western, not to speak of what is Latin, Gothic, Impressionist, Expressionist, the Hohenstaufen, the Hapsburg, Charlemagne—till they alone are left, perhaps with Henry the Lion and Snow White thrown in. On these odds and ends they base their Chambers of Culture, their esthetic Sing-Sing.

The artist is reincorporated in the guild order from which he freed himself about 1600. He is regarded as an artisan, a particularly senseless and corruptible artisan, patronized by the cell leader or the Soldiers' Home. Artisans are not supposed to care about the era's political or social decisions; only Kultur-Bolsheviks and traitors do. Anyone daring to say that artistic creation presupposes a measure of inner freedom is called before the Chamber; anyone mentioning the word style gets a warning; mental hospitals and institutions are consulted on the question of contemporary art. As filling station attendant for vital contents, the Propaganda Minister is the authority on line and counterpoint. Music must be folksongish, or else it is banned. Only generals or Party officials are subjects for portraiture: in clear, simple colors; subtle nuances are discouraged. For establishing a bridgehead in the East you get an oil portrait, 8–12, rated according to defense value—i.e., value in defending the boss's job. Genre paintings showing fewer than five children are not to be marketed. Tragic, somber, extravagant themes

8. Reference to Hermann Göring.
9. Lake in the fashionable Westend of Berlin.
10. Lowest party official on the precinct level.

are matters for the Security Police; delicate, high-bred, languid ones for the Racial Health Court.

Personages one could never object to if they confined themselves to fattening pigs or milling flour step forward, hail "man" as ideal, organize song-fests and choir contests, and set themselves up as the measure of things. Lübzow, Podejuch County, disputes the alliterative laurels with Piepenhagen in Pomerania, while the hamlets with a population below 200 in the Schwalm region vie for the jubilee song of the Xaver Popiol S.A. Brigade. "Terpsichorean," says clubfoot; "melodious," murmurs ear-wax; skunks claim to smell of roses; the Propaganda Minister takes up relations with poetry. "Strong outlines"—no truck with the sublime! Obvious! Compared with shooting people in the neck outdoors or chair-leg fighting indoors, sublimity has a sissified, un-German look. Of course, flattening is not quite formative, but the gas station attendant does not notice. What does not take on expression stays prehistoric. Art is a buoy marking deep and shallow spots; what the Minister wants is relaxation and dash. Art among all gifted races is a profound delimiting of enhancement and transition; here they order four new pirates à la Störtebeker[11] and three freedom-fighters à la Colonel Schill.[12] Whatever style and expression a few inspired individuals achieved, over slights and abuse, among these ponderous, divided people, they have debased and falsified in their own image: the jaws of Caesars and the brains of troglodytes, the morality of protoplasm and the sense of honor of a sneak thief. All nations of quality create their own élite; now it has come to the point where being German means being hostile to any sort of differentiation and, in matters of taste, betting always on the clumsiest horse; the sensitive are given the third degree by the Gestapo. It also looks after art studios: great painters are forbidden to buy canvas and oils, and at night the block wardens go round checking on the easels. Art comes under the heading of pest control (Colorado beetle). A genius is chased screaming through the woods at night; when an aged Academy member or a Nobel Prize winner finally dies of starvation, the culture guardians beam with glee.

Vengeful underdogs, perspectival *formes frustes*—but, although

11. Klaus Störtebeker, leader of a group of buccaneers around 1400.
12. Ferdinand v. Schill, Prussian officer during the Napoleonic wars.

the occasion scarcely justifies it, one must look at it even more comprehensively. It is the centuries-old German problem that here has the chance to manifest itself so clearly, under the protection of the nation's armed criminals. It is the German substance, something outside differentiation and esthetic transformation. An historically not uninteresting, in spots even distinguished work about conditions in the pre-Reformation era points out that Dürer endangered his Germanness by turning to those mathematical problems in painting that Italian painters had formulated under the impact of the Renaissance. So Dürer was concerned with formal processes of orderly consciousness—studies in proportion—and this was already un-German, already too much. The clear sky of abstraction, which arches over the Latin world without any dehumanizing or sterilizing effect, is here unhealthy and harmful to production. This is the voice of an urge for illiteracy—but here it is genuine. It is part of their *"Lebensraum,"* their "evolution," their thought-shunning dash. The resolution of inner tensions by esthetic means is alien to them. The cathartic nature of expression in general they will always deny, for lack of any corresponding inner experience. What they lack is impressions of the constructive form of the sublime. Spiritually held down by low-grade ideas, such as that of a single, mechanical causality, they will never be able to grasp an essential, productive causality of the creative principle. What they can experience is history, a result of bacteriological research, an experiment, an economic process—they are incapable of experiencing the questing and agonized motions of a productive gene inherent even in the white race and that gene's escape into a structural element. That is why their writers wind up even short paragraphs, trivial dicta, on a moral, didactic, and, if possible, absolute note; they can find no other way of getting themselves off-stage. Their lack of any tendency towards artistic abstraction is complete—for that would require hard work, objectivity, discipline. Objectivity in turn demands decency and detachment, a moral, personal decency that is beyond riff-raff. So wherever they see things raised to the level of consciousness and find an artist revealing his own productive processes, they work off their feelings in hatred against "artistics," in rambling balderdash about formalism and intellectualism. For this people, uniovular twins are more important than geniuses: the former lend themselves to statistics, the latter contain lethal factors. This people spews out its geniuses as the sea spews out its pearls: for the inhabitants of other realms.

And so this people is caught up in the Awakening, in the "German miracle," the "recuperative movement," according to E. R. Jaentsch's book, *The Anti-Type.* (The anti-type consists not of the awakened but of the undaunted, those who go on striving for more refinement.) This movement would have us believe that the Great Migrations have just come to an end, and that we are now called upon to clear the forests. It is a miracle whose most unique and sincere quality appears when the cities have to be blacked out, when people fall silent, mists billow, and only they talk and talk and talk, until their stinking breath rolls like vast cow-pats over the suffocated fields. It is a rising, the essence of which—apart from their get-rich-quick schemes, which come so naturally to them—is a lie of lies and an anthropological unreality, excluding the achievement of any sort of identity with any age, race, or continent. This movement purges art. It does so by means of the same concept with which it glorifies and justifies itself and which thus looms gigantically, programmatically, into our field of vision: history.

Five hoplites armed with machine-guns attack a boy they had promised not to harm; then they march in somewhere—: history. Mahomet began as a robber of caravans; the ideology was a later addition. He even poisoned the wells in the desert—for centuries an unimaginable crime, but now ennobled by divine and racial needs: first theft, then religion, finally history. Under Nero, in 67 A.D., private correspondence in Rome had ceased entirely, since all letters were opened; the postmen came to the houses in the mornings bringing news by word of mouth about the latest executions: world history.

And this means: at breakfast, on mountain-tops, while breaking and entering, with filmstars—Colleoni![13] Before rabbit-hutches, cloakrooms, extra distributions of synthetic honey—Alexander! At mass murders, lootings, blackmail: geopolitics and fulfillment of destiny! Now, history may have its own methods, and one that our eyes can clearly discern is undoubtedly its use of microcephalics, but art has also proved itself in forty centuries. This essay is art's rejoinder; these are the expressions it has found to fit the epoch. It

13. Bartolomeo Colleoni (1400–1475), Italian condottiere.

finds them as naturally and sharply as the Gestapo aims its shots. It collects them and hands them on to those who will always exist, during every historical victory and during every historical doom, and whose influence will outlast both victory and doom. Art now records these expressions in the belief that there will some day be a European tradition of the mind, which Germany will also join, a tradition from which it will learn and to which, having learned, it will contribute.

(Written 1941, published 1949)   *Translated by Ernst Kaiser and Eithne Wilkins*

Pallas

A thena, who leapt fully armed and shining from Zeus's brow—blue-eyed, the motherless divinity. Pallas—delighting in battles and destruction, Medusa's head on her breastplate, the somber, joyless bird of night upon her helmet; she steps back a little and with a single movement lifts the enormous border-stone from the field against Mars, who sides with Troy and Helen. Venus bemoans her hand, wounded by Diomedes, and Pallas laughs at this blood: probably scratched herself on a golden buckle down there, fondling someone in armor. Pallas, beyond Sappho and Mary, once almost overpowered in the darkness of a cavern, always helmeted, never impregnated, a childless goddess, cold and alone.

Pallas protects matricides! It is her vote against the Erinyes that gains Orestes his acquittal. (Aeschylus, *The Eumenides*, 458 B.C., Theatre of Bacchus.) Athena says:

> Not the mother is procreator of her child,
> she only bears and nourishes the newly wakened life.

With these lines the cataclysm sets in. Woman is dethroned as the primary and supreme sex, debased into an inseminable hetaera. The accursed age begins. Plato, Aeschylus, Augustine, Michelangelo—all of the accursed age, some even paederasts. The modern champion of the maternal spirit declares: "A glorious victory, forsooth! Clytemnestra slew vicious Agamemnon, who had slaughtered her daughter Iphigenia—hers, the mother's daughter—on the sacrificial altar and who returned to Mycenae bringing his new wives along. Orestes, her son, thereupon slew Clytemnestra, his mother, who had killed his father. The Erinyes appeared to accuse the matricide, Apollo and Athena defended him and forced his acquittal. The speeches of both, in behalf of the father-idea and the permissibility of matricide, suffice to indicate the moral decline concealed by the ascendancy of the Apolline solar cult and the cult of paternity in Classical Greece." "A perverse poetic idea." "The poet-philosopher (Aeschylus) may be excused by his ignorance of biological facts." "The immoral and violent spirit of patriarchal ethics." "One of the most disastrous errors ever made by civilized man." For: "Matricide is much further beyond atonement than mariticide by a wife, which is frequent enough in Nature, as for instance among the bees."

Among the bees! The bee is the matriarchalist's favorite animal. "The religio-social miracle of bee-life." "A thousand meters above the earth, where the larks sing and the clouds drift, copulation takes place. There the strongest drone overtakes the queen, clutches her honey-scented body, and gives life to her womb, himself dying immediately afterwards. It is, as it were, heaven itself that fertilizes the queen in the solitude of blue space." Thus pleads our modern matriarchalist. After the bees come the ants. "Males survive only for a short time in the ant state. They take no part in community activities." And, finally, the aphids: "One might call it a law that all state forms not constituted in the matriarchal spirit will not rise above the principle of aphid swarms." The insects against Pallas!

Isis, Demeter—those were the days! Ishtar-Madonna, Our Lady with the cow, the milk-giver, as a symbol of maternity; and then the fatherless condition of all Near Eastern saviors—certain God-men were sent back into the womb five times. Yet even Diotima would comb her hair, using Socrates' bald head as a mirror; whatever he may have been thinking inside it, he held it still for her anyway. But then the cataclysm! Pallas! Now her great bronze statue stands in the open place between the two temples. And what was Socrates up to right afterwards by the Illyssus, with Phaedo? That did not please the Great Mother! The tide of procreative life, exclusively destined for her womb, dialectically frozen under the hands of philosophizing old men of pockmarked countenance! (Our matriarchalist!)

Pallas, man's protectress, Pallas the ever-clear, though all should remain primal ground, primal womb, primal darkness, and primal murmurings! Pallas, who brought Achilles, Theseus, Heracles to success, and likewise that potency with the lion's face, the roaring cosmic bull—if he does not get the heifer instantly, his vengeful cunning makes him think with horns and testicles! First he thinks as a scent-atomizer, a seducer by means of fragrance, an evaporator of cerebral perfume—all honor to him! If only he had remained a bull, a perfume, a peacock, a little monkey, a Josephean watcher by the crib! But he became this transcendental masculine subject, this androcratic heretic, this temple-paederast, unnatural, immoral, and the cause of all crime! *Cherchez l'homme!* Why does society let him carry on? In heat he is the most infantile and dangerous of creatures, one that still goes in for tongue-clicking and whistling, he is the capercaillie revolving in love-play, and a moment later he loses his mind and kills. His thinking, primarily sheer hullabaloo, cooing, steering by tumescent organs, the paraphernalia of an exterminable species ordained to be nothing but the co-opener of the gateway of birth—this somber can-opener has made himself independent now with his systems, all negative, and his contrary delusions—all these lamas, buddhas, god-men, divine kings, saviors, and redeemers, none of whom has really saved the world—all these tragic male celibates, alien to Nature's primal material ground, averted from the secret maternal sense of things, unintentional cleavages in the formative power, impure rationality, dismal customers far inferior to the communal musical courtships of cicadas and frogs; in the highest animal societies, the lepidoptera states where everything ends normally in the act of copulation, they would be declared public enemies, to be suffered only for a while. All this was brought on by Pallas; from Pallas to schizophrenia is only one step—Pallas and nihilism, Pallas and progressive cerebralization—it all began under those plane trees, in Socrates' thick, disagreeable skull, with the first mirror-reflections and projections—ah, and once upon a time it reflected your hair and your lips, O Diotima!

II

What lives is something other than what thinks. This is a fundamental fact of our time, and we must come to terms with it. Whether it was ever different, whether some sidereal union glimmers upon us out of worlds to come, who knows? At this hour, anyway, it is not there. We must not only come to terms, we must acknowledge, defend the Orestean epoch, the world as a spiritual construction, as a transcendental apperception, existence as an intellectual edifice, the act of being as a dream of form. All this is the outcome of hard fighting and much suffering, this and much else. Pallas invented the flute—reed and wax—a little thing. Our brain also finds itself faced with a limitation of space. We can form only limited partial centers; it is not given to us to develop long perspectives horizontally and in time. Working within limited areas, chiseling planes no larger than the palm of one's hand, tight summaries, concise theses—everything beyond that lies outside the epoch.

A feast of Dionysus, wine against corn, Bacchus against Demeter, phallic congestion against the nine-month magic, the aphorism against the historical novel! A piece of writing is accomplished, paper covered with typescript, thoughts, sentences; it lies on the table. One returns from other realms, circles, professional spheres, the brain loaded with data, overflowing, repressing every flight and every dream—one returns hours later and sees the white sheets on the table. What is this? An inanimate something, vague worlds, things garnered in anguish and exertion, thought up, grouped, checked, revised, a pitiful residue, loose ends, unproved, weak—tinder, decadent nullity. The whole thing devious, a disease of the race, a somber birthmark, a confusion of connections? Then Pallas approaches, never perturbed, always helmeted, never impregnated, a slender childless divinity sexlessly born of her father.

What approaches is the law of frigidity, of minimum fellowship. It is through the blood that animals rejuvenate themselves, in the loins that Nature exhausts herself; after her—before her in the cycle of hours—the mind appeared, issuing forth for the first time in a created being and filling it with the dream of the Absolute. Dreams also generate, images weave, concepts burn things of every kind—ash the earth, cinders ourselves. Nietzsche says the Greeks were constantly regenerating and correcting themselves by way of their physiological needs; that preserved their vitality. It may have been so, but his own physiological needs were called knowledge—that was the new biology, which the mind demanded and created. Out of the futility of the material and historical process a new reality arose, created by the ambassadors of formal reason; the second reality, achieved by the slow gatherers and introducers of intellectual decisions. There is no road back. No invocation of Ishtar, no *retournons à la grand' mère*, no conjuration of the Realm of the Mother, no enthronement of Gretchen over and above Nietzsche, can do anything to change the fact that for us there is no longer any such thing as a state of Nature. Where man occurs in the state of Nature, he is of a paleontological character, a museum piece. The white, ultimate man is no longer Nature; he has taken the road he was shown by that "Absolute Reality," by gods, pregods, *prima materia, ens realissimum, natura naturans,* in short, by the heart of darkness—he has stepped out of Nature. His goal, perhaps only his transition, at any rate his existential mission, can no longer be called natural Nature; it is cultivated Nature, intellectualized Nature, stylized Nature—art.

The world of expression! In front of it Pallas stands, the childless divinity; Demeter's and all embryonic glutens' grandson keeps silence; let it all repose in primal darkness, on the knees of the gods. And the gods, eternal inspirers with breath and kneaders of clay, millepedes and multicolorists, will catch up again with time and space, and the fission-fungi and the spectra will give posterity plenty to play with and to suffer—some day! But I see the Achaeans around me. Achilles, his sword in its sheath; *not yet*—or I shall tear your yellow hair; Odysseus, man of many wiles, there the island lies, you will fetch the bow of Philoctetes. *Today! This!* Not Oceanus, not the barren waste of waters; where the ships sail, the Aegean and the Tyrrhenian Sea—*there!* Posterity! Already there are nourishing wellsprings from the Gulf Stream, the meteors provide us with savory and choice raw materials—the milk of the molluscs has been made sure of—do you now turn—fetch the bow—you alone!

Pallas pauses, it is evening, she loosens her armor, taking off the breastplate with the Gorgon's head upon it, this head in which the Babylonian dragon Tiamat and the serpent Apophis from Egypt live on, but stricken and vanquished. It is evening; there her city lies, stony land, the marble hill and the two rivers. Everywhere the olive tree, her handiwork, spreads in groves. She stands on what was once the place of judgment, the hill of Ares, the old Amazon castle that was destroyed by Theseus, lifter of stones. Before her are the steps of the altar on which sentence was uttered. She sees the Furies, she sees Orestes. She sees Apollo, her companion in the scene, and she recalls the remark of Proteus, ruler of the seals: that before long, reckoned by the hours of the gods, another would stand in this place, proclaiming the resurrection of the dead. Clytemnestra—Agamemnon; mariticide—matricide; patriarchal idea—matriarchal idea; the slain and the resurrected: all mere murmurs, mere ideas—ideas are as meaningless as facts, exactly as chaotic, regulating and illuminating no more than a fraction of the eon, either—nothing counts but the completed forms, the statues, the friezes, Achilles' shield. These are devoid of ideas, speak only of themselves, are perfect.

Among the constellations she saw the Horn of Amalthea, the Cretan goat that suckled her father as a child, as the doves brought him food and golden bees fed him with honey. Then he destroyed the amorphous, the unformed, the unlimited, along with the Titans and giants, the boundless element. This star had a bright green light, it was purer than Ariadne, next to it, whom Bacchus had flung up there in the transports of love. Pallas thought of her father. By means of a stone wrapped in goat's hair, Rhea, his mother, had saved his life, handing Saturn the stone to devour instead of the new-born divine child. That much-talked-of stone! The living, the formed had gained time to steal into the light! Then his reign began, and things moved in his course. This land, the home of poverty and the ancestrally inherited custom of acquiring advantages only by work and understanding—there now were the ivory and gold statues of the gods, there now the ghostly white colonnades of the Propylaea. In these things a nation saw itself, created itself. How long was it since Helios' rays struck not only the backs and fins of the downward-looking but an answering fire, since a mortal walking upright came to behold himself, interpreting himself and thinking and introvertly returning his own essence to himself in utterances and works: now—here? Pallas turned away and paced toward the city. And the city was a-glimmer with olive twigs and red thistles; tomorrow's players billowed through the streets, throngs of pilgrims and the crowd of onlookers. It was the evening before the Panathenaea. People came from the springs, from the terraced slopes of the mountains, from the sepulchral mounds in the marshes near Marathon; those who came from the sea had sailed for the flashing spear of Athena Promachos—that had been their beacon. Tomorrow they would step before the images and the statues and the masks made ready for the drama. All the Hellenes! The Hellenes of the plane trees, the chisel-wielding, the Orestean Hellenes! From among them Pallas now vanished, the motherless goddess, once more armored and alone.

(Written 1943–1944, published 1949) Translated by Ernst Kaiser and Eithne Wilkins

Pessimism

M an is not solitary, but thought is solitary. True, man is densely cloaked in mournfulness, but many share in this mourning, and it is popular with all. But thought is ego-bound and solitary. Perhaps primitive man thought collectively—the Red Indians, the Melanesians, most markedly the Negroes—here a number of things might be interpreted as an intensification of mass-participation; on the other hand, even on this level the figures of magicians, medicine-men, and saviors indicate the individually isolated nature of the intellectual manifestation. As for the white race, I do not know whether its life is happiness, but at any rate its thought is pessimistic.

Pessimism is the element of its creativeness. Admittedly we live in an epoch when pessimism is considered degenerate. There have been times—for instance, in the fourth and fifth centuries, before the great migrations could have any influence at all—when pessimism was an almost universal, at least theoretically admissible, attitude. It was pessimism that created the monasteries of Egypt and Palestine. A mass movement, incidentally: at the time of Jerome, the Easter festival at Tabenna was celebrated by 50,000 monks and nuns, all from the Nile area. They lived in rocky caves, in tombs between the sea and the marshes, in cottages built out of reeds, abandoned citadels, with snakes around them as they knelt, the mirages of the desert around them in their ecstasies—wolves and foxes went leaping by while the saint was at prayer. What impelled them was denial of the world, of the *saeculum*. The consequences are with us to this day: monotheistic religion at its purest, the literature of Antiquity, the philosophy of ideas and images; in short: the West would not exist without them.

Pessimism is not a Christian motif. The Choruses of Sophocles tell us that it is best never to be born, and that if you live, the next best thing is to go swiftly whence you came. That we are such stuff as dreams are made on was taught, 2,000 years before the Swan of Avon, by Buddhism—the embodiment of all that pessimism ever said and meant. Modern nihilism goes directly back to this, via Schopenhauer: "extinction"—"fading out," "a juggler's tricks"—"the starless void." It is very striking that this first authentic, one might even say popular, pessimism to appear in the history of the world as a system and a mass conviction, did not originate among India's oppressed lower castes, but among the mighty Brahmins. It was from a principality tropically luxuriant in pleasures and possessions that Shakyamuni came, the hermit "son of the Shakyas" (born 623 before Christ). But it is still more remarkable that his teaching did not set out to abolish any evils, any social, moral, or physical states of suffering but to abolish *existence itself*, the very substance of being. Life as such cast that handful of dust into the air, into the cycle of growth, before Sansara's wheel—so extinguish it—blow away all thirst of desire—no gods—the void. At the beginning there is a form of pessimism that denies all historical achievement, the state, any community—an *existential* pessimism frankly aimed at germ destruction.

And its germ-destroying trend culminates in *Schopenhauer's* dictum "Paederasty is a stratagem of Nature driven to the wall by her own laws—a *pons asinorum* that she has constructed in order to choose the lesser of two evils." And: "Life is continuous deception; it keeps no promise and gives so as to take." Here we have neither consciousness nor the unconscious, neither substance nor causality, neither reality nor dream, only fathomless, blind will, incapable of cognition. Behind this there stands *Schelling,* for whom the human head was only "Creation's tail-end," man "an amusing beast," death's-heads behind the ogling masks, even the stars full of bones and worms. He says: "It is all nothing, all choking and greedily gulping itself down, and this very self-devouring is the sly pretense that something exists—since, if the choking were to stop, nothingness itself would be so clearly manifest as to appall them." And *Byron* stands behind it: "Accursed be he who created life"; "the deeds of Athens' great men are the fable of an hour, a schoolboy's tale." *Stendhal:* "History is a collection of misdeeds; there is scarcely one virtuous act to a thousand crimes." *Diderot:* "To be born in helplessness and dependence, with pain and cries; to be the plaything of ignorance, error, need, sickness, of vileness and the passions; step by step from the moment when one begins to stammer to the moment of departure, when one raves; to live among rogues and charlatans of every kind; to pass away between one who feels our pulse and another who confounds us, not knowing whence one comes, why one has come, whither one is going—this is what is called the most precious gift we receive from our parents and from Nature: life." Here too are the Romans. *Pliny:* "Hence Nature has given man nothing better than brevity of life." *Marcus Aurelius:* "Man's nature is fluid, his feelings dim, the substance of his body tending to corruption, his soul comparable to a spinning top, his destiny hard to define, his reputation a matter of uncertainty." "Dream and rapture—war and journeying—his epitaph: oblivion." "Mayflies both he who remembers and he who is remembered." "Yesterday a bubble, tomorrow an embalmed corpse, then a heap of ashes." "Life is spent in bad company, in the frail body; what should deserve our love and striving in all the filth and corruption of circumstances, in the eternal interchange of essence and form, in the incalculable way things take their course, is more than man can see." "The sole consolation is going towards the dissolution of all things." *Septimius Severus,* gazing back over the road he had traveled from a low position in life up to imperial greatness, summed up: *"Omnia fui et nihil expedit*—I have been everything, and it was all for nothing." *Charles the Fifth,* on the road to St. Just, said that the greatest happiness he had enjoyed had always been associated with such manifold unhappiness that he must truthfully say he had never known a pure pleasure, never an unmixed delight.

These last three were emperors, wearing the diadem and wielding the power of the world. Evidently he who wants to accomplish things mistakes the action; in any case, the action takes a course different from that of their dream: *omnia fui et nihil expedit.* To be extinguished—to fade out—Hispanic monks, open the door for me! But what are we to make today of these words in *Wilhelm Meister's Travels:*[1] "Once one knows what really matters, one tends

1. Novel by Goethe.

to stop talking." Again a turn towards silence, away from participation and fellowship; words that are sheer rejection—was even he who wrote this, and who confessed to Eckermann that for him life had been the perpetual heaving of a boulder that had to be shifted again and again, that in seventy-five years he had not known four weeks of real ease—was even he *pre-nihilistic?* And what had happened to life's most strenuous glorifier, to that great prober and summarizer—what had Nietzsche lost that the world became a gateway to "a thousand deserts mute and cold"? Is there any possible interpretation of those weighty verses entitled "In Isolation," other than the assumption that their writer had lost all belief in fellowship, in the strong man's will to something higher and his ability to reach it, in biology, in race, in the "blond beast" ("Caesar with the soul of Christ")—was it perhaps here that the breakdown began, the fall into those ten years of sickbed-Nirvana after so many gigantic visions of a superior breed of men?

Omnia fui et nihil expedit. The game is not worth the candle. *Vulnerant omnes, ultima necat*—"All of them wound, the last one kills"—an inscription on the face of a medieval sundial, referring to the hours. And the ancient waterclock in the German Museum in Munich, the nymph weeping away the hours, the minutes, tear by tear—all this is the prelude to European nihilism. In a word, *pessimism is a legitimate spiritual principle,* a very ancient one which found genuine expression in the white race and which it will interweave with the future, supposing it still to possess the metaphysical power to incorporate and assimilate, the power of integration and of giving form. In this direction, too, points the strange passage in a letter of Burckhardt's, written in 1875, which says that the global battle between optimism and pessimism still remains to be fought. Victory, we may add today, can be won only in the sign of pessimism; negation alone will help to create that new world which not only man but Nature herself inclines to, in which she senses her transformation: the world of expression.

(1949)   *Translated by Ernst Kaiser and Eithne Wilkins*

Induced Life

I

Years ago a film was running in Berlin, a film about Negroes, *Hosanna,* in which one saw blacks arriving at a state of intoxication by singing together. Their special nature predisposed them for this kind of experience; the process itself took place on a sensual as well as a conscious level. Similar things are told about American Indians; in the Great Night-Song, one of their main festivals, the men hold hands, move in a rhythmic fashion, and fall into a trance. Evidently it is part of the primitive mentality to be close to an intoxicated state and to a transition into a collectively heightened feeling of existence. The congregation induces the transition by means of rituals, movements, particular ancient songs. It is a call of the race. Its nature is religious and mythical, a stirring communion with the universe with a highly transforming effect on the individual.

In contrast to trances induced by ritual, movement, and rhythm, the intoxicant and consciousness-expanding substances derived from plants are more universally known. Several million inhabitants of the earth drink or smoke Indian hemp—countless generations, for two thousand years. Three hundred million chew betel; the great rice nations would sooner do without betel than without the Areka nut—for them, to stop chewing would be to die. The three largest continents stimulate themselves with caffeine; in Tibet, time is measured by a cup of tea and its effects; tea has been found among the remains of prehistoric people. Chemical materials with effects on the brain, transformers of consciousness—primitive man's first attention to the nervous system. How he discovered these effects is a mystery. We are presented with a primeval urge and a secret. Among a thousand roots, shrubs, trees, mushrooms, blossoms—this one! Probably countless people died of poisoning before the race had achieved its goal: intensification, expansion—induced life. Caravans with opium cross the desert; Sykone is renamed Mykone, which means poppy city. On the coffin of the sleeping Ariadne, the bearded god of sleep leaning over her is bearing poppy heads and the poppy horn. The queen of the Incas named herself after the miraculous plant *Erythroxylon coca*: Mama Cuca; coca leaves are stuffed into the left cheeks of idols to indicate their divinity; standing around everywhere are the bottle-shaped gourds in which the leaf was preserved, mixed with calcium and the ashes of plants, ready for eating; the point of the long needle with which it is ingested is moistened with the mouth. The effect of one portion of coca lasts forty minutes = three kilometers on level territory, two kilometers on mountain terrain, that is the measure of dosage.

In the dreamers' ranch of Ecuador, in tents, to the beat of the magician's drum, in empty cellars with stone ledges alongside the walls for the guests to sit on, on festive occasions or every day, to the exclusion of women or by their side, the potion is ingested: the "black drink," the "white water," the "joy pills," or the "herb of graves" which brings communion with the spirits. Stages of excitation, stages of dreaming—one is beside oneself, but one feels, one learns from twitches and disturbances of the breath, one receives apathy and mobility, as one wishes. From concealed centers, from the depths, it rises: to rest, never to move again—supine, regression, aphasia. Hours fulfilled with satisfied cravings for a drowsing and substanceless life. He who calls this bestial misjudges the situation: it is lower than the animal, far below the reflexes, down to the level of root, lime, and stone. This cannot be racial exhaustion, degeneration, for these are early peoples; this is something primary: defense against the beginnings of consciousness, against its senseless imperative projects—hence the urge to alter the spatial dimensions, to extinguish time, to blow out the horrible flow of its hours.

Insofar as the brain, as an organ of serial organization, has assembled a fund of memories, civilizations—to forget! In front of the bistro these pinstriped types, owner-occupied idealisms, worn-off childhood kingdoms, curves without amplitude, standardized refuse—ah!—waiter, another glass of cocaine-pulque or in the bathroom a pinch of snuff upon the mucous membrane of the anus or a saturated filling stuffed into a carious tooth specially prepared for this purpose—ah!—already the vistas are opening up; it's incessantly bubbling out from crisscross lines, snaking and slithering—Helen served nephentes, surely an opiate, to the heroes at their meals, when the mood had declined, or before a battle—ah! my battle too is beginning—first come fields, multicolored like jewels, then red birds—*a reality made purely of cerebral cortex*—cruciform designs are especially frequent—"Jewelers or artists should see that; they could take their designs from it"; the colors become subtler; strings hang from the surfaces; miracles gaze out of things.

The I disintegrates, the loci of disintegration are the former contact surfaces. Galactic coldness, supernal and icy, develops in the structure, red heat in the central axis; sensations of lengthening and contracting limbs, feelings of swelling to club-shaped proportions; at the same time, subtilization of threshold phenomena: assault of impressions, susceptibility to the alien and unknown, projected at something universal, a sense of Allness—"Feeling of Noon." The senses confuse their functions: "At the stroke of the clock I saw purple rising"—impressions of confluence and, alternately, of separation; thwartings of the ego stance, affectless smiles, reasonless tears. Feelings of capacity: "The solution of vaguely intuited problems seems imminent"—"Everywhere the tremendous jubilation of a powerful harmony"—"Lord, let me blossom" (Bucke's "cosmic emotion").

Another: "A great tension came over me. Something great would have to reveal itself to me. I would behold the essence of all things, all the problems of world history would be revealed. I was desensualized." A god walking by the banks of the Po. "Golden late afternoon light." Then: "Only beauty in the eternal recombining of forms and colors. An increasing feeling of liberation overcame me. Everything would have to be resolved in this, *for ultimately the life of the cosmos resided in rhythm*." (Klages[1] came to this

1. Ludwig Klages (1872–1956), German philosopher and psychologist.

conclusion as well, just not as eruptively, but at the end of a long life and with the aid of many books. And the quantum theory says basically the same thing.)

Strange penetration of the ground, magma-osmosis: "I need time to complete my world view, the frame of which already stands on that single sentence: *God is a substance.*" God is a substance, a drug! An intoxicant closely related to the human brain. It's certainly possible, and at any rate more likely than his being an electrostatic generator or a Spemannian triton larva developed by transplanting tadpole tissues into the mouth region. . . .

Complexity becomes brittle, one can see through the cracks: "I had a very peculiar muscular sensation. *I could have removed every single muscle separately from my body.*" (Long, long ago! The "muscle soul" arising, its contribution to the development of consciousness.) The cortex losing its late-gained possession of specific sensory qualities (seeing, hearing, smelling, tasting), responding instead in forms of general resonance. The "outer" is not there yet; there are grounds, but these are hunting and fishing grounds—the prehistory of "reality."

II

The formation of the concept "reality" introduced the crisis, the premorbid stage, its depth, its nihilistic existence. Indo-Javanese art (the pedestal of Borobudur) still evinced the other stage 800 years after Christ. Its almost obscene proliferations of limbs and forms, the endless reliefs of animals, plants, humanoid growths, bears, flowers, bayaderes, hermits, turtles, jackals, monkey kings, all depicted without exaggeration, unseparated and inexhaustible—the people all of the same roundish smooth full-bodied kind with relatively small heads, all built the same way, all naked—all this expresses the *Tat twam asi*, "Thou art that," of the Hindu doctrine; expresses the ethical and physiological promiscuity, the quondam unisexuality of the primitive creature which executed the processes of seed-formation and breeding and fruition within itself, but it also speaks of an inner world that is still accessible to everyone, a serene and gentle circularity of intertwining forms, a world which still knows a coherence, a unity that perpetually forms and renews itself around a spiritual nucleus. It is from here that the Great Day- or Night-Song arises, the Great Pedestal Song of prelogical worlds that are yet capable of fulfillment.

Thirteen hundred years before this pedestal, in the south of our continent, the concept of reality began to develop. The Helleno-European principle of the agonal, of the overcoming of Adversity by achievement, slyness, stealth, gifts, force—Greek in the form of the arena, late European in Darwinism and the Superman—had a decisive formative influence upon it. The ego emerged, stepped down, fought; and for this, means were needed, matter, power. The ego approached matter differently, removing itself sensually but entering into a closer formal relationship with it. It analyzed matter, experimenting, distinguishing: weapon, exchange object, ransom; purified it by isolation; reduced it to formulas; tore pieces out of it; distributed them. The brutality and lowness of this attitude as against the gently undulating Javanese feeling of being is self-evident. It was avenged by the separation of ego and world, the schizoid catastrophe, the fatal neurosis of the Western world: reality. A tortuous concept, and it tortured everyone, splitting the intelligence of countless generations. Nemesis of a concept with which the West wrestled without ever grasping it, to which it brought sacrifices in hecatombs of blood and happiness, a concept whose tensions and breaks could no longer be filtered back to the essential unitary quietude of prelogical existence, either by a natural way of seeing or by any methodical epistemology. At a particular critical moment, Kant tried to introduce certain formal safeguards, but this only accelerated the process, for now the reality concept comprised only the results of causal analysis, including those of biological experimentation, while everything else was the product of dreams, animism, psychogenic arabesque. The only publicly verifiable case of a man overcoming the problem for several decades was Goethe; here was a healing that lasted, but it was of a purely personal nature. No one else has overcome the concept of reality and no one can; instead, its cataclysmic character has become more and more evident, for example, in Nietzsche's case. He took reality so literally at face value that he wanted to "penetrate" it in a highly forceful manner with ideas and eugenic speculations, and he sent out Zarathustra "to create the creator," a task that was surely very alien to this ancient Ormuzd- and Ahriman-dualist. Presumably he would have cast one glance at the impenetrable sun and then gazed at the poppies sown among the rose fields of Shiraz and lightly touched the ground with his forehead: thou gavest the Shire-Teriak and I partake of it! A state, finally, a social order, a public morality for which life is nothing but economically utilizable life, is in no position to meet the destructive inroads of the reality concept. A community whose hygiene and racial self-maintenance are a modern ritual founded on the hollow experiences of biological-statistical research is incapable of any viewpoint other than that of the superficial mass viewpoint, for whose sake it can wage wars, incessantly, since reality is merely regarded as raw material while its metaphysical background remains hidden. But all the foregoing treats of this background and connects it with the problems of sublimation, Janet's[2] *émotions sublimes,* that is to say, with phenomena of intensified consciousness and expressive values.

III

The issue is the mythical collectivity as a vital foundation, as a nonreflexive feeling of existence, whatever remnants of it are still left us, and the processes that bring them about. In contrast to the tribal life of the primitives, which is the fruit of an inner endowment, in contrast to the image-saturated faiths of Asia, there can be no doubt but that the vital contents expressed by denatured European brains in their professional transactions, pressure groups, clannish riotings, summer excursions, and so-called festivals represent the ultimate in conventionality and exhaustion known to the memory of man, and the few elemental crimes that may occur in a decade do not suffice to restore one's faith in the race's moral endowment. There is a particular lack of any systematic educational work in the direction of a conscious increase of vitality, since the epoch lacks any true principles altogether. If this were not the case, we would by now have considered the possibility of allowing the race to avail itself of an influx of realization and spirit, perhaps through mescaline and hashish, that might release a new period of creativity.

2. Pierre Janet (1859–1947), French philosopher and psychiatrist.

Or we might have struck upon the idea of using hypnosis (which today is exclusively in the hands of causal-analytical doctors drilled in the precepts of normative psychology) not just for life-affirming purposes in the sense of industrial productivity, but also in order to attempt to liberate unconscious, that is, ineffectual, organic functions as well as archaic mechanisms: surprising experiential results would be gained. Instead of pumping pervitine into bomber pilots and bunker pioneers, it could be used in higher education for the deliberate purpose of producing cerebral oscillations. To some this may sound like a deviant route, but it is merely the natural continuation of one idea of humanity. Whether by rhythm, by drugs, by modern autogenic training—it is the ancient human desire for release from tensions that have become intolerable, such as the tension between outside and inside, God and non-God, self and reality—and for the ancient and new human knowledge of how to achieve this transcendence. Buddha's systematic "prayerful breathing," the ritual prayer positions of the early Christian hesychasts, Loyola's inhalation before every word of the Lord's Prayer, the dervishes, the yogis, the Dionysians, the Mysteries—they are all of one family and their relationship is called religious physiology. German mysticism—according to Jakob Böhme,[3] "the reversion of natural selfhood to Nothingness" (remarkably enough, it's to Nothingness, not to God)—this mysticism, which a modern scholar calls "an almost experimental religious psychology of the most ruthless kind," was nothing different in essence. What we have here, then, is induced religion.

All these are historical facts; they are widely known and can be experienced, even if one regards them from a purely biological standpoint: psychological facts. And yet the contemporary state apparatus regards them with the utmost suspicion. It recently founded an antinarcotics center, an organization whose biologists regard themselves as the vanguard of our times. It would be difficult to persuade the state that the relationship between this antinarcotics organization and the problem of humanity is approximately that of the mailman to the problem of cosmopolitanism. This modern state does not fail to entrust physiologists with the task of investigating the possibility of increasing the human organism's capacity

---

3. German philosopher of mysticism, 1575–1624.

to withstand heights by testing the influence of great quantities of medicine on mountain climbers, but it doesn't consider the possibility of heightening the formal-esthetic functions. It cultivates centers for the collection of mothers' milk, one of which, according to recent reports, was supplied by twelve hundred mothers from Frankfort on the Main with an exemplary 10,000 liters, one mother alone delivering 753 liters, and another, after the birth of her sixth child, 460 liters. But potent brains are not fortified by milk but by alkaloids. Such a small and vulnerable organ, which succeeded in not only approaching but creating and imagining pyramids and gamma rays, lions and icebergs, cannot be sprinkled with ground water like a forget-me-not; it's more than sufficiently supplied with stagnant matter as it is. *Existence is nervous existence,* that is, irritability, discipline, enormous factual knowledge, art. To suffer means to suffer consciousness, not bereavements. Work is intensification of consciousness for the making of intellectual forms. In short: *Life is induced life.*

Of course there is the immediate objection that this might be *harmful,* both to the individual and to the race. Drugs, intoxications, ecstasies, spiritual exhibitionisms—to the national community this sounds infernal. But the concept of harmfulness belongs, first of all, to the conceptual systems called "causal analysis" and "biology," and partakes of their very relative validity. But even within these systems, the state is not entitled to remonstrate about harmfulness so long as it wages wars that cause the deaths of three million men within three years, doubtless a greater damage to individual and collective interests than could be inflicted by experiments that test the consciousness-expanding effects of drugs. So the issue is not harmfulness but principles and how one wishes to define these. If one regards the concept of harmfulness in an even more general way, it is extremely interesting to note that when harms of a universal nature befall a race, they can bring compensations that are of far greater vital value than what was lost. The loss of skin pigmentation, for instance, which singled out the white race, represented at first a most life-threatening deprivation of defense reactions against the unimaginable impact of radiation, but then our common primary sprout-leaf, the ectoderm, put forth another shoot in compensation and developed the overarching defensive nervous system which culminates in us. On the basis of this original damage, or at least following it in time, there developed the white human brain. Therefore, when one uses the word *harmful*, one must always indicate the immediate context. Whether or why, in this context, the European brain could be damaged at all as it sinks in its mire, would require some further definition.

No one will gain any knowledge in this area if his meditations in the proximity of the brain are too expedient and too short-term. The brain is a perfect test case for the pygmy character of causal theories, for it accomplished its journey with thoroughly acausal steps, and all biological hypotheses fail to explain it. The works of Versluys, Poetzl, and Lorenz appear to have proven that it developed by a discontinuous doubling of neurons and a simultaneous rearticulation of the cortical regions. "Intermediate forms are lacking." Not a trace of adaptation, of a summing up of the smallest stimuli, of a gradual rotting and ripening until an expedient adjustment was reached—*what was always present were crises of creativity*. The brain is the mutative, that is, revolutionary organ par excellence. Not content but form was always its essence; its instrument was consciousness expansion; its desire was for stimuli. From the beginning, this shelter of rudiments and catacombs brought along its own equipment, it didn't depend on impressions, and it produced itself when it was called. It did not by preference turn to "life," but also to lethal factors, hunger, fasting, walking on nails, singing to snakes, magic, bionegativity, death.

Mens sana in corpore sano[4] was a figure of speech among the Roman warrior caste which found its modern resurrection in Friedrich Ludwig Jahn[5] and Bavarian leather jerkins. Judging by the mind's standards, the extravagant body achieved more than the normal body: its bionegative qualities created and sustain the human world. By these standards, there is no reality at all, and no history either, but certain brains realize their dreams at certain intervals, dreams that are images of the great original dream, a remembrance of it. This realization takes place in "stone, verse, flute song," and art develops; sometimes just in thought and in ecstasy. A wonderful sentence in one of Thornton Wilder's novels defines the situation: "We come from a world in which we knew unbelievable standards

4. "A healthy mind in a healthy body."
5. (1778–1852), nicknamed "Turnvater," advocated physical education as a basis for military fitness.

of perfection, and, vaguely remembering the beauties we were never able to hold fast, we return to that world." Plato distinctly looms in from the shadows; endogenic images are the last chance at happiness left for us to experience.

(Written 1943, published 1949)   *Translated by Joel Agee*

Future and Present

The way of an intellectualist. . . . An intellectualist, I take it, is someone rather cool in human affairs, someone who loves clear words and defends himself with concepts sharper than bread knives. He may be a still unbalanced rudiment of a *sapiens* type whose later forms will no longer have affective or humane or even historic problems, because he thinks in terms of order and regulation, feels his mission in those, and fulfills it under the aegis of great, supranational complexes that will be comparatively just but unsentimental. All this has yet to grow, and I hope that Europe will then be in on it.

The past century was bursting with the notion, and the word, "collective." The paleologists taught that the mythical collective was at an end; the social scientists opined that the social one was beginning—"no, the racial one," snarled the Third Reich, and the Eastern office neon-lighted the active, quota-fulfilling, progressive, constructive one; you could not make head or tail of all the collectives. This dream is finished. Collective—that was sheer illusion, a fable to fill the ineffable emptiness of our robot existence, and the explanation of our inability to put a modern state conception into practice. Now the states have broken down under the joint pressure of victories and defeats, and the new, supranational complexes no longer need this auxiliary construction; they drain and involve the individual in other directions and replenish it with other necessities.

But these questions more or less concern the future, and the future, as I often wrote, is not important to the living. Their serious concern is with the present, with their own inner being, their self.

So I will take another look at my circles, and do so in aphorisms.

1. My generation still had certain literary residues from earlier ones to latch on to: father-and-son problems, Antiquity, adventure, travel, social issues, *fin de siècle* melancholia, marital questions, themes of love. Today's generation has nothing in hand any more, no substance and no style, no education and no knowledge, no emotions and no formal tendencies, no basis whatever—it will be a long time until something is found again.

Addendum: confusion and bad writing alone does not make one a surrealist.

2. Actually, what my generation discussed and excogitated— what, one might say, it suffered or, one might also say, it harped upon—had all been already expressed, exhausted, definitely phrased by Nietzsche; what came after him was exegesis. His dangerously stormy, flashing manner, his restless diction, his renunciation of idyls and universal reasons, his establishment of instinctual psychology, constitutional motivation, physiology as dialectics—"cognition as affect"—the whole of psychoanalysis, the whole of existentialism, all this is his work. More and more clearly we see in him the far-reaching giant of the post-Goethean epoch.

Addendum: after Nietzsche, Spengler. Not because of his assumption of decline, but because he propounded the concept of a morphology of cultures, a not only interesting but guiding and regulating idea in the confused historic world.

3. One may doubt and ridicule science, including genetics and paleontology, but the sciences are telescopes; now and then we put our eyes to them, and then we see that there have been infinities of human and extra-human development and formation before us, without us, far from us. Our bit of latitude, our bit of climate, our clothing, the nutrition of our momentary little continent, and our evaluations, moods, tendencies, ideals, philosophies—what does it all amount to? What I miss is a treatise on the domesticity of axioms, a geography of apriority, the climatical excuse for so much dust.

4. Estrangement from nature. Nature is a strange milieu; if you leave your room, even the ordinary air feels alien. A flowering shrub in a city street will do it, or again a look at the sky, a gray sky with a bird flying in it—no special bird, just a starling—and then the night begins. We are creatures of giant cities; it is in the city, and there only, that the Muses exult and grieve.

5. In the beginning was the word. It is amazing and has cost me a great deal of thought that this was in the beginning. In the beginning, when animism and totemism and cave-scraping and beasts and magic masks and rain-rattles kept the field and the world—the Jews were probably very old when they said this, and knew much. Truly, it is in the word that the earth centers; there is nothing more revealing than the word. It has always fascinated me to see experts in their fields, even profound philosophers, suddenly faced with the free word—the word that yields no tirades, no systems, no facts of external, historically buttressed observation, and no commentaries; that produces one thing only: form. How they operate there! Utterly at a loss. Little idyllicists, crickets, small boys. In the beginning, in the middle, and at the end is the word.

Addendum: there really are now only two verbal transcendencies, the theorems of mathematics and the word as art. The rest is business speech, bar parlance.

6. How many good starters were seen to fall by the wayside! At first, big avant-garde, some indeed divinely gifted—and at forty they take the family tramping through Andalusia and detail the bullfights, or they discover Hindu introversion on a Cook's tour. What breaks them, according to my observations, is premature fame, allowing themselves to be typed by critics and admirers. Only if you break yourself again and again, if you forget yourself, go on and pay for it, live under burdens, let no one talk you into occasions to write, but make your own reasons for writing—then, perhaps, then, if a great deal of disappointment and self-denial and forced abandonment is added—then, eventually, you will perhaps have advanced the Pillars of Hercules by a few worm-lengths—perhaps.

7. No work can come to be save in a closed space. What people call dynamic and imagine as being revolutionary, tempestuous, frontier-smashing belongs to other realms of existence. Those are premises, and art is static. Its content is a balance between tradition and originality, its procedure the equilibrium of mass and point of support. This fact explains the peculiar proximity of everything artistic in the cycle of civilization, from early Egyptian sculpture to Picasso drawings, from the hymns of the Middle Kingdom and the Hebrew psalms to the poems of Ezra Pound. Yet this fact separates art from all other realms—a thesis that we see ever more plainly

emerging, a thesis that cannot be made plain enough, in order to take in what follows.

What follows came out of an interview with a gentleman from the radio and a gentleman of the press. They both asked what I had to say about the numerous reviews of my new books. "What are the objections of your critics, and what is your position?" My first answer was: I greatly admire my critics, when they agree with me as well as when they object, since hardly any of them fails to grasp the essence of my literary manner, to set his sights in the direction of my style, and to digest my opinions. From this I infer, to my own surprise, that the inner currents I am trying to express are much more widespread in European letters than is casually assumed—that certain tensions in the productive sphere of present Western man have built up to a degree of condensation and have created pressures for discharge that will soon make undreamed-of psychic transformations understandable, even to those who are more remote and not artistically active.

As for the rest, I'll summarize that in aphorisms again. I am aware of the peculiar acuity of my phrasings, also of reiterating things already said in the first part of this book, that of 1934. As for the acuity, I think that in the intellectual world more damage has been done by flabbiness than by rigor.

1. *The Crisis of Foundations*
Thought clashes with thought—Marxist with Western, Faustian with Mediterranean, collective with isolationist, biological with psychological, critical with empirical, social with aristocratic. These encounters can be most exciting, suspenseful, and moving, but they all occur in the same setting of dialectics, ratio, and ideology. The thought that advances today will be beaten tomorrow; the idea we identify with our time will be obsolete and void after the next counter-movement; some motifs last for hundreds or thousands of years, like those of Nazareth or of Antiquity, but the dialectic defensive-offensive milieu remains. The feeling of this actual or potential relativity of the world of European thought, the loss of certainty and absoluteness, is the present stigma of our civilization. It is an immensely widespread and general, an already popular, feeling. Everywhere you see societies that discuss it, circles which

some city pays to reason about it; academies mushroom; clubs debate the hopeless situation—there is a rabbit warren of analyses and prognoses, a rabbit warren of introversions and incantations as well as evasions and blights all over the continent. Can you blame a man for saying: Fine, all right, I guess it must be that way, but without me, please—for the brief span of my days without me, please—for I know a sphere without this sort of mobility, a sphere that rests, that can never be set aside, that is conclusive: the esthetic sphere.

2. Artistics

When you announced your visit, you promised not to ask me if I am a nihilist. The question is, indeed, as immaterial as it would be to ask whether I skate or collect postage stamps. For the point is *what you make of your nihilism.* Sonia Henie and Maxi Herber[1] doing *pas des patineurs,* the golden Suaheli in philately, and expression in the world of the mind: always the purest, always the nearly perfect. Style is superior to truth, for it carries the proof of existence in itself. Form: in form is distance, is duration. "Thought is always the scion of want," says Schiller—in whose work we see, after all, a very conscious shift of emphasis from ethics to esthetics; he means that thought is always close to utility, to the satisfaction of urges, to axes and clubs, that thought is nature. And Novalis goes on to speak of "art as the progressive anthropology."

The epochs end in art, and the human race will end in art. First came the saurians, the lizards, and then the species with art. Love and hunger—that's paleontology, and even insects have all kinds of government and division of labor; but our species made gods and art, and then art alone. We live in a late world underset with preliminary stages, early forms of existence; everything ripens in it. All things are reversed, all concepts and categories change character as soon as we view them as art, when it faces them, when they face it. A novel attitude, a novel affection. It is an hour from Homer to Goethe, and twenty-four hours from Goethe to this day—twenty-four hours of change, of dangers that only he who acts according to his own legalities can meet. People now ask often for a "correct" image of Goethe, but there will be no such thing; we must be

---

1. Famous ice-skaters.

satisfied with the knowledge that here something was launched that confuses, that is incomprehensible but scatters seed on barren shores—and that is art.

3. *Religion and Humility*

A great new tide of piety engulfs the continent. Döblin,[2] once avant-garde, Franz Biberkopf of Alexanderplatz, is now a strict Catholic proclaiming *ora et labora*,[3] Toynbee is Christian, so is Eliot; Jünger[4] plays the Christian humanist—all of them reach backwards. Fine pose, but style relaxation, conformism. I forego this reaching; it is another question I can only view artistically. "God is a bad rule of style," I once wrote, and, "Gods in the first verse is something other than gods in the last verse"—meaning, I either turn myself inside out or someone else does; I can't have it both ways. If you were to ask me whether I believe, I should say that believing would already put me outside the substance I work in, would separate me from the essence of my mission and my involvement; the nature of this mission and involvement is more obscure to me than it has ever been. I regard prayer and humility as arrogant and pretentious. Their premise is that I am anything at all—which is just what I doubt; there is only something that goes through me. A Catholic newspaper, after praising me highly in detail, concluded, "Out with this man; he derides God and despises the religions." What misjudgment! I despise humans who cannot handle their own affairs and therefore ask help from another quarter—a quarter that can scarcely know them, these shadows of nothing, these rabbits, these wormwood drops left in the dregs, who reform for ten cents and whose main hope should be to go to their graves before long and get out of the sight of the Great Being. This Great Being—a subject by itself! Consider what it has done to us: it certainly has not endowed me well enough to find my way; it has veiled much that would matter to me; I must take plenty and end up knowing no more than when I started. Result: I must go through everything alone, through my breakdowns, through the study of myself, through the phenomenology of my remaining ego—should I then suddenly grow humble at the decisive moment and say, "I'm sorry, I didn't

2. Alfred Döblin (1878–1957), author of *Berlin Alexanderplatz*.
3. "Pray and work."
4. Ernst Jünger (1895–   ), novelist and essayist.

mean it?" Where would that leave the individualism our West is said to live by, if it suddenly sawed off and threw away its façade and humbled itself? Humility as a broadening motif, a mood, a vacuum for lock-opening and novelty-admitting purposes—all right; but as a moralistic and religious overcast it merely confuses the style. This Great Being certainly should have elaborated its situation more distinctly before making precise claims.

4. Principles of Art

cannot be publicly and politically generalized. It is provincial immaturity on the artist's part to expect the public to care about him, to support him financially, and to celebrate his sixtieth birthday with banquets and floral tributes. He rampages within himself—who should thank him for it? Remember, too, how many "Egmont" and "Leonore" overtures have thundered over the average politician's head at inaugurations and other festive occasions, without effecting a change in him. I agree, therefore, with Monet's maxim, *"Il faut décourager les arts,"* and with James Joyce's paraphrase of a Talmud saying, "We Jews are like the olive, giving our best when we are crushed, when we collapse under the burden of our labors"—in Joyce's view this applies to artists. Those are healthy ideas! Let us at last distinguish between art carriers and culture carriers, as I proposed in one of my books fifteen years ago. The art carrier is statistically asocial, living only with his inner material, utterly disinterested in expansion, broad effect, increased reception, and culture. He is cold; his material must be kept cold, since his task is to chill and harden the idea—the warmth to which others may humanly yield—so as to give stability to softness. He is mostly very sober and does not even claim to be anything else, while the idealists sit among the culture carriers and money-makers. Thus I wrote some fifteen years ago; and it is not half of what will be revealed by the future. . . .

(1950)   *Translated by E. B. Ashton*

Artists and Old Age

... Last winter in Berlin I went to a lecture at the Kant-Gesellschaft given by a Kant scholar on Kant's posthumous work. This work, the *Opus posthumum,* the original of which was lost in Northern Germany during the last war, exists in the form of transcripts which, with notes and commentary, were made available to the limited public of the philosophically interested about twenty years ago; it is apparent that Kant never got to the point of working it over and finishing it completely. The *Opus posthumum* was written during the years 1797–1803; Kant's great earlier works had been published some twenty years before that time. It has now become evident that some of his fundamental theses look very different in the light of the later work, which contains passages in contradiction to the *Critique of Pure Reason,* and the lecturer raised the question which propositions were to be considered valid, the earlier or the post-humous ones; for the two were scarcely reconcilable. The lecturer did not attempt to settle the question, but suggested that some of the earlier theses were cancelled out by some of the later. Behind this question of the comparative validity of Kant's earlier or later work, there looms up the problem of early and late works in general, the problem of the continuity of the creatively productive person-ality, of the transformations it undergoes and the breaks that occur. The particular case is that of a philosopher, but the problem is one that occurs in the case of artists, too.

It was about the same time that I read in a newspaper a review of an exhibition of the work of Lorenzo Lotto that had been held in Venice the previous summer. In this review was the sentence: "The works of the last decades strike one as being unsure, in the same marked way as one notices it in the German artists Baldung and Cranach." So these great masters became unsure of themselves in their last period of creative productivity. While I was pondering on this, I came across the following dictum by Edward Burne-Jones in a work on the history of art: "Our first fifty years are squandered on committing great errors; then we grow timid and scarcely dare to set our right foot before the left any longer, so well are we aware of our own weakness. Then there follow twenty years of toil, and only now do we begin to understand what we are capable of and what we have to leave undone. And then there comes a ray of hope and a trumpet-call, and away we must go from the earth." Here then is the opposite of Lotto's case; here it is youth that is uncertain, and certainty comes with old age, when it is too late. This is reminiscent of the scene from "Titian's Death" by the twenty-year-old Hofmannsthal, where Titian lies on his death-bed, but still goes on painting—I think the picture was "Danae"—and suddenly he starts up and asks for his earlier pictures to be brought before him.

He says that he must see them,
Those old, and wretched, pale ones,
must now compare them with the new ones he is painting;
for now, he says, things very hard to grasp are clear to him,
he understands, as earlier he never dreamt he could,
that up to now he was a feeble blunderer.

So here, too, we have it, seen through the artist's own eyes: only in his ninety-ninth year does he cease to be a feeble blunderer.

To my surprise, I found similar trends of thought in the East. Hokusai (1760–1849) says: "I have been mad about drawing since I was six years old. By the time I was fifty I had given the public a vast number of drawings, but nothing of what I did before my seventy-third year is worth mentioning. At about the age of seventy-three I had come to understand something of the true nature of animals, plants, fishes, and insects. It follows that by the age of eighty I shall have made further progress, by the age of ninety I shall see into the mystery of things, and if I live to be one hundred and ten everything I do, even if it is no more than a stroke or a dot, will be alive." Here we come up against the question that has occasionally been aired in literature—what would the world have thought of certain men had they died earlier than they did in fact? In this particular case it is the question what would have been left of Hokusai if he had died before his seventy-third year.

"All Eastern and all Western lands/Tranquil lie within His Hands"—so I took counsel with our Olympian great-granfather, Goethe, and studied his *Maxims and Reflections,* a book that everyone who has his troubles should dip into for a few hours each week. There I found the following aphorisms:

1. Growing old means entering into a new business; all the circumstances change, and one must either entirely cease to act or take over the new role with purposefulness and deliberation.

2. When one is old one must do more than when one was young.

3. On the guillotine itself Madame Roland asked for writing materials in order to write down the quite special thoughts that had occurred to her on her last journey. What a pity it was denied her—for at the end of life there come to the resigned and courageous soul thoughts that were hitherto unthinkable, and they are like blissful spirits, settling radiantly on the peaks of the past.

Blissful spirits—on the way to the guillotine! Very Olympian, very gigantic!—and indeed this great-grandfather of ours, with his many talents and possessions of every kind, was quite the man to start upon a new business at any moment. All the same, this was scarcely of a generally illuminating nature. However, in the same volume there was the fragment *Pandora,* and I found myself considering the strange figure of Epimetheus:

> For Epimetheus I was called by my progenitors,
> he who muses on things past, and traces back,
> in the laborious play of thoughts, the quick deed
> to the dim realm of form-combining possibilities.

To muse, to trace back, in the laborious play of thoughts, to the dim realm of form-combining possibilities—perhaps this Epimetheus was the patron of old age, a twilight figure, sombre, backward-glancing, in his hand the torch already lowered.

At this point you may, perhaps, say to yourself that you are listening to someone making extensive use of quotations, alert for whatever he can pick up, on the lookout for advice and information, like a young girl travelling alone, and you may ask yourself: What is he after, what is he getting at? Is there something personal hidden behind all this? Yes, indeed, that is precisely the case, there *is* something personal behind it all, but it does not take up undue space in what is to follow. All the same, just for a moment, if you please, imagine a writer with an unquiet past, in unquiet times, who began his vocation together with a whole circle of others of the same age from all countries of the world, and who also underwent that same stylistic development which was known by various names—Futurism, Expressionism, Surrealism—and still keeps discussion alive today, since it is a stylistic development of decidedly revolutionary character—admittedly, and let us get this said once and for all—no more revolutionary, in our author's opinion, than such earlier stylistic developments as Impressionism, Baroque, or Mannerism—but still, for this century, it certainly was revolutionary. This author sailed under various colors in his life: as a poet and as an essayist, as a citizen and as a soldier, as a hermit in the country and as a man of the world in this or that great metropolis—and for most of the time under criticism and attack. Well, now this writer is getting on in years, and he still goes on publishing things. And if he has not entirely quenched the volcanic element in himself, not entirely lost the dash and vigor of youth, what it comes to is that the critics nowadays exclaim: "Good heavens, why can't the man be quiet? Isn't it time he got down to writing something classical and preferably with something of a Christian tinge? Surely it's high time for him to ripen and mellow as befits his years!" But if, for once, he does write something rather more mellow and glowing and, so far as he has it in him, classical, the cry is: "Oh, the fellow's completely senile! He was moderately interesting when he was young, in his storm-and-stress period, but now he's a mere hanger-on desperately trying to keep up with himself. He hasn't anything to say, so why can't he have the decency to shut up?"

So far, so good. When an individual book of a writer's is reviewed, whether it is panned or praised, he can feel proud or annoyed, according to his mood. But the situation changes when the writer has got on so far in years that books begin to appear about him, when the younger generation begins to write theses on him for their doctorates, at home and abroad, analyzing him, classifying him, cataloguing him—theses in which a comma that he put in thirty years ago, or a diphthong that he produced one Sunday afternoon after the first World War, is treated as a fundamental stylistic problem. The studies in themselves are interesting, the linguistic and stylistic analysis is superb, but for the writer under discussion it is like watching himself being vivisected. Others have seen what he is like, and so now he himself sees what he is like. For the first time in his life he recognizes himself; up to now he was utterly a stranger to himself, he had to grow old in order to see himself.

And supposing that this writer has at some time in his life uttered opinions that are later considered impossible, then good care is taken that these opinions should drag along behind him like the harrow after a farm horse, and everyone is delighted to see them continually hitting him on the heels. Well, that's part of the game—the writer says to himself—nothing can be done about that. If one were to write nothing but what turned out to be opportune fifteen years later, presumably one would never write anything at all. One little example of what I mean, and then I shall leave this writer of ours for some time. In a conversation, a very serious conversation between three old men, this writer once wrote the sentence: "To be mistaken and yet be compelled to go on believing what one's own innermost being tells one—that is man and his glory begins yonder, beyond victory and defeat." From our author's point of view this declaration was a sort of anthropological elegy, a cyphered melancholy; but his critics thought differently. It shocked them to the core. Here they said was a blank check for every conceivable political crime. At first the author did not know what these critics meant, but then he said to himself: Oh well, in the nineteenth century the natural sciences made an onslaught on poetry, Nietzsche was fought by the theologians, today it is politics that gets mixed up with everything—all right, let's leave it at that—"dim realm of form-combining possibilities." But all this together, the theoretical and the practical, caused our author to look into the question of how other old men had fared and what old age and the process of aging mean for the artist.

First of all, my inquiry is not concerned with the physiology of aging. What medicine has to say on this subject doesn't amount to much. Its current formula is that aging is not a process of wear-and-tear but of adaptation, and I must say this doesn't convey much to me. It goes on, as I have discovered from its journals, to deplore the lack of unprejudiced, systematic psychological examination of old people who are not in psychiatric clinics. I don't know how many of you will also deplore this. Nor am I going to say anything about rejuvenation cures, or about the celebrated Bogomoletz serum either. What I am more concerned with is the question at what age aging actually begins.

The forty-six years after which Schiller died, the forty-six years after which Nietzsche fell silent forever, the forty-six years after which Shakespeare had done his work and retired for five years more of life as a private citizen, or the thirty-six years after which Hölderlin became insane—such, surely, is no great age. But mere arithmetic will, of course, get us nowhere. There can be very little doubt that foreknowledge of an early death compensates, in terms of inner life, for decades of physical life and the process of aging that goes with them. Such seems to have been the case with those who suffered from tuberculosis, for instance Schiller, Novalis, Chopin, Jens Peter Jacobsen, Mozart, and others. The early death of so many men of genius—something that the bourgeois-romantic ideology likes to connect with the notion of the consuming and devouring character of art—will have to be looked at a little more closely in each individual case. Some of these young men died of acute diseases. Schubert and Büchner died of typhus. Raphael, if one goes by Vasari's description, died of influenza at thirty-seven. Accident or war caused the deaths of Shelley, Byron, Franz Marc, Macke, Apollinaire, Heym, Lautréamont, Pushkin, Petöfi. Kleist, Schumann, and van Gogh committed suicide. In short, the ranks become thinner in relation to a direct causal connection between art and death. And looking at the dates when men of genius died, one makes a very odd observation of an entirely different kind, which I pass on to you, not as the result of deep thought or as something of a metaphysical nature, but simply because it is interesting. It is this: it is astonishing, indeed quite amazing, how many old and even *very* old men one finds among the famous. Let us take as our basis the figures that Kretschmer and Lange-Eichbaum[1] give for those who have been regarded as people of genius or of extraordinary gifts during the last four hundred years in the West;

---

1. See note 1 on page 87 above.

there are between a hundred and fifty and two hundred of them. Now it turns out that of these men and women of genius almost half have lived to be very old indeed. Our lifespan is seventy years, so let us waste no time on that. Let us begin rather with those who lived more than seventy-five years. I think you will be surprised, as I was. Here now is a list, merely with the names and ages, beginning with painters and sculptors: Titian ninety-nine, Michelangelo eighty-nine, Franz Hals eighty-six, Goya eighty-two, Hans Thoma eighty-five, Liebermann eighty-eight, Munch eighty-one, Degas eighty-three, Bonnard eighty, Maillol eighty-three, James Ensor eighty-nine, Donatello eighty, Tintoretto seventy-six, Rodin seventy-seven, Käthe Kollwitz seventy-eight, Renoir seventy-eight, Monet eighty-six, Menzel ninety. Among the living: Matisse eighty-four, Nolde eighty-six, Gulbransson eighty-one, Hofer, Scheibe over seventy-five, Klimsch eighty-four.

Among poets and writers: Goethe eighty-three, Shaw ninety-four, Hamsun ninety-three, Maeterlinck eighty-seven, Tolstoy eighty-two, Voltaire eighty-four, Heinrich Mann eighty, Ebner-Eschenbach eighty-six, Pontoppidan eighty-six, Heidenstamm eighty-one, Victor Hugo eighty-three, Tennyson eighty-three, Swift, Ibsen, Björnson, and Rolland seventy-eight, Ricarda Huch eighty-three, Hauptmann eighty-four, Lagerlöf eighty-two, Gide eighty-two, Heyse eighty-four, d'Annunzio seventy-five, Spitteler, Fontane, and Freytag seventy-nine, Frenssen eighty-two, and among the living: Claudel eighty-five, Thomas Mann, Hesse, Rudolf Alexander Schröder, Alfred Döblin, and Hans Carossa over seventy-five, Emil Straub eighty-seven.

There are, admittedly, fewer great composers. Let me mention Verdi eighty-eight, Richard Strauss eighty-five, Pfitzner eighty, Heinrich Schütz eighty-seven, Monteverdi seventy-six, Gluck and Handel seventy-four, Bruckner seventy-two, Palestrina seventy-one, Buxtehude and Wagner seventy, Georg Schumann eighty-one, Cherubini eighty-two, Reznicek eighty-five, Auber eighty-four; and among the living: Sibelius eighty-eight.

My list is by no means complete. I did not set about compiling it systematically, but only picked up whatever I happened to come across when I was looking into this matter in general. I am convinced the list could be extended further. If one wanted to explain this phenomenon, there are two points one could bring up. First, there is the sociological point that it is primarily those who live long who become great and famous, because they have a long time in which to produce their works. Secondly, there seems to be a quite reasonable biological explanation: regarded from one point of view art is, after all, a phenomenon of liberation and relaxation, a cathartic phenomenon, and such phenomena are closely associated with the physical organism itself. This assumption accords quite well with Speranski's theory, now finding its way into pathology, that both the state and the threat of illness are regulated and warded off by central impulses to a far higher extent than was hitherto supposed. There can scarcely be any doubt about it that art is a central and primary impulse. In saying this I don't want to make far-reaching assertions, but it does seem to me that such great age is particularly remarkable in view of the fact that so many of these people lived in times when the general expectancy of life was far lower than it is today. As you know, the expectation of life for new-born children has almost doubled since 1870.

Now the question what aging means for an artist is a complex one, in which subjective and objective elements cut across each other; on the one hand, we have moods and crises, on the other, history and description. Never again to be able to reach the height once attained, in spite of struggling for decades, is one fate. It was, for instance, Swinburne's; at the age of twenty-nine he was a sensation, and from then on he went on writing, ceaselessly, until when he died at the age of seventy-two he was a fertile, stimulating man, writing poetry. Something similar could be said of Hofmannsthal: the way from the poems written by the twenty-year-old Loris to the political confusions of *Der Turm* of the fifty-year-old author was the way from the feeding of the five thousand to the gathering up of the crumbs. It is the same again with George and Dehmel. All these men are lyrical poets in whom hard work and determination took the place of the intuitive glimmerings they had known in youth. Now I shall turn from these introspective allusions to an entirely concrete question on the objective side of our problem, namely: what do art history, literary history, and art criticism generally mean by a "late" work? How do they define the formal transition from an artist's youthful work to the style of his "late" period?

It is difficult to get a straight answer to this question. Some critics

resort to such terms as gentleness, serenity, toleration, a noble mel-
lowness, liberation from the vanities of love and passion; others
speak of weightlessness, a floating beyond the things of earthly life—
and then they come out with the word "classical." Others again
see the characteristic of the artist's old age as lying in ruthlessness,
in a radical honesty—which makes one think of Shaw's dictum that
old men are dangerous because they don't care about the future.
Commenting on a painting by Franz Hals, Pinder introduces a new
concept by saying that the style is recognizably that of an eighty-
four-year-old painter, for only such a man could produce this petrified superabundance of experience and history, this conscious
awareness of the proximity of death. Petrified—here now is a contradiction to "weightless" and "floating." Someone else writes of
Dürer that he died too early, for one feels a downright need of a
loosening of the formal power through the workings of a broad,
gentle spirituality. At this point analysis of works of art becomes
nothing less than wishful thinking, the desire to see a confirmation
of the idea that broad, gentle spirituality is what constitutes a late
style.

And now to take an example from literature, where the word
"late" has become very fashionable—one is always reading articles
about the late Rilke, the late Hofmannsthal, the late Eliot, or the
late Gide. I am thinking now of a book by a well-known literary
historian who specializes in the late Rilke. His book contains excellent, even profound observations, but the tendency is clearly as
follows: phase 1: the phase of experiment, effort, and beginnings,
then phase 2: "fulfillment" and "the true form." It is only in phase
2 that Rilke really became "what in the beginning he believed he
was but in fact was not." What then is "the true"? There is too
much eschatology, too much ideology, too much old-fashioned evolutionary theory, behind this term for my liking. Our friend the
literary historian insists on seeing Rilke striving towards an ideal
state, that is, his own, the literary historian's, ideal; but this seems
to me particularly inappropriate in the case of Rilke, from whose
early phase we have poems of such perfect beauty that no "true"
anything can outshine them. I sometimes think that the urge, to be
found among the learned, to see and represent the artist in "phases"
must be one that is specifically German-idealist.

One of the most important books on our subject is Brinckmann's

Spätwerke grosser Meister. Brinckmann tries to define the structural
changes in creative minds by the aid of his antithesis between relation and fusion. These two concepts are the grappling-irons he
uses in dealing with the problem. Relation, which is the first phase,
means seeing and representing the relations between people, actions,
objects in space, and colors. Fusion, the later phase, is that in which
the colors fuse into one ground-tone and the elements that were
previously treated individually and contrastingly are subordinated
to the structural totality, often becoming elusive and intangible—
and now Brinckmann speaks of "the abandonment of a state of
tension in favor of a higher freedom." Wherever the word "freedom" crops up it all becomes obscure, and at this point I have
difficulty in following him. However, Brinckmann has made an
extremely fascinating analysis of several painters who painted a
subject first in their youth and then again in old age. He places the
periods of change in the structure of productivity in the thirty-fifth
and sixtieth years, and in this claims to be following Freud. Brinckmann is, furthermore, the only writer who, still following Freud,
touches on the relationship between sexuality and artistic productivity. Although this problem is, at this moment and at this point,
rather a digression, I should like to mention it. Such a relationship
does undoubtedly exist, although it is extremely obscure. Everyone
knows there are a great many artists of the first rank who are
homoerotic and in whose work this divergence from normal sexuality does not become apparent. Take four of the greatest minds
in all Western culture, say Plato, Michelangelo, Shakespeare, and
Goethe: two were notoriously homosexual, one may have been,
and only Goethe seems to have been free from abnormality. And
then, on the other hand, there is the asexual type of genius: you
may remember Adolf Menzel's celebrated testament, from which
it appears that in all his ninety years of life he never once had
intercourse with a woman. We still know nothing about the link
between the lessening of the sexual urge and the falling off of
creativeness. We all know that, at the age of seventy-five, Goethe
fell in love with Ulrike and wanted to marry her. Or there is the
almost grotesque situation that Gide describes in his journals: in
Tunis, at the age of seventy-two, he fell in love with a fifteen-year-
old Arab boy, and he describes the rapturous nights that reminded
him of the fairest years of his youth. There is something positively

embarrassing about his enraptured confession that when he first saw the boy, who was a servant in his hotel, he was so overcome by his exquisiteness and shyness that he did not dare to speak to him. Gide at seventy-two in a Gretchen situation![2] The problem is interesting, but there is as yet no way of deciding whether the fading of the sexual urge paralyzes the mind or, as others contend, lends it wings.

A special case, and one that I was continually coming across in these investigations, is that of Michelangelo's Rondanini "Pietà," which he produced at the age of eighty-nine, but did not finish. Eminent art historians hold such conflicting views about this "Pietà" that one is forced to assume that here is a case of decisive structural change in the artist. One art historian writes of the work's sublime inwardness and spirituality. Another says it radiates a deep emotion that cannot be gainsaid, something spiritualized and ethereal, a sort of floating upwards in which a last sigh mingles with the first faint glimpses of redemption. The other school of thought asserts that in this work of his old age Michaelangelo turned his back on all that had constituted the fame of his youth. Simmel[3] goes so far as to say: "In this work Michelangelo disowned the vital principle of his art; it is a betrayal, a tragedy, the final proof of his inability to reach salvation by the road of artistic creation, which is centered in the vision of the senses. It is the ultimate tragic failure." Here, it seems, we have a case in which a great man abandoned his former methods and techniques of controlling his mode of experience, unable to make any further use of them, presumably because they had come to seem obsolete and conventional, and who nevertheless had no new mode of expression for his new mode of experience, and so gave up, let his hands sink. Perhaps this is an example of what Malraux means in a deeply significant passage in his *Psychology of Art:* "First they invent their language, then they learn to speak it, often inventing another one as well. When they are touched by the style of death, they remember how in their youth they broke with their teachers, and now they break with their own work." And Malraux goes on: "The most complete embodiment of the artist is based equally on rejection of his masters and on the destruction of all that he once was." These are weighty words, and I

2. Reference to Goethe's *Faust.*
3. Georg Simmel (1858–1918), German philosopher.

should like to apply them to a man who carried a whole century upon his shoulders and whose fame is a meridian in our scheme of values.

In conclusion of this section I should like to speak of a book that confronted me with another question arising out of the subject. It is Riezler's book on Beethoven,[4] the final chapter of which is called "The Last Style." The description of this last style is fascinating, convincing, and imbued with tremendous knowledge. But—I said to myself—first of all, the writer of the book has to translate his musical impressions and analyses into language, expressing in words something that the music itself, by its very nature, does not contain. These words, which are intended to embody the essence of Beethoven's last style, are notably "authority," "power," "monumentality," "gigantic," "tectonic solidity," and, on the other hand, "weightless," "floating," "ethereal," "ultimate spirituality"—i.e., all words belonging to the emotive vocabulary we found in descriptions of the late works of painters and which we should presumably also come across now and then in descriptions of great works by younger men. Riezler begins this last chapter of his with the assertion that it is possible to find general terms for the description of a characteristic late style in all the arts throughout all periods, since "the modes of expression used in the various arts are all subordinate to the supreme fact of the 'universal artistic principle.' " And what is this universal artistic principle, this final hieroglyph? Would it not be just as easy to say that, quite apart from music, painting, and poetry, there is a linguistic medium that serves the purposes of criticism, providing the learned with the terminology they need in order to set up their systems?

But now another question—what is it like for the artist himself to grow old, to be old? How does he experience it himself? Take Flaubert—there in his house on the high ground, in Rouen, not leaving his room for days on end, and night after night the light from his windows shining out on the river, so that the Seine boatmen take their bearings from it. He is not old, he is only fifty-nine, but he is worn out, he has bags under his eyes and his eyelids are wrinkled with bitter scorn—scorn of the *gent épicière*, those shop-

4. Walter Riezler's general biography *Beethoven* first appeared in 1936.

keepers, the middle classes—to be sure, the court did not pronounce *Madame Bovary* immoral, but it did recommend him to exercise his gifts of observation on nicer people, people with more goodness of heart. And did that make him write about goodness of heart? When his *Education sentimentale* was published, they wrote: A cretin, a pimp, one who dirties the water in the gutter where he washes.

In his youth he wrote that anyone who wanted to create something permanent must take care not to laugh at fame. But how was it later on? Was there anything he did not laugh at? And most of all it was himself he laughed at; he could not look at himself in the mirror while shaving without bursting into laughter. And now he was drawing up a list of follies of those of the dead whose names constitute what we call humanity. Should he put on yet another record: Sit yet again in the *bistro* downtown, tense with concentration visually and acoustically, in order to penetrate into the object, to slip behind those faces? Should he once again make that superhuman effort of observation, an effort so tragic in every instant, picking up expressions, collecting phrases, things one could take one's stand on?—For there they all sit in the bar, all after money, all after love, while what he is after is *expression,* a sequence of sentences, and these two worlds must embrace. Put on another record? Realism, Artism, Psychologism—they say I am cold—well, coldness is not such a bad thing, I'd rather be cold than go in for singing and interpreting—for whom? For what? So do you believe in anything, Flaubert? Come on, say yes or no. Yes, I do believe, for after all believing only means being made in a particular way so that you can accept this and that. No, I don't believe, *je suis mystique et je ne crois à rien.*

Such was Flaubert when he was old.

And there's Leonardo in the little chateau of Ducloux on the Loire, when Italy was no longer a place for him, all his patrons dead or imprisoned. What does he think of in those evenings? The king is out hunting, and all is still, there is nothing to be heard but the metallic clang of the clock on the bell-tower and the cry of the wild swans on the water. By the river there are poplars, like those in Lombardy long ago. The king has offered him four thousand guilders for the "Gioconda," but he cannot bring himself to part with her. The king goes on insisting, and the old man throws himself at the king's feet, weeping, making himself a laughing-stock before the guests, offering the king his latest picture, a "St. John the Baptist," but not the "Gioconda," not that, that picture is his life. Five long years he worked at it, five years he bent over it, silent, growing old, not letting anyone see it. In the room where he painted it there were fragments of Greek statues, dog-headed Egyptian gods in black granite, Gnostic gems with magical inscriptions, Byzantine parchments hard as ivory, lost, clay potsherds bearing Assyrian cuneiform script, Persian magical writings bound in iron, papyri from Memphis, transparent and delicate as the petals of flowers. . . . He had had to transform himself into all that, to lose himself in it, perhaps even to succumb to it. And in this way he lived for five years, dedicated to his inner vision, his one vision. The king and the court thought him a poor fool, but still, he had managed to keep the picture in his room. The spiral staircase up to his bedroom was narrow and steep, and as he climbed it he suffered attacks of dizziness and breathlessness. Then his right side became paralyzed, and though he could still draw with his left hand, he could not paint. Then he spent the evenings with a monk, playing games with little blocks of wood, or cards. Then his left side became paralyzed, too. And he had just managed to say "Arise and cast yourself into the sea" when he died and lay there, at rest, like a weight that has fallen. After his death a Russian ikon-painter who lived nearby came and stood before the easel with his "St. John" and exclaimed: "What unheard-of shamelessness! Can this debauched fellow who is naked like a whore, and has neither beard nor moustache, be the forerunner of Christ? Diabolical sight, away, sully not my eyes!"

Such was Leonardo da Vinci when he was old.

Evenings of life—oh, these evenings of life! Most of them are spent in poverty, coughing, crook-backed—drug-addicts, drunkards, some even as criminals, almost all unmarried, almost all childless—the whole bio-negative Olympic assembly, a European, cis-Atlantic team of Olympians that has borne the glory and the sadness of post-Classical man for hour hundred years. Those born under a lucky star managed, perhaps, to get themselves a house, as Goethe and Rubens did, and those whose lot was meager went on painting to the end of their days without a penny in their pockets, painting their wavy olives, and those who live in the age of the conquest of space look out of a back-room window on a rabbit-hutch and two hortensias. Making a survey of them all, one can discover only one thing—they were all under some compelling urge that they could not escape from. "If I don't tremble as the adder does in the snake-tamer's hand, I am cold. Anything I ever did that was any good at all was done in that condition," Delacroix said. And Beckmann wrote: "I would gladly live in sewers and crawl through all the gutters of the world if that were the only way I could go on painting." Adders, gutters, sewers—that is the overture to life's evening.

I am not wallowing in the macabre for its own sake, nor amusing myself with an obsolete picture of things dating from the days of the *poètes maudits*. These psychopathological and sociological studies of the lives of men of genius, and of their last days, are none of my making; they are the work of others. The trend of thought may seem a little disconcerting nowadays, when the artist has acquired some of the outer trappings of the solid, respectable citizen and adopts the airs of a functionary; and indeed he feels that he *is* a functionary, in a definite position, which forces him to seek government commissions and external security. Routine criticism, the reviewing of exhibitions and books commissioned and paid for by newspapers and publishers, has dragged the artist into public life, into the general hotch-potch in which individualism is coming to an end in our epoch. But let there be no mistake about it: he who is under that compelling urge remains inwardly untouched. In a helicopter painted arsenic-green he goes on climbing back into his esoteric studio. It is only a short while since the eighty-three-year-old Degas said: "A picture is something that needs just as much smartness and viciousness as crime does—forgery with a dash of Nature thrown in."

Perhaps the image of the arsenic-green helicopter is a trifle banal. All the same, let us get into that helicopter for a moment so that we can look down on what we can't take with us of mankind and the earth.

It is not an ascent that is made with very much love for humanity. Think, for instance, of that self-portrait of Tintoretto's, a late work (I don't remember where it hangs, I only know it from reproductions)—there's a thing one can't forget, and there is only one word for it: rancid. Or think of Rembrandt's last self-portraits—reserved, wary, cold, and as though they were saying: count me out. None of the great *old* men was an idealist. They got along without idealism. What they could do and what they wanted were the things that are possible. It is only dilettantes who dream of the impossible.

Art—these men say—art *must* put into the picture the relationship there is between the world and the absolute. Art must restore the center, but without losing in depth. Art must represent man as being made in the image of God—and is there anything at all that is not made in the image of God?—for if there is, I haven't heard of it—and I don't exclude even the tiger. And what it comes to finally is that there is no "must" where art is concerned. There's a radio in this helicopter of ours, and right now it's playing a hit from the film *Moulin Rouge*. It makes me shiver with excitement. For a first-rate dance-tune sometimes has more of the century in it than a motet, and a word may weigh heavier than a victory.

Ah, these old men! What I see is not so much something lofty, but simply the century and the compulsion. A rose-pink century—right, then, let's paint pastoral idylls, and above all let us stick to the center. But supposing it's a black century—what do we paint then? Something technical perhaps, in keeping with our habit of holding conferences? After all, it's technical things that people sit round talking about; "technology" and "integration" are the watchwords. Everything must be in keeping with everything else: poetry with the Geiger-counter, inoculation-serums with the Church Fathers, and so on, and don't leave anything out or global coalitionism is endangered. Language must be assimilated to the technical, too—though I must say this is an idea I should never have had on my own. The only sort of language that bears, that grows, that works, is the language that lives on its own resources, spontaneously procreating, absorbing, but integrating according to its own immanent law, the few expressions it takes over from physics and the automobile industry. These few miserable splinters it absorbs into its body, and the place heals over; the transcendence of language is never disturbed.

Up and up we go in our helicopter—earth dwindles away, but we can still make out those colossal complexes, those collectives, those things called institutes and institutions. "I made my way through them, too," one of the old men might say nowadays. "I suffered from depressions, I entered an institution and went to a psychoanalyst. And he said: 'You are suffering from oral-narcissistic deficiency, you lack an adequate intake of external objects. You are introverted—I suppose you know what I mean by that!' I replied that introverted and extroverted seemed pretty crude basic concepts to me. There are those who bear a hereditary burden and those who bear none. There are those who are fettered and those who are free. And the first are the more interesting. 'Contactual insufficiency,' the therapist said, pressing into my hand a booklet entitled: *You and the Libido,* and thereupon fell into a trance."

"Then I heard," one of those old masters would say today, "that thought makes you free, thought makes you happy. And so I entered another institution and went to the thinkers. But sociology, phenomenology, and the theory of types—it all sounds just like Puccini. Ontology—where, I ask you, is there any existence of anything outside my pictures? And what is all this stuff about things, anyway? Things come into existence because one admits their existence, that's to say, one formulates them, paints them. If one doesn't grant them their existence, they vanish into the realm of unreality and insubstantiality. These thinkers with their grounds of existence that no one can see, which is utterly formless—all these contributions and contributors—they turn on the faucet and what comes out is generally a spurt of Plato. Then they take a quick shower, and then the next one steps into the tub. None of them ever finishes anything. *I* have to finish *my* things! They're all idealists, and they think the whole thing only starts with them. They're all optimists, and at the age of seventy-five they go and have a new jacket made to measure. Schopenhauer was a well-off man, I believe, independent, and did some real thinking all the same—his thought was interesting, it was sublime, it was far-reaching. But none of these gentry nowadays really *thinks*—unless one excepts Wittgenstein, who said: 'The limits of language are the limits of my world,' and 'What the picture represents is what it means.' There's sound thinking, there's concrete thinking! No loose ends there! There is a systematic self-limitation to the thinking of propositions. That is painterly thinking, that is Lethe, and there myth comes to an end."

And so what is the situation like? Desperate? Send me up some fresh supplies of libido and a guaranteed pre-Spenglerian civilization. The exploration of outer space hasn't yet reached the stage where we could start to feel something again at the sight of the stars. Oh, why didn't I become a landscape-painter, professionally busy dashing from the Teutoburger Wald to Astrachan, and all by aid of the Volkswagen that we have these days? Then I could have some springy woodland earth underfoot!

"How queer the nations are," our old man goes on thinking. "They want interesting minds, but they also want to be the ones who decide what the interesting minds are to be interesting about. They want internationally famous names, but anyone who writes a word against their pet ideas is instantly crossed off the list. They want to be delivered of works of universal significance, but it is they who organize the midwives and provide them with textbooks on confinement. Kleist's *Penthesilea* would never have been written if a vote had been taken on it first. Strindberg, Nietzsche, El Greco would never have appeared on the scene. But conformism would have existed all right! It has always been there, only *it* would never have created the four hundred years of Western civilization." Surely there's no writer who hasn't often envied painters: they can paint oranges and asphodels, pitchers, even lobsters and other crustaceans, and nobody reproaches them with not having got in anything about the housing problem. But obviously the trade unions have their rights in the case of anything written. Anti-social is the word. "Art *must* . . ." It's probably a waste of time pointing out that Flaubert gave us a description of the artist's predicament, of his inability to express all he feels and yearns for, and how he can only express what it is given to him to express within the limitations of word and form.

Twenty-three thousand feet above sea level is the death line. Only thirty-three hundred more and we shall have reached it. The traveler glances down. When the diamond-dealer Salomon Rossbach jumped off the Empire State Building, he left a mysterious message: "No more above, no more below, and so I leap off." A good message, the traveler says: no more above, no more below, the center is damaged, the compass-needle and the quarters of heaven are no longer valid, but the species is rampant and keeps going by means of pills. The body has grown more morbid, with modern medicine positively offering it thousands of diseases, and they break out of it with scientific vigor—oh, no slur on the doctors, a very fine lot of men, I only mean that in the old days if you were bitten by a mosquito you scratched the place, but today they can prescribe a dozen different ointments and not one of them helps—still, that's life, it keeps things moving. Our bodies are more morbid than they used to be, but they live longer. A roman during the time of the Caesars had a life expectancy of 25 years but he was carried by the Roman concept of virtue. Today they are weakened by preventive medical care and can hardly make it home between visits to their physicians.

The brain lives longer, but where there was once power of resistance there are now empty places developing—or can you, down there on the earth, look out of your window and still imagine a God in it all, a God who created anything as gentle as plants and trees? Rats, plague, noise, desperation—yes—but flowers? There is a fourteenth-century picture called "The Creation of the Plants," with a small, crooked, black-bearded figure of God standing there, his right hand, which is much too big for the rest of him, raised as though he were pulling the two trees out of the ground, and there they are beside him—apart from them the whole place is still pretty empty. Can you imagine that kindly Creator today? Vice, worms, maggots, sloths, and skunks—that, yes; masses of it, ever new installments of it, fresh deliveries every day, 100 per cent genuine, continual new editions—but an affectionate little God who pulls two trees out of the ground? No trees, no flowers—but electronic brains, artificial insemination for cows and women, chicken farms with music laid on to increase productivity, artificial doubling of the chromosomes bringing about giant hybrids, deep freezing, overheating—you've sown a seed, have you? Well, jump, quick! Else the shoot will get you in the leg!

Well, so here we are. The old man enters his studio—a bare room, a big table covered with slips of paper and sheets of notes. He goes up to it, saying to himself: "Now what shall I do with this?—essay, poem, dialogue? The notion that the form is born together with the content is just another illusion hatched by philosophies of art— I can use this here or there, coloring, weaving, fixing it up, all just as I feel like it, I went through my beginning and I am going through my end, *moira*, my allotted part. Only one thing is certain: When a thing's finished it must be complete, perfect. Though of course there's the question: And what then?"

Take another look at the most famous "late" works—what are they like? For instance, there's Goethe's *Novelle*—a menagerie catches fire, the booth burns down, the tigers escape, the lions are loose! And it all works out harmoniously. No, this earth is scorched and bare, flayed by lightning, and today the tigers bite. Or what about the second part of *Faust?* Undoubtedly this is Germany's most mysterious gift to the world. But all those choruses, gryphons, lamias, pulcinellos, ants, cranes, and empusae, the whole thing humming and buzzing away, singing to itself, away off to where the fairy rings are and the crowns of stars and the angelic boys—where does it all come from anyway? Let's face it, the whole thing hovers in the realm of pure imagination, it's all table-rapping, telepathy, hocus-pocus. There's someone standing on a balcony, unreal, motionless, blowing bubbles—some bright, some dark—conjuring forth more and more clay pipes and straws to blow his iridescent bubbles with—oh, a magnificent God on the Balcony, inoculated with the spirit of the Classical and the Baroque, with miracles and mysteries dangling from his coat tails. But in our day the eye is slightly moist when one looks that way, and that's all there is to it. That's how it stands with such works nowadays.

Around the greatest of all, the translators and interpreters keep on circling for a few centuries, but soon there is no one left who understands their language. What then? Primitives, the Archaic, the Classical, the Mannerists, the Abstractionists, in a word, the Quaternary Period. But what then? Spaces that are much too big have been opened up to us, and too many spheres, and feelings too weighty—perhaps the making of art is, after all, a rather shallow reaction? Isn't it perhaps *profounder* simply to suffer the human substance in silence? What was it the Lord Jehova put into our essential nature, what was the fate he gave us? Was creative salvation to be our lot, or were we meant to go for the still point, to sit under the Bo-tree, immobile, waiting to meet Kama-Mara, the god of love and death? How many hours of life I have spent pondering on a certain saying of the Balcony God's, turning it this way and that—the saying that: "On its highest peak poetry seems to be completely external. The more it withdraws inwards, the further it sinks." What does that mean? Am I supposed to disown my inner being, cheat it, make a fool of it—is *that* the pre-condition for poetry? And what else is it? A conjuror's act, the rope-trick, mere nothingness with a glaze over it? And from the East I hear them harping on the same tune. The Master Kung Dsi, speaking of painters, says: "He is crude in whose work the meaning has more weight than the line." In other words, for him, too, the higher thing is the manipulated thing, the manufactured thing, style. On the other hand, there's Guardini[5] saying that "behind every work of art, as it were, something opens up. . . ." Well, and what is it that as it were opens up? After all, we are supposed to cover it up with paint and hide it. Or what of a great philosopher's dictum that "art is the self-manifestation and operation of truth"? What truth, anyway? A truth made up of sketches and designs, a manufactured truth? Or is truth only mentioned in order to let philosophy make a showing, for of course art isn't concerned with truth at all, only with expression. And then finally we come to the question: What is this expression that thrusts its way in in front of depth? Is expression the same as guilt? It might be.

Still, I dare say I'm too old to unravel these problems. Mists of weariness and melancholy cloud my mind. I can remember having heard Pablo Sarasate playing his violin and Caruso singing at the Metropolitan Opera House, with the Astors sitting in the diamond horseshoe. I have watched Bergmann operating, and I stood on parade before the last Emperor. I began studying by the light of an oil-lamp, with Haeckel's *Riddles of the Universe* for my forbidden reading. I rode horses and flew in planes, but I have also seen the great sailing-ships upon the seas that no man had ever yet flown across—but that's all past and gone—all over now: And today I say it was all much more heavily charged than one thought at the time; everything was much more predestined than it seemed. And the oddest thing of all is that one was much more *in the air* then than one dreamed, believing as one did in one's autonomy. To take just one example: there were painters who spent their whole life painting in tones of silver or of yellow, and another one who always stuck to brown, and there was a generation that wrote poetry mainly in nouns. It wasn't a literary caprice, it was in the air—in the air of entirely heterogeneous dimensions. A short time ago I read the following story about Clemenceau. He had just engaged a new private secretary, and on the first day he was showing him what the job consisted of. "Some letters," Clemenceau said, "you will have to draft by yourself. Now listen: a sentence consists of a noun

5. Romano Guardini (1885–1968), Catholic theologian (Tübingen), essayist.

and a verb. If you want to use an adjective, come and ask me first."
Come and ask me first! It's exactly the same advice that Carl
Sternheim[6] gave me when we were both young. "When you've
written something," he said to me, "go through it again and cross
out the adjectives. Your meaning will be much clearer then." It
turned out to be true. Indeed, the leaving out of explanatory, pad-
ding-out adjectives became a sort of compulsion-neurosis with my
generation.

My generation! But of course the next one is here by now, the
young people, the youth of our time! God preserve their imitative
urge for them, and then it wouldn't be long before the whole thing
stops of its own accord. But supposing they were to produce a new
style—*evoe!* A new style is a new type of man. Now, though genetics
haven't produced very much that is clear, one thing seems to be
certain: a new generation means a new sort of brain, and a new
sort of brain means a new sort of reality and new neuroses, and
the whole thing is called evolution, and that's the way civilization
goes on spreading. If I were to give this younger generation of ours
some advice, talking down to them from my pulpit of old age, it
would be this: "When you have published four of those rhymed or
unrhymed things that are called poems, or have drawn a goat more
or less true to nature, don't expect that from now on every time
you have a birthday the Mayor of your town will call. After all,
it's only human handiwork you're doing. You would do well to
think occasionally of how when Schubert was twenty-nine someone
advised him to buy unlined paper and draw the lines himself, since
that was cheaper. What impudence! everyone says nowadays when
they hear of it, but of course the same thing keeps on happening
all over again, and it isn't everyone who by the age of thirty-one
has reached a stage where he doesn't need to spend money any
more."

Gentlemen of the rising generation, allow me to be provoking.
I do it in the hope of making you tough. Toughness is the greatest
blessing an artist can have—the ability to be hard on himself and
on his work. Or as Thomas Mann said: "It is better to ruin a work
of art and make it useless for giving to the world than not to go

6. German expressionist writer, 1878–1942.

all out at every point." Or as I tried to put it a moment ago: One thing is certain, when a thing is finished it must be complete, perfect. And in this connection don't for a moment forget the questionable and devious nature of your undertaking, the dangers and the hatred that surround your activities. Don't lose sight of the cold and ego- tistical element in your mission. Your art has deserted the temples and the sacrificial vessels, it has ceased to have anything to do with the painting of pillars, and the painting of chapels is no longer anything for you either. You are using your own skin for wallpaper, and nothing can save you. Don't let yourself be tempted by "se- curity"—312 pages, cloth-bound, price 13 marks 80. There is no turning the clock back. The things of the mind are irreversible; they go right along their road to the end, right to the end of the night. With your back to the wall, care-worn and weary, in the gray light of the void, read Job and Jeremiah and keep going. Formulate your principles without regard for anything else, because there will be nothing left of you but your words when this epoch comes to an end, making an end of all singing and chanting of poetry. What you don't say will not exist. You will make enemies, you will be alone, a tiny boat on the vast ocean, a tiny boat in which there are dubious clatterings and clankings going on and shivering that comes 0021from your own dismay at your undertaking. But don't send out an SOS. First of all, there's no one to hear you, and secondly, after so many voyages your end will be a quiet one.

Ladies and gentlemen, the portrait of old age is finished. We have left the studio. The helicopter is about to land. There are still many questions one might raise, for instance: should one disavow the works of one's youth, rewrite them, adjust them to one's new in- sights, provided one has any. Should one pretend to be an old gazelle if one was a young jackal. Too late to think about it—the helicopter is about to land. Out of the cabin there steps an *homme du monde,* wearing a gray tie and a black homburg, who disappears in the hustle and bustle of the airport. The airport is out in the country, and this gentleman strolls up to the edge of it, where he sees poplars like those on the banks of the Loire and like those long ago in Lombardy, and sees the river a ribbon winding away into the dis- tance like the Seine, where once the bargemen looked out for that lighted window in the dark. The same things recur for as long as there is sameness. And when some day nothing is like anything else any more at all and the great rules change—even then some kind of order will persist.

"To be mistaken and yet be compelled to go on believing what one's own innermost being tells one—that is man, and his glory begins yonder, beyond victory and defeat. . . ." Yes, he would write that same sentence yet once again, if he had to start all over again, even if it were misleading, even if it were a falsification. After all, what dictum is blameless? Face to face with the Western world, I did my work; I lived as if the day had come—my own day. I was the man that I shall be. And so at the end I take my stand on all the Church Fathers, all those ancient men with centuries behind them: *non confundar in aeternum*—I too shall not be condemned eternally.

(1954)   *Translated by Ernst Kaiser and Eithne Wilkins*

Part Three

POEMS

Mann und Frau gehn durch die Krebsbaracke

Der Mann:
Hier diese Reihe sind zerfallene Schöße
und diese Reihe ist zerfallene Brust.
Bett stinkt bei Bett. Die Schwestern wechseln stündlich.

Komm, hebe ruhig diese Decke auf.
Sieh, dieser Klumpen Fett und faule Säfte,
das war einst irgendeinem Mann groß
und hieß auch Rausch und Heimat.

Komm, sieh auf diese Narbe an der Brust.
Fühlst du den Rosenkranz von weichen Knoten?
Fühl ruhig hin. Das Fleisch ist weich und schmerzt nicht.

Hier diese blutet wie aus dreißig Leibern.
Kein Mensch hat so viel Blut.
Hier dieser schnitt man
erst noch ein Kind aus dem verkrebsten Schoß.

Man läßt sie schlafen. Tag und Nacht.—Den Neuen
sagt man: hier schläft man sich gesund.—Nur sonntags
für den Besuch läßt man sie etwas wacher.

Nahrung wird wenig noch verzehrt. Die Rücken
sind wund. Du siehst die Fliegen. Manchmal
wäscht sie die Schwester. Wie man Bänke wäscht.

Hier schwillt der Acker schon um jedes Bett.
Fleisch ebnet sich zu Land. Glut gibt sich fort.
Saft schickt sich an zu rinnen. Erde ruft.

1912

Man and Woman Go through the Cancer Ward

The man:
Here in this row are wombs that have decayed,
and in this row are breasts that have decayed.
Bed beside stinking bed. Hourly the sisters change.

Come, quietly lift up this coverlet.
Look, this great mass of fat and ugly humours
was precious to a man once, and
meant ecstasy and home.

Come, now look at the scars upon this breast.
Do you feel the rosary of small soft knots?
Feel it, no fear. The flesh yields and is numb.

Here's one who bleeds as though from thirty bodies.
No one has so much blood.
They had to cut
a child from this one, from her cancerous womb.

They let them sleep. All day, all night.—They tell
the newcomers: here sleep will make you well.—But Sundays
one rouses them a bit for visitors.—

They take a little nourishment. Their backs
are sore. You see the flies. Sometimes
the sisters wash them. As one washes benches.—

Here the grave rises up about each bed.
And flesh is leveled down to earth. The fire
burns out. And sap prepares to flow. Earth calls.—

Babette Deutsch

Nachtcafe

824: Der Frauen Liebe und Leben.
Das Cello trinkt rasch mal. Die Flöte
rülpst tief drei Takte lang: das schöne Abendbrot.
Die Trommel liest den Kriminalroman zu Ende.

Grüne Zähne, Pickel im Gesicht
winkt einer Lidrandentzündung.

Fett im Haar
spricht zu offenem Mund mit Rachenmandel
Glaube Liebe Hoffnung um den Hals.

Junger Kropf ist Sattelnase gut.
Er bezahlt für sie drei Biere.

Bartflechte kauft Nelken,
Doppelkinn zu erweichen.

B-moll: die 35. Sonate.
Zwei Augen brüllen auf:
Spritzt nicht das Blut von Chopin in den Saal,
damit das Pack drauf rumlatscht!
Schluß! He, Gigi!—

Die Tür fließt hin: Ein Weib.
Wüste ausgedörrt. Kanaanitisch braun.
Keusch. Höhlenreich. Ein Duft kommt mit.
                       Kaum Duft.
Es ist nur eine süße Vorwölbung der Luft
gegen mein Gehirn.

Eine Fettleibigkeit trippelt hinterher.

1912

Night Café

824: The Love and Life of Women.
The 'cello has a quick drink. The flute
belches throughout three beats: his tasty evening snack.
The drum reads on to the end of the thriller.

Green teeth, pimples on his face,
waves to conjunctivitis.

Grease in his hair
talks to open mouth with swollen tonsils,
faith hope and charity round his neck.

Young goiter is sweet on saddle-nose.
He stands her three half pints.

Sycosis buys carnations
to mollify double chin.

B flat minor: sonata op. 35.
A pair of eyes roars out:
Don't splash the blood of Chopin round the place
for this lot to slouch about in!
Hey, Gigi! Stop!

The door dissolves: a woman.
Desert dried out. Canaanite brown.
Chaste. Full of caves. A scent comes with her. Hardly scent.
It's only a sweet leaning forward of the air
against my brain.

A paunched obesity waddles after her.

Michael Hamburger

Blinddarm

Alles steht weiß und schnittbereit.
Die Messer dampfen. Der Bauch ist gepinselt.
Unter weißen Tüchern etwas, das winselt.

„Herr Geheimrat, es wäre soweit."

Der erste Schnitt. Als schnitte man Brot.
„Klemmen her!" Es spritzt was rot.
Tiefer. Die Muskeln: feucht, funkelnd, frisch.
Steht ein Strauß Rosen auf dem Tisch?

Ist das Eiter, was da spritzt?
Ist der Darm etwa angeritzt?
„Doktor, wenn Sie im Lichte stehn,
kann kein Deibel das Bauchfell sehn.
Narkose, ich kann nicht operieren,
der Mann geht mit seinem Bauch spazieren."

Stille, dumpf feucht. Durch die Leere
klirrt eine zu Boden geworfene Schere.
Und die Schwester mit Engelssinn
hält sterile Tupfer hin.

„Ich kann nichts finden in dem Dreck!"
„Blut wird schwartz. Maske weg!"
„Aber—Herr des Himmels—Bester,
halten Sie bloß die Hacken fester!"

Alles verwachsen. Endlich: erwischt!
„Glüheisen, Schwester!" Es zischt.

Du hattest noch einmal Glück, mein Sohn.
Das Ding stand kurz vor der Perforation.
„Sehn Sie den kleinen grünen Fleck?—
Drei Stunden, dann war der Bauch voll Dreck."

Appendectomy

Everything white and sterile and gleaming.
Under a sheet a moan and a stir.
Abdomen painted. Scalpels are gleaming.
"We are ready when you are, Sir."

The first incision. Like cutting of bread.
"Clips!" A gusher of crimson red.
Deeper. The muscles flaming and fresh,
a garland of roses the vibrant flesh.

Is this pus that started to spurt?
Have the intestines perhaps been hurt?
"Doctor, if you stand in the light,
how can I keep that omentum in sight?
Anesthetist, I cannot work,
the guy is making his belly jerk."

Through the silence of mist and gore
the clatter of scissors dropped to the floor.
The patient nurse, with watchful eye,
keeps sterile tampons in supply.

"I can't see a thing in all this rot!"
"Off with the mask! Blood starts to clot."
"For Heaven's sake! Hey, Mister, please,
a little more pressure upon the knees!"

Everything tangled. Finally found.
"Cautery, nurse!" A hissing sound.

Boy, I should say you were fortunate.
The thing was about to perforate.
"See this green spot? Three hours, I guess,
and the mesentery would have been a mess."

Bauch zu. Haut zu. „Heftplaster her!
Guten Morgen, die Herrn."
      Der Saal wird leer.
Wütend klappert und knirscht mit den Backen
der Tod und schleicht in die Krebsbaracken.

         1912

Gesänge

      I
O daß wir unsere Ururahnen wären.
Ein Klümpchen Schleim in einem warmem Moor.
Leben und Tod, Befruchten und Gebären
glitte aus unseren stummen Säften vor.

Ein Algenblatt oder ein Dünenhügel,
vom Wind Geformtes und nach unten schwer.
Schon ein Libellenkopf, ein Möwenflügel
wäre zu weit und litte schon zu sehr.

      II
Verächtlich sind die Liebenden, die Spötter,
alles Verzweifeln, Sehnsucht, und wer hofft.
Wir sind so schmerzliche durchseuchte Götter
und dennoch denken wir des Gottes oft.

Die weiche Bucht. Die dunklen Wälderträume.
Die Sterne, schneeballblütengroß und schwer.
Die Panther springen lautlos durch die Bäume.
Alles ist Ufer. Ewig ruft das Meer—

         1913

"Sutures! Bandage! Jolly good show."
Everything closed. They wash up and go.
Raging, rattling her bony sword,
Death sneaks off to the cancer ward.

Karl F. Ross

Songs

I

O that we were our primal ancestors.
A little clump of slime in a warm bog.
Then life and death, then pregnancy and birth
From our dumb lymph would issue for that quag.

A leaf of alga or a simple dune,
Windshaped yet weighted by its rooted clutch.
A gull's wing, the head of a dragonfly
Were all too long and suffering too much.—

II

Despicable, the lovers and the mockers,
Despair, longing, the hopeful, all are vile.
We are such sickly, such corrupted gods,
Yet our thoughts turn godwards every little while.

The gentle inlet. The woods' darkling dreams.
The grave stars, huge as blossoming snowballs.
The panthers leap soundlessly through the trees.
And all is shore. And always the sea calls.—

Babette Deutsch

Untergrundbahn

Die weichen Schauer. Blütenfrühe. Wie
aus warmen Fellen kommt es aus den Wäldern.
Ein Rot schwärmt auf. Das große Blut steigt an.

Durch all den Frühling kommt die fremde Frau.
Der Strumpf am Spann ist da. Doch, wo er endet,
ist weit von mir. Ich schluchze auf der Schwelle:
laues Geblühe, fremde Feuchtigkeiten.

Oh, wie ihr Mund die laue Luft verpraßt!
Du Rosenhirn, Meer-Blut, du Götter-Zwielicht,
du Erdenbeet, wie strömen deine Hüften
so kühl den Gang hervor, in dem du gehst!

Dunkel: nun lebt es unter ihren Kleidern:
nur weißes Tier, gelöst und stummer Duft.

Ein armer Hirnhund, schwer mit Gott behangen.
Ich bin der Stirn so satt. Oh, ein Gerüste
von Blütenkolben löste sanft sie ab
und schwölle mit und schauerte und triefte.

So losgelöst. So müde. Ich will wandern.
Blutlos die Wege. Lieder aus den Gärten.
Schatten und Sintflut. Fernes Glück: ein Sterben
hin in des Meeres erlösend tiefes Blau.

1913

Subway Train

Lascivious shivers. Early bloom. As if
from warm furred skins it wafted from the woods.
A red swarms up. The great strong blood ascends.

Through all of Spring the alien woman walks.
The stocking, stretched, is there. But where it ends
is far from me. I sob upon the threshold:
sultry luxuriance, alien moistures teeming.

O how her mouth squanders the sultry air!
You brain of roses, sea-blood, goddess-twilight,
you bed of earth, how coolly from your hips
your stride flows out, the glide that is in your walking.

Dark: underneath her garments now it lives:
white animal only, loosed, and silent scent.

A wretched braindog, laden down with God.
My forehead wearies me. O that a frame
of clustered blooms would gently take its place,
to swell in unison and stream and shudder.

So lax, adrift. So tired. I long to wander.
The ways all bloodless. Songs that blow from gardens.
Shadows and Flood. Far joys: a languid dying
down into ocean's deep redeeming blue.

Michael Hamburger

Ikarus

I

O Mittag, der mit heissem Heu mein Hirn
zu Wiese, flachem Land und Hirten schwächt,
dass ich hinrinne und, den Arm im Bach,
den Mohn an meine Schläfe ziehe—
o du Weithingewölbter, enthirne doch
stillflügelnd über Fluch und Gram
des Werdens und Geschehns
mein Auge.
Noch durch Geröll der Halde, noch durch Land-aas,
verstaubendes, durch bettelhaft Gezack
der Felsen—überall
das tiefe Mutterblut, die strömende
entstirnte
matte
Getragenheit.

Das Tier lebt Tag um Tag
und hat an seinem Euter kein Erinnern,
der Hang schweigt seine Blume in das Licht
und wird zerstört.

Nur ich, mit Wächter zwischen Blut und Pranke,
ein hirnzerfressenes Aas, mit Flüchen
im Nichts zergellend, bespien mit Worten,
veräfft vom Licht—
o du Weithingewölbter,
träuf meinen Augen eine Stunde
des guten frühen Voraugenlichts—
schmilz hin den Trug der Farben, schwinge
die kotbedrängten Höhlen in das Rauschen
gebäumter Sonnen, Sturz der Sonnen-sonnen,
o aller Sonnen ewiges Gefälle—

Icarus

I

O noon that with hot hay reduce
my brain to meadow, shepherds and flat land,
so that I flow away, my arm immersed
in the stream's water, and to my brow
draw down the poppies—noon that's vaulted wide,
now mutely winging above the curse and grief
of all that is and will be,
unbrain my eye.
Still through the hillside boulders, still through land-carrion,
turning to dust, through beggarly sharp shapes
of rocks—still everywhere
deep mother-blood, this streaming
deforeheaded
weary
drifting away.

The animal lives only for the day
and in its udder has no memory,
the slope in silence brings its flower to light
and is destroyed.

I only, with a sentry between blood and claw,
mere brain-devoured carrion, shrieking and cursing plunged
into annihilation, bespat with words,
guyed by the light—
O noon that's vaulted wide,
but for one hour infuse my eyes
with that good light which was before eyes were—
melt down the lie of colors, hurl
these cavities pressed by filth into the roar
of rearing suns, whirl of the sun of suns,
O everlasting fall of all the suns—

II

Das Hirn frisst Staub. Die Füsse fressen Staub.
Wäre das Auge rund und abgeschlossen,
dann bräche durch die Lider süsse Nacht,
Gebüsch und Liebe.
Aus dir, du süsses Tierisches,
aus euern Schatten, Schlaf und Haar,
muss ich mein Hirn besteigen,
alle Windungen,
das letzte Zwiegespräch—

III

So sehr am Strand, so sehr schon in der Barke,
im krokosfarbnen Kleide der Geweihten
und um die Glieder schon den leichten Flaum—
ausrauschst du aus den Falten, Sonne,
allnächtlich Welten in den Raum—
o eine der vergesslich hingesprühten
mit junger Glut die Schläfe mir zerschmelzend,
auftrinkend das entstirnte Blut—

1915

Das späte Ich

I

O du, sieh an: Levkoienwelle,
der schon das Auge übergeht,
Abgänger, Eigen-Immortelle,
es ist schon spät.

Bei Rosenletztem, da die Fabel
des Sommers längst die Flur verließ—
moi haïssable,
noch so mänadisch analys.

II

The brain eats dust. Our feet devour the dust.
If but the eye were round and self-contained
then through the lids sweet night would enter in,
brushwood and love.
From you, the sweetly bestial,
from out your shadows, sleep and hair,
I must bestride my brain,
all loops and turns,
the ultimate duologue—

III

So near the beach, so much embarked already,
dressed in the victim's crocus-colored garment,
and round your limbs the light and delicate down—
O sun, you rustle forth from out your folds
each night new universes into space—
O, one of these, obliviously scattered here
with its young glow is melting down my temples,
drinks my deforeheaded blood.

Michael Hamburger

The Late Ego

I

Gilliflower billow, see it swell,
moist-eyed already, and abate,
drop-out, and auto-immortelle,
for it is late.

At rose-recession, when the fable
of summer long has left the mead—
moi haissable,
though now maenadically surveyed.

II

Im Anfang war die Flut. Ein Floß Lemuren
schiebt Elch, das Vieh, ihn schwängerte ein Stein.
Aus Totenreich, Erinnern, Tiertorturen
steigt Gott hinein.

Alle die großen Tiere: Adler der Kohorten,
Tauben aus Golgathal—
alle die großen Städte: Palm- und Purpurborden—
Blumen der Wüste, Traum des Baal.

Ost-Gerölle, Marmara-Fähre,
Rom, gib die Pferde des Lysippus her—
letztes Blut des weißen Stiers über die schweigenden
                                              Altäre
und der Amphitrite letztes Meer—

Schutt. Bacchanalien. Propheturen.
Barkarolen. Schweinerein.
Im Anfang war die Flut. Ein Floß Lemuren
schiebt in die letzten Meere ein.

III

O Seele, um und um verweste,
kaum lebst du noch und noch zuviel,
da doch kein Staub aus keinen Feldern,
da doch kein Laub aus keinen Wäldern
nicht schwer durch deine Schatten fiel.

Die Felsen glühn, der Tartarus ist blau,
der Hades steigt in Oleanderfarben
dem Schlaf ins Lid und brennt zu Garben
mythischen Glücks die Totenschau.

Der Gummibaum, der Bambusquoll,
der See verwäscht die Inkaplatten,
das Mondchâteau: Geröll und Schatten
uralte blaue Mauern voll.

II

At the beginning was the Flood. A lemur raft
by Elk, the beast, is pushed, made pregnant by a stone.
Out of death's kingdom, memory, animals tortured, cleft
God enters in.

All the great animals: eagles of the cohorts,
doves from Golgatha Vale—
all the great cities: palm and purple borders—
flowers of the desert, dream of Baal.

Scree of the Orient, ferry of Marmara,
Rome, set the horses of Lysippus free—
last blood of the white bull over silent altars
and Amphitrite's final sea—

Rubble. And bacchanalia. Prophetcraft.
Barcarolles. And filthy stuff.
In the beginning was the Flood. A lemur raft
into the last seas pushes off.

III

O soul, putrescent through and through,
hardly alive but still too much,
when not one grain of dust from glades,
when not one leaf from any forest
but leaden hurtles through your shades.

The rocks are glowing, Tartarus is blue,
Hades ascends in oleander hues
into sleep's eyelid, burning into sheaves
of mythic bliss the autopsy.

Bamboo tumescence, rubber tree,
lake water licks the Inca scrawls,
the moon château: shadows and scree
clutter the blue archaic walls.

Welch Bruderglück um Kain und Abel,
für die Gott durch die Wolken strich—
kausalgenetisch, haïssable:
das späte Ich.

1922

Wer bist Du—

Wer bist du—alle Mythen
zerrinnen. Was geschah,
Chimären, Leda-iten
sind einen Kniefall da,

gemalt mit Blut der Beeren
der Trunkenen Schläfe rot,
und die—des Manns Erwehren
die nun als Lorbeer loht,

mit Schlangenhaar die Lende
an Zweig und Thyrsenstab,
in Trunkenheit und Ende
und um ein Göttergrab—

was ist, sind hohle Leichen,
die Wand aus Tang und Stein,
was scheint, ist ewiges Zeichen
und spielt die Tiefe rein—

in Schattenflur, in Malen,
das sich der Form entwand—:
Ulyss, der nach den Qualen
schlafend die Heimat fand.

1925

Fraternal bliss of Cain and Abel
for whom God cleft the clouds, in spate—
aetiologic, haïssable:
the ego, late.

Michael Hamburger

For another version see page 274.

Who Are You

Who are you—all the legends
are vanishing. What was—
chimeras, Leda's kindred
in genuflecting pass,

painted with blood of berries,
the scarlet drunkards, she—
the masculine-defying—
a fiery laurel tree,

with serpent hair the haunches,
by branch and thyrsus staff,
in drunken fit, finale,
and round a holy grave—

What is, are hollow corpses,
the rock and seawrack screen,
what seems, eternal token
that plays the whole depth clean—

in phantom fields, portrayal
inhabiting no form—:
Odysseus past affliction
who sleeping found his home.

Christopher Middleton

Qui sait

Aber der Mensch wird trauern—
solange Gott, falls es das gibt,
immer neue Schauern
von Gehirnen schiebt
von den Hellesponten
zum Hobokenquai,
immer neue Fronten—
wozu, qui sait?

Spurii: die Gesäten
war einst der Männer Los,
Frauen streiften and mähten
den Samen in ihren Schoß;
dann eine Insel voll Tauben
und Werften: Schiffe fürs Meer,
und so begann der Glauben
an Handel und Verkehr.

Aber der Mensch wird trauern—
Masse, muskelstark,
Cowboy und Zentauern,
Nurmi als Jeanne d'Arc—:
Stadionsakrale
mit Khasanaspray,
Züchtungspastorale,
wozu, qui sait?

Aber der Mensch wird trauern—
kosmopoler Chic
neue Tempelmauern
Kraftwerk Pazifik:
die Meere ausgeweidet,
Kalorien-Avalun:
Meer, das wärmt, Meer, das kleidet—
neue Mythe des Neptun.

Qui Sait

Yet mankind shall mourn
while God—if that exists—
moves ever newly born
brain waves into the lists
from the Hellesponts
to Hoboken's quay,
opens ever new fronts—
what for? *Qui sait?*

Spurii: being sowed
used to be men's meed;
women stripped and mowed,
into their womb the seed;
then came an isleful of pigeons
and wharves: ships for the sea,
and thus began the religions
of commerce and industry.

Yet mankind shall mourn—
masses; muscular mark;
cowboy, Centaur reborn;
Nurmi as Joan of Arc—:
sacred arenas of speeding
with DeVilbiss spray;
pastorals of breeding—
what for? *Qui sait?*

Yet mankind shall mourn—
cosmopolitan styles,
temple walls adorn
Pacific power piles;
eviscerated oceans,
calorific Avalon:
sea heat, costuming lotions—
Neptune's new pantheon.

Bis nach tausend Jahren
einbricht in das Wrack
Geißlerscharen,
zementiertes Pack
mit Orang-Utanhauern
oder Kaiser Henry Clay—
wer wird das überdauern,
welch Pack—qui sait?

1927

Aus Fernen, aus Reichen

Was dann nach jener Stunde
sein wird, wenn dies geschah,
weiss niemand, keine Kunde
kam je von da,
von den erstickten Schlünden
von dem gebrochnen Licht,
wird es sich neu entzünden,
ich meine nicht.

Doch sehe ich ein Zeichen:
über das Schattenland
aus Fernen, aus Reichen
eine grosse, schöne Hand,
die wird mich nicht berühren,
das lässt der Raum nicht zu:
doch werde ich sie spüren,
und das bist du.

Und du wirst niedergleiten
am Strand, am Meer,
aus Fernen, aus Weiten:
„—erlöst auch er;"
ich kannte deine Blicke
und in des tiefsten Schoss

Until a thousand years later
rabidly penitent
gangs invade the crater,
rabble cast in cement,
ape fangs dripping saliva
or Emperor Henry Clay—
and who'll be the survivor?
Which gang—*qui sait?*

E. B. Ashton

From Far Shores, from Kingdoms

What were that moment over
shall be, and were this done,
cannot be told, no message
came thence, not one,
from breathless gorges can it,
from rays that, broken, slant,
can it be resurrected,
I think it can't.

Yet I discern a token:
over the shadow-land
from far shores, from kingdoms
a large, beauteous hand,
it cannot touch me ever,
no space will let it through:
you feel it I shall surely,
and it is you.

And you will come down gliding
borne landward by the wave
from far shores, from distances:
"—him too I save";
your eyes I knew, their glancings
deepest where gathered are,

sammelst du unsere Glücke,
den Traum, das Los.

Ein Tag ist zu Ende,
die Reifen fortgebracht,
dann spielen noch zwei Hände
das Lied der Nacht,
vom Zimmer, wo die Tasten
den dunklen Laut verwehn,
sieht man das Meer und die Masten
hoch nach Norden gehn.

Wenn die Nacht wird weichen,
wenn der Tag begann,
trägst du Zeichen,
die niemand deuten kann,
geheime Male
von fernen Stunden krank
und leerst die Schale
aus der ich vor dir trank.

1927

Dennoch die Schwerter halten

Der soziologische Nenner,
der hinter Jahrtausenden schlief,
heißt: ein paar große Männer
und die litten tief.

Heißt: ein paar schweigende Stunden
in Sils-Maria-Wind,
Erfüllung ist schwer von Wunden,
wenn es Erfüllungen sind.

Heißt: ein paar sterbende Krieger
gequält und schattenblaß,

gathered by you, our gladness,
vision, and star.

A day is now ended,
the children's hoops are gone,
the song of night
two hands play on, play on,
and from the room where fading
dark chords from keys resound,
watch now how mast and ocean
move northward bound.

When the night shall vanish,
and come the day,
tokens you bring with
meanings that none can say,
cryptic, stigmata
of distant time's disease,
the cup I drank you drink
and drain the lees.

Christopher Middleton

And Yet, with Swords at the Ready

Sociology's modifier,
behind millennia asleep,
means: men we have learned to admire,
whose suffering ran deep.

Means: all that a wind-swept hill meant
in alpine solitude
to someone seeking fulfillment
in an afflicted mood.

Means: cheeks that are pallid and hollow,
of soldiers about to die;

sie heute und morgen der Sieger—:
warum erschufst du das?

Heißt: Schlangen schlagen die Hauer
das Gift, den Biß, den Zahn,
die Ecce-homo-Schauer
dem Mann in Blut and Bahn—

heißt: so viel Trümmer winken:
die Rassen wollen Ruh,
lasse dich doch versinken
dem nie Endenden zu—

und heißt dann: schweigen und walten,
wissend, daß sie zerfällt,
dennoch die Schwerter halten
vor die Stunde der Welt.

1933

Einst

Einst, wenn der Winter begann,
du hieltest von seinen Schleiern,
den Dämmerdörfern, den Weihern
die Schatten an.

Oder die Städte erglommen
sphinxblau an Schnee und Meer—
wo ist das hingekommen
und keine Wiederkehr.

Alles des Grams, der Gaben
früh her in unser Blut—:
wenn wir *gelitten* haben.
ist es *dann* gut?

1934

tomorrow the victor will follow—
Thou hast ordained it: why?

Means: drinking of hemlock's chalice
as snakes sink poisonous fangs
into one's veins, oozing malice
and Ecce Homo pangs.

Means: so many ruins remind you
the races are longing for peace.
Go, leave all that behind you,
sink to unending release.

And then means: quietly holding steady,
knowing the end is nigh,
and yet, with swords at the ready,
looking the world in the eye.

Karl F. Ross

Yesteryear

Yesteryear: winter came down,
You would hang onto the shadows
Left by the ponds and meadows
And twilight towns.

Sphinx-blue the cities would glimmer,
Marking the ocean-snow track—
Where has that gone now, I wonder?
There's no way back.

Those ancient gifts and that grieving
Which always made us so tough—
If we have *truly suffered,*
Is *that* enough?

Alexandra Chciuk-Celt

Leben—niederer Wahn

Leben—niederer Wahn!
Traum für Knaben und Knechte,
doch du von altem Geschlechte,
Rasse am Ende der Bahn,

was erwartest du hier?
immer noch eine Berauschung,
eine Stundenvertauschung
von Welt und dir?

Suchst du noch Frau und Mann?
ward dir nicht alles bereitet,
Glauben und wie es entgleitet
und die Zerstörung dann?

Form nur ist Glaube und Tat,
die erst von Händen berührten,
doch dann den Händen entführten
Statuen bergen die Saat.

1936

Wer allein ist—

Wer allein ist, ist auch im Geheimnis,
immer steht er in der Bilder Flut,
ihrer Zeugung, ihrer Keimnis,
selbst die Schatten tragen ihre Glut.

Trächtig ist er jeder Schichtung
denkerisch erfüllt und aufgespart,
mächtig ist er der Vernichtung
allem Menschlichen, das nährt und paart.

Life—What a Vulgar Delusion!

Life—what a vulgar delusion!
Dream fit for striplings and slaves,
But you, of a family that's ancient,
Of a race at the end of its days,

What can you have in view?
Yet one more surge of elation,
A moment's exchange of station
Between the world and you?

Still looking for woman and man?
Had you not all preparation,
Faith and its slow separation
And dissolution then?

Form alone is faith and is deed.
Only what hands first mold,
Taken then from hands that enfold:
Statues salvage the seed.

Robert M. Browning

For another version see page 275.

He Who's Alone

He who's alone, the secret's around him:
images begotten in their flow,
budding, constantly surround him,
mark the shadows, even, with their glow.

Every stratum means gestation
thought to term and stored up in his mind;
his power of annihilation
touches coupling, nursing humankind.

Ohne Rührung sieht er, wie die Erde
eine andere ward, als ihm begann,
nicht mehr Stirb und nicht mehr Werde:
formstill sieht ihn die Vollendung an.

1936

Einsamer nie—

Einsamer nie als im August:
Erfüllungsstunde—im Gelände
die roten und die goldenen Brände,
doch wo ist deiner Gärten Lust?

Die Seen hell, die Himmel weich,
die Äcker rein und glänzen leise,
doch wo sind Sieg und Siegsbeweise
aus dem von dir vertretenen Reich?

Wo alles sich durch Glück beweist
und tauscht den Blick und tauscht die Ringe
im Weingeruch, im Rausch der Dinge—:
dienst du dem Gegenglück, dem Geist.

1936

Astern

Astern—schwälende Tage,
alte Beschwörung, Bann,
die Götter halten die Waage
eine zögernde Stunde an.

He is unaffected by his seeing
how the earth has changed from what he knew;
"Die" and "Become" no longer: Being,
Perfect Form at rest holds him in view.

Joseph B. Dallett

For other versions see pages 276–77.

Never More Lonely

Never more lonely than in August: 'tis
a time of plentitude—of lands
ablaze with red and golden brands—
and yet, where is your garden's bliss?

Lakes shine, soft is the heavens' roof,
the fields are clean and gently lambent,
yet in the realm you represent,
where is the triumph and the proof?

Where luck alone proves all mankind
and glances are exchanged and rings
in wine smell, in the lust of things:
you serve the counter-luck—the Mind.

E. B. Ashton

Asters

Asters, and days that smoulder,
Old incantation, spell,
The gods hold the scales in balance
A hesitant moment still.

Noch einmal die goldenen Herden
der Himmel, das Licht, der Flor,
was brütet das alte Werden
unter den sterbenden Flügeln vor?

Noch einmal das Ersehnte,
den Rausch, der Rosen Du—
der Sommer stand und lehnte
und sah den Schwalben zu,

noch einmal ein Vermuten,
wo längst Gewißheit wacht:
die Schwalben streifen die Fluten
und trinken Fahrt and Nacht.

1936

Turin

„Ich laufe auf zerrissenen Sohlen",
schrieb dieses große Weltgenie
in seinem letzten Brief—dann holen
sie ihn nach Jena—Psychiatrie.

Ich kann mir keine Bücher kaufen,
ich sitze in den Librairien:
Notizen—dann nach Aufschnitt laufen:—
das sind die Tage von Turin.

Indes Europas Edelfäule
an Pau, Bayreuth und Epsom sog,
umarmte er zwei Droschkengäule,
bis ihn sein Wirt nach Hause zog.

1936

Once more the herds of heaven,
All golden, the light, the fields—
Old Becoming, what do your brooding
Slow dying wings conceal?

Once more all that I longed for:
Rapture, the roses' "you"—
The slanting summer stood there
And watched the swallows too.

Once more a vain supposing
When certainty's found its mark:
The swallows are skimming the waters
And drinking flight and dark.

Robert M. Browning.

For other versions see pages 277–79.

Turin

"On torn, on worn-out soles I trundle",
wrote this great cosmic genius
in his last letter—then they bundle
him off to Jena—mental case.

I can't afford to buy new books,
I sit in public libraries:
take notes—then shop, cold meat for snacks:—
That's how he spent his Turin days.

While Europe's top putrescence savoured
Bayreuth and Epsom, Pau and Rome,
with hugs two hackney nags he favoured,
until his landlord dragged him home.

Michael Hamburger

Gedichte

Im Namen dessen, der die Stunden spendet,
im Schicksal des Geschlechts, dem du gehört,
hast du fraglosen Aug's den Blick gewendet
in eine Stunde, die den Blick zerstört,
die Dinge dringen kalt in die Gesichte
und reißen sich der alten Bindung fort,
es gibt nur ein Begegnen: in Gedichte
die Dinge mystisch bannen durch das Wort.

Am Steingeröll der großen Weltruine,
dem Ölberg, wo die tiefste Seele litt,
vorbei am Posilip der Anjouine,
dem Stauferblut und ihrem Racheschritt:
ein neues Kreuz, ein neues Hochgerichte,
doch eine Stätte ohne Blut and Strang,
sie schwört in Strophen, urteilt im Gedichte,
die Spindeln drehen still: die Parze sang.

Im Namen dessen, der die Stunden spendet,
erahnbar nur, wenn er vorüberzieht
an einem Schatten, der das Jahr vollendet,
doch unausdeutbar bleibt das Stundenlied—
ein Jahr am Steingeröll der Weltgeschichte,
Geröll der Himmel, und Geröll der Macht,
und nun die Stunde, deine: im Gedichte
das Selbstgespräch des Leides und der Nacht.

                                            1941

Poems

In cognizance of Him Who grants the hours,
entangled in your generation's ways,
you gazed upon a moment that devours
your unassuming introspective gaze.
Reality, torn loose from its foundation,
thrusts coldly forth, demanding to be heard:
there is but one—the poem's—confrontation
that bans reality with mystic word.

Beyond the rubble of the World's cadaver,
Mount Olives, where the deepest soul did bleed,
pass Anjou castles on Vesuvio's lava,
the spiteful strut on Barbarossa's breed:
Another Cross, another Condemnation,
and just one refuge free from blood and hate—
the oath of verse, the poem's judication,
the silent turning of the wheels of Fate.

In cognizance of Him Who grants the hours,
sensed only when His shadow moves along
to terminate another year of ours,
but never fathomed in the moment's song—
a year's debris of global fragmentation,
debris of Heavens and debris of Might.
This hour is yours: a poem's inspiration,
the monologue of tragedy and night.

Karl F. Ross

Ein Wort

Ein Wort, ein Satz—: aus Chiffren steigen
erkanntes Leben, jäher Sinn,
die Sonne steht, die Sphären schweigen
und alles ballt sich zu ihm hin.

Ein Wort—ein Glanz, ein Flug, ein Feuer,
ein Flammenwurf, ein Sternenstrich—
und wieder Dunkel, ungeheuer,
im leeren Raum um Welt und Ich.

1941

Monolog

Den Darm mit Rotz genährt, das Hirn mit Lügen—
erwählte Völker Narren eines Clowns,
in Späße, Sternelesen, Vogelzug
den eigenen Unrat deutend! Sklaven—
aus kalten Ländern und aus glühenden,
immer mehr Sklaven, ungezieferschwere,
hungernde, peitschenüberschwungene Haufen:
Dann schwillt das Eigene an, der eigene Flaum,
der grindige, zum Barte des Propheten!

Ach, Alexander und Olympias Sproß
das wenigste! Sie zwinkern Hellesponte
und schäumen Asien! Aufgetriebenes, Blasen
mit Vorhut, Günstlingen, verdeckten Staffeln,
daß keiner sticht! Günstlinge:—gute Plätze
für Ring—und Rechtsgeschehn! Wenn keiner sticht!
Günstlinge, Lustvolk, Binden, breite Bänder—
mit breiten Bändern flattert Traum und Welt:
Klumpfüße sehn die Stadien zerstört,
Stinktiere treten die Lupinenfelder,

A Word

A word, a phrase—: from Cyphers rise
Life recognized, a sudden sense,
The sun stands still, mute are the skies,
And all compacts it, stark and dense.

A word—, a gleam, a flight, a spark,
A thrust of flames, a stellar trace—,
And then again—immense—the dark
Round world and I in empty space.

Richard Exner

Monologue

Their colons fed with mucus, brains with lies
these chosen races, coxcombs of a clown,
in pranks, astrology and flight of birds
construing their own ordure! Slaves—
from icy and from burning territories,
gross with vermin more and more slaves come,
hungry and whiplash-driven hordes of them:
Then all that's personal, the downy cheek,
with scurf and scab, swells to a prophet's beard!

Ah, Alexander and Olympia's offspring,
that least of all! They wink whole Hellesponts,
and skim all Asia! Puffed up, pustules
with vanguard, covert squadrons and with minions
that none may prick them! Minions; the best seats
for wrestling and in court! Let no man prick them!
Minions, joyriders, bandages, broad streamers—
broad streamers fluttering from dream and world:
the clubfoot sees the stadiums destroyed,
skunks trample under foot the lupin fields

weil sie der Duft am eigenen irremacht:
Nur Stoff vom After!—Fette
verfolgen die Gazelle,
die windeseilige, das schöne Tier!
Hier kehrt das Maß sich um:
Die Pfütze prüft den Quell, der Wurm die Elle,
die Kröte spritzt dem Veilchen in den Mund
—Hallelujah!—und wetzt den Bauch im Kies:
Die Paddentrift als Mahnmal der Geschichte!
Die Ptolemäerspur als Gaunerzinke,
die Ratte kommt als Labsal gegen Pest.
Meuchel besingt den Mord. Spitzel locken
aus Psalmen Unzucht.

Und diese Erde lispelt mit dem Mond,
dann schürzt sie sich ein Maifest um die Hüfte,
dann läßt sie Rosen durch, dann schmort sie Korn,
läßt den Vesuv nicht spein, läßt nicht die Wolke
zu Lauge werden, die der Tiere Abart,
die dies erlistet, sticht und niederbrennt—
ach, dieser Erde Frucht- und Rosenspiel
ist heimgestellt der Wucherung des Bösen,
der Hirne Schwamm, der Kehle Lügensprenkeln
der obgenannten Art—die maßverkehrte!

Sterben heißt, dies alles ungelöst verlassen,
die Bilder ungesichert, die Träume
im Riß der Welten stehn und hungern lassen—
doch Handeln heißt, die Niedrigkeit bedienen,
der Schande Hilfe leihn, die Einsamkeit,
die große Lösung der Gesichte,
das Traumverlangen hinterhältig fällen
für Vorteil, Schmuck, Beförderungen, Nachruf,
indes das Ende, taumelnd wie ein Falter,
gleichgültig wie ein Sprengstück nahe ist
und anderen Sinn verkündet—

because the scent makes them suspect their own:
Nothing but excrement! The obese
course after the gazelle,
the windswift one, the lovely animal!
Inverse proportion enters everything:
The puddle plumbs the source, the worm the ell,
toad squirts his liquid in the violet's mouth,
and—hallelujah!—whets his pot on stones:
The reptile horde as history's monument!
The Ptolemaic line as tic-tac language,
the rat arrives as balm against the plague.
Most foul sings murder. Gossips wheedle
obscenity from psalms.

And this earth whispers discourse with the moon,
then round its hips it hangs a Mayday feast
then lets the rose pass, then stews the corn,
forbids Vesuvius erupt, won't let the cloud
become a caustic that would prick and shrivel
the beasts' base form whose fraud contrived this state—
oh, all the play on earth of fruit and rose
is given up to evil's usury,
brain-fungus, and the gorge's speckling lies
of the above-named sort, proportion inverse!

To die means leaving all these things unsolved,
the images unsure, and hungry dreams
abandoned in the rifts between the worlds—
but action means: to serve vulgarity,
aid and abet iniquity, means loneliness
and dropping furtively the great solution
that visions are and the desire of dreams,
for gain, for gold, promotion, posthumous fame,
while giddily like a moth, indifferent
as a petard the end is near and bodes
a meaning that is different—

—Ein Klang, ein Bogen, fast ein Sprung aus Bläue
stieß eines Abends durch den Park hervor,
darin ich stand—: ein Lied,
ein Abriß nur, drei hingeworfene Noten
und füllte so den Raum und lud so sehr
die Nacht, den Garten mit Erscheinungen voll
und schuf die Welt und bettete den Nacken
mir in das Strömende, die trauervolle
erhabene Schwäche der Geburt des Seins—:
ein Klang, ein Bogen nur—: Geburt des Seins—
ein Bogen nur und trug das Maß zurück,
und alles schloß es ein; die Tat, die Träume . . .

Aus einem Kranz scharlachener Gehirne,
des Blüten der verstreuten Fiebersaat
sich einzeln halten, nur einander:
„unbeugsam in der Farbe" and „ausgezähnt
am Saum das letzte Haar", „gefeilt in Kälte"
zurufen, gesalzene Laken des Urstoffs:
Hier geht Verwandlung aus: Der Tiere Abart
wird faulen, daß für sie das Wort Verwesung
zu sehr nach Himmeln riecht—schon streichen
die Geier an, die Falken hungern schon—!

1941

Verlorenes Ich

Verlorenes Ich, zersprengt von Stratosphären,
Opfer des Ion—: Gamma-Strahlen-Lamm—
Teilchen und Feld—: Unendlichkeitschimären
auf deinem grauen Stein von Notre-Dame.

Die Tage gehn dir ohne Nacht und Morgen,
die Jahre halten ohne Schnee und Frucht
bedrohend das Unendliche verborgen—
die Welt als Flucht.

A sound, a curve, a chink of blue almost,
reverberated through the park one night
as I stood there—: a song,
only an outline, casual, three notes heard,
and occupied all space and made the night
so full, the garden full of apparitions,
created so the world and bedded me
prostrate within the stream of things, the sad
sublime infirmity of being's birth—:
a sound, only a curve—: but being's birth—
only a curve, proportion it restored
and comprehended all things, act and dreaming . . .

A garland intertwined of scarlet brains
whose flowers grown from scattered fever-seed
shut to each other, keeping separate:
'the coloration form' and 'edges frayed,
the last thread snapping' and 'a hard cold contour,'
these spicy pickles of the protoplasm,
Here transformation starts: the beasts' base form
shall so decay the very word corruption
will smell for it too much of heaven—the vultures
are gathering now and famished hawks are poised!

Christopher Middleton

Forsaken I

Forsaken I, in rout from stratospheres,
The ion's victim—: radiation's sacrificial lamb—
Particle and field—: infinity's chimeras
On those grey stones of your new Notre Dame.

Your days go by without a night or morning,
The years conceal, no snow, no fruit in sight,
The infinite's dark threatening warning—
The world as flight.

Wo endest du, wo lagerst du, wo breiten
sich deine Sphären an—Verlust, Gewinn—:
ein Spiel von Bestien: Ewigkeiten,
an ihren Gittern fliehst du hin.

Der Bestienblick: die Sterne als Kaldaunen,
der Dschungeltod als Seins- und Schöpfungsgrund,
Mensch, Völkerschlachten, Katalaunen
hinab den Bestienschlund.

Die Welt zerdacht. Und Raum und Zeiten
und was die Menschheit wob and wog,
Funktion nur von Unendlichkeiten—
die Mythe log.

Woher, wohin—nicht Nacht, nicht Morgen,
kein Evoë, kein Requiem,
du möchtest dir ein Stichwort borgen—
allein bei wem?

Ach, als sich alle einer Mitte neigten
und auch die Denker nur den Gott gedacht,
sie sich dem Hirten und dem Lamm verzweigten,
wenn aus dem Kelch das Blut sie rein gemacht,

und alle rannen aus der einen Wunde,
brachen das Brot, das jeglicher genoß—
o ferne zwingende erfüllte Stunde,
die einst auch das verlorne Ich umschloß.

1943

Where will you end, where pitch your camp, where see
Your spheres outspread—all's one, or loss or gain—
A game where only wild beasts win: eternities
Along whose bars you flee in vain.

The bestial glaze: the stars as internalia,
The jungle death as being and creation's ground,
Man, Leipzig's slaughter, Catalaunias,
Down the beasts' maw, all down.

World thought to bits. Space and the ages,
And what mankind groped for as guide,
Infinities are now their gauges—
The myth has lied.

Where from, where to—no night, no morning,
No evoë, no requiem,
A cue might satisfy your yearning,
But who can cue you in?

Oh, when all wholly to one center tended
And even thinkers only thought of God
With Shepherd and with Lamb all lives were blended
And from His cup He cleansed them with His blood,

And all mankind from that one wound seemed welling,
Breaking the bread that each one might partake—
Oh distant hour, fulfilling and compelling,
That even the forsaken I did not forsake.

Robert M. Browning

For another version see page 279.

Welle der Nacht

Welle der Nacht—Meerwidder und Delphine
mit Hyakinthos leichtbewegter Last,
die Lorbeerrosen und die Travertine
wehn um den leeren istrischen Palast,

Welle der Nacht—zwei Muscheln miterkoren,
die Fluten strömen sie, die Felsen her,
dann Diadem und Purpur mitverloren,
die weiße Perle rollt zurück ins Meer.

1943

Die Züge deiner—

Die Züge deiner, die dem Blut verschworen,
der Menschheit altem, allgemeinen Blut,
die sah ich wohl und gab mich doch verloren,
schlummerbedeckt und schweigend deiner Flut.

Wave of the Night

Wave of the night—sea-ram and dolphin seen
with Hyakinthos' airy weight borne high,
where laurel roses and the Travertine
around the empty Istrian palace sigh,

Wave of the night—two chosen shells it bore,
in tidal stream from cliffs incessantly,
then, diadem and purple lost once more,
the white pearl rolls into the sea.

Christopher Middleton

The Wave of Night

The wave of night—the dolphin trails meander,
with Hyacinthus' easy-floating host,
around the palace, ringed with oleander,
that stands deserted on the rocky coast.

The wave of night—two oysters bob and billow,
swept inland past the cliffside by the swirl;
then, torn from diadem and purple pillow,
back to the ocean rolls a shiny pearl.

Karl F. Ross

Those Traits of Yours

Those traits of yours, to ties of blood committed,
humanity's old, universal blood,
I saw them well and nonetheless submitted
in slumber's sweep and silence to your flood.

Trugst mich noch einmal zu des Spieles Pforten:
die Becher dunkel und die Würfel blind,
noch einmal zu den Letzten süßen Worten
und zum Vergessen, daß sie Träume sind.

Die Vesten sinken und die Arten fallen,
die Rasse Adams, die das Tier verstieß,
nach den Legionen, nach den Göttern allen,
wenn es auch Träume sind—noch einmal dies.

1943

Chopin

Nicht sehr ergiebig in Gespräch,
Ansichten waren nicht seine Stärke,
Ansichten reden drum herum,
wenn Delacroix Theorien entwickelte,
wurde er unruhig, er seinerseits konnte
die Notturnos nicht begründen.

Schwacher Liebhaber;
Schatten in Nohant,
wo George Sands Kinder
keine erzieherischen Ratschläge
von ihm annahmen.

Brustkrank in jener Form
mit Blutungen und Narbenbildung,
die sich lange hinzieht;
stiller Tod
im Gegensatz zu einem
mit Schmerzparoxysmen
oder durch Gewehrsalven:

Once more you led me to the gates of gambling,
of faceless dice rolled from a hidden sleeve;
once more to tender words so sweet and rambling
and to forgetting they are make-believe.

The stirpes vanish and the strongholds crumble;
the race of Adam—barred from Fauna's door. . . .
Let all the heroes, all the idols tumble:
Though it be make-believe—just this, once more.

Karl F. Ross

Chopin

Not very forthcoming in conversation,
opinions were not his forte,
opinions don't get to the center;
when Delacroix expounded a theory
he became restive, he for his part was unable
to explicate his Nocturnes.

Weak as a lover;
shadows at Nohant,
where George Sand's children
would not accept
his pedagogic advice.

Consumptive, of the kind
with hemorrhages and cicatrization,
the kind that drags on for years;
quiet death
as opposed to one
with paroxysms of pain
or one by the firing-squad:

man rückte den Flügel (Erard) an die Tür
und Delphine Potocka
sang ihm in der letzten Stunde
ein Veilchenlied.

Nach England reiste er mit drei Flügeln:
Pleyel, Erard, Broadwood,
spielte für zwanzig Guineen abends
eine Viertelstunde
bei Rothschilds, Wellingtons, im Strafford House
und vor zahllosen Hosenbändern;
verdunkelt von Müdigkeit und Todesnähe
kehrte er heim
auf den Square d'Orléans.

Dann verbrennt er seine Skizzen
und Manuskripte,
nur keine Restbestände, Fragmente, Notizen,
diese verräterischen Einblicke—
sagte zum Schluß:
„Meine Versuche sind nach Maßgabe dessen vollendet,
was mir zu erreichen möglich war."

Spielen sollte jeder Finger
mit der seinem Bau entsprechenden Kraft,
der vierte ist der schwächste
(nur siamesisch zum Mittelfinger).
Wenn er begann, lagen sie
auf e, fis, gis, h, c.

Wer je bestimmte Präludien
von ihm hörte,
sei es in Landhäusern oder
in einem Höhengelände
oder aus offenen Terrassentüren
beispielsweise aus einem Sanatorium,
wird es schwer vergessen.

They moved his grand piano (Erard) up to the door
and Delphine Potocka
sang for him at his dying hour
a violet song.

To England he went with three pianos:
Pleyel, Erard, Broadwood,
gave for twenty minutes
fifteen-minute recitals
at Rothschild's, the Wellingtons, at Stratford House,
and to countless garters;
darkened by weariness and approaching death,
he went home
to the Square d'Orléans.

Then he burnt his sketches
and manuscripts;
no residues please, no fragments or notes,
they grant such revealing insights—
and said at the end:
"My endeavors are as complete
as it was in my power to make them."

Every finger was to play
with the force appropriate to its structure;
the fourth is the weakest
(mere siamese twin to the middle finger).
When he began they rested
on E, F sharp, G sharp, B, C.

The man who has ever heard
certain Preludes by him,
whether in country houses or
in a mountain landscape
or on a terrace, through open doors,
a sanatorium's for instance,
will hardly forget it.

Nie eine Oper komponiert,
keine Symphonie,
nur diese tragischen Progressionen
aus artistischer Überzeugung
und mit einer kleinen Hand.

1945

September

I

Du, über den Zaun gebeugt mit Phlox
(vom Regenguß zerspalten,
seltsamen Wildgeruchs),
der gern auf Stoppeln geht,
zu alten Leuten tritt,
die Balsaminen pflücken,
Rauch auf Feldern
mit Lust and Trauer atmet—

aufsteigenden Gemäuers,
das noch sein Dach vor Schnee und Winter will,
kalklöschenden Gesellen
ein: „ach, vergebens" zuzurufen
nur zögernd sich verhält—

gedrungen eher als hochgebaut,
auch unflätigen Kürbis nackt am Schuh,
fett and gesichtslos, dies Krötengewächs—

Ebenen-entstiegener,
Endmond aller Flammen,
aus Furcht- und Fieberschwellungen
abfallend, schon verdunkelten Gesichts—
Narr oder Täufer,

Never composed an opera,
no symphony,
only these tragic progressions
out of artistic conviction
and with a slender hand.

Michael Hamburger

For *another version see page 281.*

September

I

You leaning there over the fence with phlox
(splintered by rainstorm,
with a strange animal smell),
who are pleased to walk over stubble
and to accost old folk
gathering balm apples,
breathe with joy and sadness
smoke over ploughland—

rising walls want there
a roof before the snow and winter come,
to shout a "You're wasting your time"
at lime-slaking laborers,
but, hesitant, restrain yourself,

thickset rather than tall in build,
with dirty pumpkin also bare at your shoe,
fat and faceless this toady growth—

Risen from the plains,
ultimate moon of all flames,
from tumescences of fruit and fever
dropping, darkened your face already—
fool or baptist,

des Sommers Narr, Nachplapperer, Nachruf
oder der Gletscher Vorlied,
jedenfalls Nußknacker,
Schilfmäher,
Beschäftigter mit Binsenwahrheiten—

vor dir der Schnee,
Hochschweigen, unfruchtbar
die Unbesambarkeit der Weite:
da langt dein Arm hin,
doch über den Zaun gebeugt
die Kraut- und Käferdränge,
das Lebenwollende,
Spinnen and Feldmäuse—

II

Du, ebereschenverhangen
von Frühherbst,
Stoppelgespinst,
Kohlweißlinge im Atem,
laß viele Zeiger laufen,
Kuckucksuhren schlagen,
lärme mit Vespergeläut,
gonge
die Stunde, die so golden feststeht,
so bestimmt dahinbräunt,
in ein zitternd Herz!

Du:—anderes!
So ruhn nur Götter
oder Gewänder
unstürzbarer Titanen
langgeschaffener,
so tief eingestickt
Falter und Blumen
in die Bahnen!

summer's fool, echoer, necrologue,
or foresong of glaciers,
anyway nutcracker,
sedge-cutter,
ponderer of platitudes—

Snowfall ahead of you,
high silence, barren
the far unplantable distance;
that far your reach extends,
but, leaning over the fence,
throngs of beetles and plants now,
all life-desiring things,
spiders and field mice—

II

You, rowan-veiled
by early autumn,
stubblephantom,
cabbage-whites in your breath,
let many clock-hands turn,
cuckoo-clocks call,
clamor with vesper bells,
gong
the golden presistent hour
that so firmly continues to tan,
into a trembling heart!

You:—world of difference!
Only gods rest thus
or the robes
of untoppleable Titans
long-created,
so deeply embroidered
the butterflies and flowers
into their orbits!

Oder ein Schlummer früher Art.
als kein Erwachen war,
nur goldene Wärme und Purpurbeeren,
benagt von Schwalben, ewigen,
die nie von dannen ziehn—
Dies schlage, gonge,
diese Stunde,
denn
wenn du schweigst,
drängen die Säume herab
pappelbestanden und schon kühler.

1945

Quartär—

I
Die Welten trinken und tränken
sich Rausch zu neuem Raum
und die letzten Quartäre versenken
den ptolemäischen Traum.
Verfall, Verflammen, Verfehlen—
in toxischen Sphären, kalt
noch einige stygische Seelen,
einsame, hoch und alt.

II
Komm—laß sie sinken und steigen,
die Zyklen brechen hervor:
uralte Sphinxe, Geigen
und von Babylon ein Tor,
ein Jazz vom Rio del Grande,
ein Swing und ein Gebet—
an sinkenden Feuern, vom Rande,
wo alles zu Asche verweht.

Or a slumber of pristine kind,
when no awakening was,
only golden warmth and purple berries,
nibbled by swallows, eternal ones,
that never fly away—
This note strike, gong
this hour,
for
when you fall silent,
downward the forest-edges press,
thick with poplars, already cooler.

Christopher Middleton

Quaternary

I

Worlds at the trough and drinking,
Getting drunk for another space,
The last quaternaries are sinking
The dream of Ptolemy's place.
Decay, conflagration, dispelling—
In toxic spheres and cold
A few stygian souls are dwelling,
Lonely, aloof, and old.

II

Come—let them keep sinking and rising,
Don't ages in cycles appear?
Sphinxes, fiddles, all man's devising,
And a gate of Babylon here,
Jazz from K.C. and New Orleans,
Swing by B.G. and a prayer—
By sinking campfires' last gleaming—
Ashes and nothing else there.

Ich schnitt die Gurgel den Schafen
und füllte die Grube mit Blut,
die Schatten kamen und trafen
sich hier—ich horchte gut—,

ein jeglicher trank, erzählte
von Schwert und Fall und frug,
auch stier- und schwanenvermählte
Frauen weinten im Zug.

Quartäre Zyklen—Szenen,
doch keine macht dir bewußt,
ist nun das Letzte die Tränen
oder ist das Letzte die Lust
oder beides ein Regenbogen,
der einige Farben bricht,
gespiegelt oder gelogen—
du weißt, du weißt es nicht.

III

Riesige Hirne biegen
sich über ihr Dann and Wann
und sehen die Fäden fliegen,
die die alte Spinne spann,
mit Rüsseln in jede Ferne
und an alles, was verfällt,
züchten sich ihre Kerne
die sich erkennende Welt.

Einer der Träume Gottes
blickte sich selber an,
Blicke des Spiels, des Spottes
vom alten Spinnenmann,
dann pflückt er sich Asphodelen
und wandert den Styxen zu—
laß sich die Letzten quälen,
laß sie Geschichte erzählen—
Allerseelen—
Fini du tout.

1946

I cut the sheep through their windpipes
And filled up the pit with their blood,
Shades came trooping of all stripes—
I listened and half understood.
Each one drank and recounted
The tale of its death and its pain;
Women once by bull and swan mounted
Wept in this train.

Quaternary cycles—sweeping—
But not one to set you right
Whether the end is weeping
Or whether the end is delight
Or if both a rainbow illusion
Refracting colors for show,
Mirage perhaps, delusion—
You know that you do not know.

III

Gigantic brains are bending
Over their Now and Then,
They watch the filaments wending
That the ancient spider span;
With snouts in the distance leading
On all things that must die
Depositing seed for breeding
The world that will know its I.

One of the dreams of the Maker
Observed itself for a span
With looks both playful and scornful
Like those of the Spider-Man,
Then picking some wild asphodel
That by stygian waters grew:
"Leave the Last Ones to their hell,
Let History of them tell,
All Hallows Eve and all's well—
Fini du tout."

Robert M. Browning

Epilog 1949

Die trunkenen Fluten fallen—
die Stunde des sterbenden Blau
und der erblaßten Korallen
um die Insel von Palau.

Die trunkenen Fluten enden
als Fremdes, nicht dein, nicht mein,
sie lassen dir nichts in Händen
als der Bilder schweigendes Sein.

Die Fluten, die Flammen, die Fragen—
und dann auf Asche sehn:
„Leben ist Brückenschlagen
über Ströme, die vergehn."

1949

Epilogue

The drunken torrents are falling—
the blueness is dying now
and the corals are pale as the water
round the island of Palau.

The drunken torrents are broken,
grown alien, to you, to me,
our only possession the silence
of a bone washed clean by the sea.

The floods, the flames, the questions—
till the ashes tell you one day:
"Life is the building of bridges
over the rivers that sweep away."

Michael Hamburger

Epilog 1949

The quivering flames are failing—
the hour of the vanishing blue,
of corals fading and paling
along the isle of Pelew.

The quivering flames are waning,
for you and for me remote;
they leave us nothing remaining
but memory's silent note.

The qualms, the questions, the quivers—
then ashes, barren and sere:
life is a bridging of rivers
whose waters disappear.

Karl F. Ross

Fragmente

Fragmente,
Seelenauswürfe,
Blutgerinnsel des zwanzigsten Jahrhunderts—

Narben—*gestörter Kreislauf der Schöpfungsfrühe,*
die historischen Religionen von fünf Jahrhunderten
                                    zertrümmert,
die Wissenschaft: Risse im Parthenon,
Planck rann mit seiner Quantentheorie
zu Kepler und Kierkegaard neu getrübt zusammen—

aber Abende gab es, die gingen in den Farben
des Allvaters, lockeren, weitwallenden,
unumstößlich in ihrem Schweigen
geströmten Blaus,
Farbe der Introvertierten,
da sammelte man sich
die Hände auf das Knie gestützt
bäuerlich, einfach
und stillem Trunk ergeben
bei den Harmonikas der Knechte—

und andere
gehetzt von inneren Konvoluten,
Wölbungsdrängen,
Stilbaukompressionen
oder Jagden nach Liebe.

Ausdruckskrisen und Anfälle von Erotik:
das ist der Mensch von heute,
das Innere ein Vakuum,
die Kontinuität der Persönlichkeit
wird gewahrt von den Anzügen,
die bei gutem Stoff zehn Jahre halten.

Fragments

Fragments,
Refuse of the soul,
Coagulations of blood of the twentieth century:

Scars—interrupted cycle of early creation,
The historic religions of five centuries pulverized.
Science: cracks in the Parthenon,
Planck with his quantum theory merging
In the new confusion with Kepler and Kierkegaard—

Yet there were evenings that went in the colors
Of the Father of all, dissolute, far-gathering,
Inviolate in their silence
Of coursing blue,
Color of the introvert:
Then one relaxed
With the hands caught up round the knee
Peasant-wise, simple,
And resigned to the quiet drink
And the sound of the servants' concertina—

And others
Provoked by inner scrolls of paper,
Vaulted pressures,
Constrictions in the building of style
Or pursuits of love.

Crises of expression and bouts of eroticism,
That is the man of today,
His inwardness a vacuum;
The survival of personality
Is preserved by the clothing
Which, where material is good, may last ten years.

Der Rest Fragmente,
halbe Laute,
Melodienansätze aus Nachbarhäusern,
Negerspirituals
oder Ave Marias.

1950

Reisen

Meinen Sie Zürich zum Beispiel
sei eine tiefere Stadt,
wo man Wunder and Weihen
immer als Inhalt hat?

Meinen Sie, aus Habana,
weiß und hibiskusrot,
bräche ein ewiges Manna
für Ihre Wüstennot?

Bahnhofstraßen und Rueen,
Boulevards, Lidos, Laan—
selbst auf den Fifth Avenueen
fällt Sie die Leere an—

Ach, vergeblich das Fahren!
Spät erst erfahren Sie sich:
bleiben und stille bewahren
das sich umgrenzende Ich.

1950

The rest fragments,
Half tones,
Snatches of melody from neighbor's houses,
Negro spirituals
Or Ave Marias.

Vernon Watkins

Travel

Zurich you think for example
Must be a place more profound
Where wonders and wisdom are always
A part of the daily round?

You think that out of Havana,
White and hibiscus red,
Must break forth eternal manna
For you in your desert of lead?

Bahnhofsstrassen and rues,
Boulevards, Lidos, and Quais,
On even the Fifth Avenues
Emptiness comes and holds sway.

Travel's a vain undertaking!
In the end you meet only yourself:
Stay put and hold in safekeeping
The I that delimits itself.

Robert M. Browning

For other versions see page 283.

Destille

I

Schäbig; abends Destille
in Zwang, in Trieb, in Flucht
Trunk—doch was ist der Wille
gegen Verklärungssucht.

Wenn man die Seele sichtet,
Potenz und Potential,
den Blick aufs Ganze gerichtet:
katastrophal!

Natürlich sitzen in Stuben
Gelehrte zart und matt
und machen aus Tintentuben
ihre Pandekten satt,

natürlich bauten sie Dome
dreihundert Jahre ein Stück
wissend, im Zeitenstrome
bröckelt der Stein zurück,

es ist nicht zu begreifen,
was hatten sie für Substanz,
wissend, die Zeiten schleifen
Turm, Rose, Krypte, Monstranz,

vorbei, à bas und nieder
die große Konfession,
à bas ins Hühnergefieder
konformer Konvention—

abends in Destillen
verzagt, verjagt, verflucht,
so vieles muß sich stillen,
im Trunk Verklärungssucht.

Bistro

I

Shabby: evenings in bistros
There's a thirst I have to slake—
Drink—but what is will power
When transfiguration's at stake?

Examine the souls' potentials,
Its patent, its latent force:
Not much in the way of credentials,
In fact it could hardly be worse.

Sitting of course in their study
Are scholars, tender and pale,
Though their ink makes tomes as ruddy
As though they were drinking ale,

And of course they built cathedrals—
Three hundred years for each—
Knowing full well that those walls
Had but a limited lease.

Can we, I ask, presume then
To understand their trance?
Knowing that time would consume them:
Tower, rose-window, monstrance?

Past, à bas, gone forever
The Athanasian creed,
A bas in the chicken feathers
Of conforming word and deed.

Evenings off to the bistro,
Disheartened, expelled, accursed;
Drink stills many a longing
And for tranfiguration, the thirst.

II

Es gibt Melodien und Lieder,
die bestimmte Rhythmen betreun,
die schlagen dein Inneres nieder
und du bist am Boden bis neun.

Meist nachts und du bist schon lange
in vagem Säusel und nickst
zu fremder Gäste Belange,
durch die du in Leben blickst.

Und diese Leben sind trübe,
so trübe, du würdest dich freun,
wenn ewig Rhythmenschübe
und du bliebest am Boden bis neun.

IV

Ich will mich nicht erwähnen.
doch fällt mir manchmal ein
zwischen Fässern und Hähnen
eine Art von Kunstverein.

Die haben etwas errichtet,
eine Aula mit Schalmei,
da wird gespielt und gedichtet,
was längst vorbei.

Ich lasse mich zerfallen,
ich bleibe dem Ende nah,
dann steht zwischen Trümmern und Ballen
eine tiefe Stund da.

1953

II

There are some songs and hit tunes
With a certain rhythm and rime,
They get to your gizzard too soon
And you're out on the floor till nine.

Most nights—soused already—
You sit vaguely blinking and nod
To other bar flies' proposals
And the paths their lives have trod,

And these lives are horribly dismal,
So dismal you'd like it fine
If rhythm and rime kept throbbing
And you stayed on the floor till nine.

IV

I don't like to point to my person,
But still I'm reluctant to scrub
As I lounge in lower class barrooms
The thought of an artists' club.

They have, you see, erected
A hall with an organ too,
What there through art is perfected
Time cannot undo.

I'll let myself go to the devil,
I'll stay here close my end,
One night there'll stand in some bistro
A profounder moment again.

Robert M. Browning

Was schlimm ist

Wenn man kein Englisch kann,
von einem guten englischen Kriminalroman zu hören,
der nicht ins Deutsche übersetzt ist.

Bei Hitze ein Bier sehn,
das man nicht bezahlen kann.

Einen neuen Gedanken haben,
den man nicht in einen Hölderlinvers einwickeln kann,
wie es die Professoren tun.

Nachts auf Reisen Wellen schlagen hören
und sich sagen, daß sie das immer tun.

Sehr schlimm: eingeladen sein,
wenn zu Hause die Räume stiller,
der Café besser
und keine Unterhaltung nötig ist.

Am schlimmsten:
nicht im Sommer sterben,
wenn alles hell ist
und die Erde für Spaten leicht.

1953

Viele Herbste

Wenn viele Herbst sich verdichten
in deinem Blut, in deinem Sinn
und sie des Sommers Glücke richten,
fegt doch die fetten Rosen hin,

What's Bad

When you do not know English
and hear of a good English detective novel
that has not been translated into German.

To see when you're hot
a beer that you can't afford.

To have a new thought without being able
to make it sound like a line by Hölderlin
as the professors do.

On a journey by night to hear waves beating
and to think: they do that all the time.

Very bad: to be invited out
when at home it is quieter,
the coffee is better,
and you've no need to be amused.

Worst of all:
not to die in summer,
when everything is bright,
and the earth is easy on the spade.

Christopher Middleton

Many Autumns

When many autumns coalesce
Within your blood, within your brain,
And judge this summer's happiness—
Then throw out all the stale champagne,

den ganzen Pomp, den ganzen Lüster,
Terrassennacht, den Glamour-Ball
aus Crêpe de Chine, bald wird es düster,
dann klappert euch das Leichtmetall,

das Laub, die Lasten, Abgesänge,
Balkons, geranienzerfetzt—
was bist du dann, du Weichgestänge,
was hast du seelisch eingesetzt?

1953

Nur zwei Dinge

Durch so viel Formen geschritten,
durch Ich und Wir und Du,
doch alles blieb erlitten
durch die ewige Frage; wozu?

Das ist eine Kinderfrage,
Dir wurde erst spät bewußt,
es gibt nur eines: ertrage
—ob Sinn, ob Sucht, ob Sage—
dein fernbestimmtes: Du mußt.

Ob Rosen, ob Schnee, ob Meere,
was alles erblühte, verblich,
es gibt nur zwei Dinge: die Leere
und das gezeichnete Ich.

1953

The faded roses' luxury,
The garden-party tinsel-fuss,
It will turn gloomy presently,
You'll hear creaky tinplate rust,

A mangy-flowered balcony,
A dried-up branch, leftover tunes—
What has your moral input been,
You rotten kindling picayune?

Alexandra Chciuk-Celt

Two Things Only

Through so many forms of existence,
through "you" and "we" and "I,"
and always with persistence
the age-old question: Why?

That is a children's query.
But later you understand:
One bears—no matter how weary—
the evil, the odd and the eerie
by far-ordained command.

The snow, the sea, the carnation,
whatever once bloomed, fell apart.
Two things have remained: The frustration
and the mark of a haunted heart.

Karl F. Ross

Aber Du –?

Flüchtiger, du mußt die Augen schließen,
denn was eindringt, ist kein Großes Los,
abends im Lokal ist kein Genießen,
selbst an diesem Ort zerfällst du bloß.

Plötzlich sitzt ein Toter an der Theke,
Rechtsanwalt, mit rotem Nierenschwund,
schon zwei Jahre tot, mit schöner Witwe,
und nun trinkt er lebhaft und gesund.

Auch die Blume hat schon oft gestanden,
die jetzt auf dem Flügel in der Bar,
schon vor fünfzig Jahren, stets vorhanden
Gott weiß wann, wo immer Sommer war.

Alles setzt sich fort, dreht von der alten
einer neuen Position sich zu,
alles bleibt in seinem Grundverhalten—
aber du—?

1954

Verliess das Haus—

I

Verließ das Haus, verzehrt, er litt so sehr,
so viele Jahre Mensch, mit Zwischendingen,
trotz Teilerfolg im Geistesringen
war keiner von olympischem Gewähr.

So ging er langsam durch die Reverie
des späten Herbsttags, kaum zu unterscheiden
von einem Frühlingstag mit jungen Weiden
und einem Kahlschlag, wo der Häher schrie.

What Are You?

Evanescer, got to close your eyes—
Really no great shakes, what you see here.
Evening cocktail lounges are a drag,
And you fall apart into your beer.

A lawyer's corpse just sat down at the bar,
Been dead two years of renal atrophy,
His widow's gorgeous, but he's drinking here
As if he were alive, quite merrily.

And this flower on the piano-bar,
Somehow it is always standing there
(I saw it half a century ago)
Anyplace there's summer—God knows where.

Everything's continuous rotation
From the old position to the new,
Faithful to its essence and behavior. . . .
What are *you?*

Alexandra Chciuk-Celt

He Left the House

I

He left, devoured and ravaged refugee—
Too many years a human, with digressions,
And all his semi-triumph cogitations
Were lacking that Olympian quality.

Outside the house, he shuffled reverie
Of late November that so much resembles
A day in spring, replete with junior meadows
And glens where bluejays chatter noisily.

So träumerisch von Dingen überspielt,
die die Natur in Lenken und Verwalten
entfernter Kreise—jüngeren und alten—
als unaufhebbar einer Ordnung fühlt—:

So trank er denn den Schnaps und nahm die Tracht
Wurstsuppe, donnerstags umsonst gereichte
an jeden Gast, und fand das angegleichte
Olympische von Lust und Leidensmacht.

II

Er hatte etwas auf der Bank gelesen
und in der letzten Rosen Grau gesehn,
es waren keine Stämme, Buschwerkwesen,
gelichtet schon von Fall und Untergehn.

Nun sank das Buch. Es war ein Tag wie alle
und Menschen auch wie alle im Revier,
das würde weiter sein, in jedem Falle
blieb dies Gemisch von Tod und Lachen hier.

Schon ein Geruch kann mancherlei entkräften,
auch kleine Blumen sind der Zeder nah—
dann ging er weiter und in Pelzgeschäften
lag manches Warme für den Winter da.

III

Ganz schön—gewiß—für Schnaps und eine Weile
im Park am Mittag, wenn die Sonne scheint,
doch wenn der Hauswirt kommt, gewisse Teile
der Steuer fehlen und die Freundin weint?

Verzehrt: wie weit darfst du dein Ich betreiben,
Absonderliches als verbindlich sehn?
Verzehrt: wie weit mußt du im Genre bleiben—
so weit wie Ludwig Richters Bilden gehn?

Inexorable and dreamy, like the laws
That Nature uses for administration
Of distant circles, recent and more ancient,
Unconsciously obedient to their cause,

He downed the sausage-soup that comes for free
With every drink on Thursdays, finding there
His asymptotic version of that rare
Olympian passion-lust and power-greed.

II

He'd read something while sitting on a ledge
And spied it in the roses' fading gray—
No tree-trunk, nothing but a gap-toothed hedge
That's marked by fall, decline, and disarray.

The book slid down. A day like any other,
The people were no different from the norm;
That wouldn't change. What's left? A mixture smothered
Of death and laughter, always true to form.

A certain odor can disarm a man,
Small flowers huddle near a sycamore—
He ambled on and saw a furrier's van
Unloading wintry warmth into the store.

III

For just a little while, it may seem fine—
A noonday park-bench in the shining sun.
It's different when your girlfriend has been crying,
The landlord knocks, some tax receipts are gone.

Devoured: How far may I then exercise
My right to Self? What's binding, and what's weird?
Devoured: How far to individualize?
How far does Norman Rockwell domineer?

Verzehrt: man weiß es nicht. Verzehrt: man wendet
sich qualvoll Einzel zu wie Allgemein—
das Zwischenspiel von Macht des Schicksals endet
glorios und ewig, aber ganz allein.

Verflucht die Evergreens! Die Platten dröhnen!
Schnaps, Sonne, Zedern—was verhelfen sie
dem Ich, den Traum, den Wirt und Gott versöhnen—
die Stimmen krächzen und die Worte höhnen—
verließ das Haus und schloß die Reverie.

1954

Tristesse

Die Schatten wandeln nicht nur in den Hainen,
davor die Asphodelenwiese liegt,
sie wandeln unter uns und schon in deinen
Umarmungen, wenn noch der Traum dich wiegt.

Was ist das Fleisch—aus Rosen und aus Dornen,
was ist die Brust—aus Falten und aus Samt,
und was das Haar, die Achseln, die verworrnen
Vertiefungen, der Blick so heiß entflammt:

Es trägt das Einst: die früheren Vertrauten
und auch das Einst: wenn du es nicht mehr küßt,
hör gar nicht hin, die leisen und die lauten
Beteuerungen haben ihre Frist.

Und dann November, Einsamkeit, Tristesse,
Grab oder Stock, der den Gelähmten trägt—
die Himmel segnen nicht, nur die Zypresse,
der Trauerbaum, steht groß und unbewegt.

1954

Devoured: Uncertainty. Devoured: You ache
In both directions: common and unique—
An ever-lonely end for Power of Fate,
That interlude of timeless majesty.

God damn the Golden Oldies' blaring drone!
What good are sun and booze and cedar-trees
Mid voices croaking jeers—you dare atone
For Self and Dream and God and Landlord's Own?
He left the house and closed the reverie.

Alexandra Chciuk-Celt

Tristesse

Shadows are turning, not only in the grove
that's fronted by the field of asphodels,
but in our midst and your embrace they move
even while sleep still cradles you, and lulls.

What is our flesh—but roses and the thorn,
what is a breast—but velvet and its folds,
and what is hair, those armpits, the forlorn
concavities, the heat our looking holds:

They bear the Once: the formerly intimate
and that Once too: by you no longer kissed,
don't even listen, for the loud and quiet
vows will fall vacant like a home that's leased.

And then November, solitude, tristesse,
grave or the stick supporting one grown lame—
only the cypress, not the wide heavens bless,
motionless, huge, the mourning tree will loom.

Michael Hamburger

Teils-Teils

In meinem Elternhaus hingen keine Gainsboroughs
wurde auch kein Chopin gespielt
ganz amusisches Gedankenleben
mein Vater war einmal im Theater gewesen
Anfang des Jahrhunderts
Wildenbruchs „Haubenlerche"
davon zehrten wir
das war alles.

Nun längst zu Ende
graue Herzen, graue Haare
der Garten in polnischem Besitz
die Gräber teils-teils
aber alle slawisch,
Oder-Neiße-Linie
für Sarginhalte ohne Belang
die Kinder denken an sie
die Gatten auch noch eine Weile
teils-teils
bis sie weitermüssen
Sela, Psalmenende.

Heute noch in einer Großstadtnacht
Caféterrasse
Sommersterne,
vom Nebentisch
Hotelqualitäten in Frankfurt
Vergleiche,
die Damen unbefriedigt
wenn ihre Sehnsucht Gewicht hätte
wöge jede drei Zentner.

Aber ein Fluidum! Heiße Nacht
à la Reiseprospekt und
die Ladies treten aus ihren Bildern:
unwahrscheinliche Beauties

Half-and-Half

In my parents' house no Gainsboroughs hung
nor was Chopin played there
a quite inartistic mental life
my father had been to the theatre once
at the turn of the century
Wildenbruch's "Crested Lark"
we lived on that
that was all.

Now ended long ago
grey hearts grey hair
the garden Polish territory
the graves half-and-half
but all Slav
Oder-Neisse-Line
irrelevant to the contents of coffins
their children think of them
spouses too for a while
half-and-half
till they have to move on
Sela, end of psalm.

Today still in a metropolitan night
café terrace
summer stars,
from the next table
the merits of Frankfurt hotels
comparisons,
the ladies dissatisfied
if their nostalgia had any weight
each would weigh three hundred pounds.

But a flux! Hot night
à la travel brochure and
the ladies step out of their pictures:
incredible beauties

langbeinig, hoher Wasserfall
über ihre Hingabe kann man sich gar nicht erlauben
nachzudenken.

Ehepaare fallen demgegenüber ab,
kommen nicht an, Bälle gehn ins Netz,
er raucht, sie dreht ihre Ringe,
überhaupt nachdenkenswert
Verhältnis von Ehe und Mannesschaffen
Lähmung oder Hochtrieb.

Fragen, Fragen! Erinnerungen in einer Sommernacht
hingeblinzelt, hingestrichen,
in meinem Elternhaus hingen keine Gainsboroughs
nun alles abgesunken
teils-teils das Ganze
Sela, Psalmenende.

1954

Das sind doch Menschen

Das sind doch Menschen, denkt man,
wenn der Kellner an einen Tisch tritt,
einen unsichtbaren,
Stammtisch oder dergleichen in einer Ecke,
das sind doch Zartfühlende, Genüßlinge
sicher auch mit Empfindungen und Leid.

So allein bist du nicht
in deinem Wirrwarr, Unruhe, Zittern,
auch da wird Zweifel sein, Zaudern, Unsicherheit,
wenn auch in Geschäftsabschlüssen,
das Allgemein-Menschliche,
zwar in Wirtschaftsformen,
auch dort!

long-legged, high waterfall
their devotion is such that it doesn't bear
thinking about.

In face of that couples fall off,
don't get there, balls hit the net,
he smokes, she twists her rings,
altogether it's worth reflecting
on how marriage bears on male achievement
paralysis or boost.

Questions, questions! Memories in a summer night
blinked, scrawled into air,
in my parents' house no Gainsboroughs hung
now it's all gone down
half-and-half the lot
Sela, end of psalm.

Michael Hamburger

For another version see page 284.

But They Are Human

But they are human, one thinks,
when the waiter goes up to a table,
an invisible one,
a regular guest's, it could be, in a corner,
but they are sensitive, hedonists in their way,
surely with feelings, too, and sufferings.

You're not all that alone
in your tangles, disquiet, trembling,
in them too there is doubt, hesitation, uncertainty,
albeit in deals made,
the generally human,
though in economic forms,
in them too!

Unendlich ist der Gram der Herzen
und allgemein,
aber ob sie je geliebt haben
(außerhalb des Bettes)
brennend, verzehrt, wüstendurstig
nach einem Gaumenpfirsichsaft
aus fernem Mund,
untergehend, ertrinkend
in Unvereinbarkeit der Seelen—

das weiß man nicht, kann auch
den Kellner nicht fragen,
der an der Registrierkasse
das neue Helle eindrückt,
des Bons begierig,
um einen Durst zu löschen anderer Art,
doch auch von tiefer.

1954

Gedicht

Und was bedeuten diese Zwänge,
halb Bild, halb Wort und halb Kalkül,
was ist in dir, woher die Dränge
aus stillem trauernden Gefühl?

Es strömt dir aus dem Nichts zusammen,
aus einzelnem, aus Potpourri,
dort nimmst du Asche, dort die Flammen,
du streust und löschst und hütest sie.

Du weißt, du kannst nicht alles fassen,
umgrenze es, den grünen Zaun
um dies und das, du bleibst gelassen,
doch auch gebannt in Mißvertraun.

Endless the heart's grief is
and general,
but whether they've ever loved
(out of bed)
burning, consumed, desert-thirsty
for a palate peach-juice
from a distant mouth,
going down, drowning
in the separateness of souls—

that one cannot know, can't
ask the waiter either
who at the till marks up
the price of a new pale ale,
greedy for his tip
so as to quench a thirst of a different
but also deeper kind.

Michael Hamburger

Poem

What does this force mean, these convergings
both pictured, reckoned, verbalized,
what is in you, how are those urgings
from feeling's quiet grief devised?

Yours is a conflux, Nothing's traces,
of potpourri, details, a blend;
ashes and flames from different places
you take to strew and quench and tend.

You cannot grasp it all, you must know;
delimit it, a fence of green
round this and that—and, while mistrust so
enthralls you, you'll remain serene.

So Tag und Nacht bist du am Zuge,
auch sonntags meißelst du dich ein
und klopfst das Silber in die Fuge,
dann läßt du es—es ist: das Sein.

1955

Kommt—

Kommt, reden wir zusammen
wer redet, ist nicht tot,
es züngeln doch die Flammen
schon sehr um unsere Not.

Kommt, sagen wir: die Blauen,
kommt, sagen wir: das Rot,
wir hören, lauschen, schauen
wer redet, ist nicht tot.

Allein in deiner Wüste,
in deinem Gobigraun—
du einsamst, keine Büste,
kein Zwiespruch, keine Fraun,

und schon so nah den Klippen,
du kennst dein schwaches Boot—
kommt, öffnet doch die Lippen,
wer redet, ist nicht tot.

1955

And so it's your move, daily, nightly,
on Sundays, too, you sculpt to free
your place, impact the silver tightly,
then leave it—it exists to *be*.

Joseph B. Dallett

Let's

Let's hold a conversation
To prove that we're alive—
Now that the flames are lapping
Our sorrow terrorized.

Let's say: come on, you blue ones,
Come on, you color red,
Intently look and listen—
This proves that we're not dead.

Alone in private deserts,
Some Gobi-shudder bleak,
You lonelify—no statues,
No women, no one speaks—

You've almost reached the boulders
In flimsy boats that glide—
Let's open up our mouths; if
We talk, we haven't died.

Alexandra Chciuk-Celt

For another version see page 286.

Menschen getroffen

Ich habe Menschen getroffen, die,
wenn man sie nach ihrem Namen fragte,
schüchtern—als ob sie gar nicht beanspruchen könnten,
auch noch eine Benennung zu haben—
„Fräulein Christian" antworteten und dann:
„wie der Vorname", sie wollten einem die Erfassung erleichtern,
kein schwieriger Name wie „Popiol" oder „Babendererde"—
„wie der Vorname"—bitte, belasten Sie Ihr Erinnerungsvermögen
						nicht!

Ich habe Menschen getroffen, die
mit Eltern und vier Geschwistern in einer Stube
aufwuchsen, nachts, die Finger in den Ohren,
am Küchenherde lernten,
hochkamen, äußerlich schön und ladylike wie Gräfinnen—
und innerlich sanft und fleißig wie Nausikaa,
die reine Stirn der Engel trugen.

Ich habe mich oft gefragt und keine Antwort gefunden,
woher das Sanfte und das Gute kommt,
weiß es auch heute nicht und muß nun gehn.

1955

Meeting People

I have met people, who,
when they were asked their names,
shyly—as if they could not even lay claim
to a name—
answered "Miss Christine," and then:
"like the given name." They wanted to make it easier to
understand:
Not a difficult name, like "Popiol" or "Babendererde"—
"like the given name," please do not burden your memory.

I have met people, who
grew up with parents and four siblings in one room,
at night, stopping their ears with their fingers,
studied in the kitchen,
came up, in appearance beautiful and refined like countesses,
and, inwardly gentle and studious like Nausikaa,
carried the pure countenance of angels.

I have often asked myself and found no answer,
where gentleness and goodness come from,
still don't know and now must leave.

Max Knight

For other versions see pages 286–88.

Kann keine Trauer sein

In jenem kleinen Bett, fast Kinderbett, starb die Droste
(zu sehn in ihrem Museum in Meersburg),
auf diesem Sofa Hölderlin im Turm bei einem Schreiner,
Rilke, George wohl in Schweizer Hospitalbetten,
in Weimar lagen die großen schwarzen Augen
Nietzsches auf einem weißen Kissen
bis zum letzten Blick—
alles Gerümpel jetzt oder gar nicht mehr vorhanden,
unbestimmbar, wesenlos
im schmerzlos-ewigen Zerfall.

Wir tragen in uns Keime aller Götter,
das Gen des Todes und das Gen der Lust—
wer trennte sie: die Worte und die Dinge,
wer mischte sie: die Qualen und die Statt,
auf der sie enden, Holz mit Tränenbächen,
für kurze Stunden ein erbärmlich Heim.

Kann keine Trauer sein. Zu fern, zu weit,
zu unberührbar Bett und Tränen,
kein Nein, kein Ja,
Geburt und Körperschmerz und Glauben
ein Wallen, namenlos, ein Huschen,
ein Überirdisches, im Schlaf sich regend,
bewegte Bett und Tränen—
schlafe ein!

January 6, 1956

No Mourning Then

In that small bed, near-crib, Droste died
(it can be seen in her museum in Meersburg),
Hölderlin on his sofa in the cabinet maker's tower,
Rilke, George most likely in Swiss hospital beds,
in Weimar Nietzsche's large black eyes
stared up from a white pillow
to the very end—
all debris now or no longer there,
unclassifiable, unreal
in painless eternal decay.

We carry in us seeds of all the gods,
the gene of death and that of lust as well—
what separated them: reality and words,
what blended them: the suffering and the site
on which they end, wooden with streams of tears,
for a short span a pitiful abode.

No mourning then. Too distant and remote,
bed and tears too insubstantial,
neither no, nor yes,
birth and the body's pain and faith
a nameless surge, a flitting by,
something unearthly, moving in its sleep,
moved bed and tears—
go to sleep!

E. L. Kanes

For another version see page 289.

The Belated I
(Das späte Ich)

I

Oh there, just look: that bed of stock that swells,
Its eye already filled with tears,
Leave-taker, its own immortelle,
Late is the year.

Last roses here, where summer's fable
Has left the fields and fallen mute—
Moi haïssable,
Maenadic still, and dissolute.

II

In the beginning was the Flood. A raft of lemures
Shoves Elk, the Beast. (A stone got him with child.)
From Realm of Death, from Memory, from tortured beasts
God enters in.

All the great animals: eagles of the legions,
Doves from Golgotha—
All the great cities: galooned with palms and purple—
Flowers of the desert, dreamt of by Baal.

The East and its scree, Bosphorus ferry,
Rome, give the stallions of Lysippus back—
White steer's blood over altars dead silent
And Amphitrite's last sea.

Rubble. Bacchanals. Prophecies.
Barcaroles. Cochonneries.
In the beginning was the Flood. A raft of lemures
Puts out for the last seas.

III

My soul, oh rotten to the core,
Hardly alive and yet too much,
Each grain of sand blown from the fields,
Each single leaf the woodland yields
Falls through your shadow at the touch.

The cliffs are glowing, Tartarus is blue,
Into sleep's eyelid Hades rises, burning
To sheaves that still a mythic yearning
The spirit ranks, all oleander-hued.

The rubber tree, the bamboo sprout,
Lake licking Incan pedigree,
The moon château: dark shade and scree
Fill ancient walls and blue redoubt.

Fraternal bliss of Cain and Abel
Who still in clouds could God espy—
Causally-minded, haïssable:
The Belated I.

Robert M. Browning

Life—A Bare Illusion
(Leben—niederer Wahn)

Life—a bare illusion
Dream for children and serfs
But you of such ancient
Race at its course's conclusion.

What is there for you to do?
One more intoxication:
Or another transposition
Of world and you?

You still want a man or a wife?
Was not all there from the start,
Faith and how it departs
And the ensuing strife?

Form is the faith and the deed
Statues which hands have first touched,
They are what carry the seed.

J. M. Ritchie

Alone
(Wer allein ist—)

Alone, you're at the mystery's center,
Stand within the endless image-flow,
Witness their begetting, see their sprouting,
Even shadows bear their glow.

Pregnant now at every level,
Mind a-teem, yet free of cares,
Gladly you'd reduce to nothing
All that's human, feeds and pairs.

How the earth has changed since you first knew it
Cannot move you, cannot change your ways,
No more dying and no more becoming:
Locked in form, behold Perfection's gaze.

Robert M. Browning

Loners
(Wer allein ist—)

Loners are aware of mystic secrets,
How an image was conceived and made,
How it's glowing at the shadows,
While among the image-flow they wade.

Solitude is multilayered-gravid,
Self-contained in thoughtful sustenance,
Mighty lord protector avid
Of man's reproductive nurturance.

Loner's watch unsentimental whole
The earth turns different from when they were made;
No more metamorphoses,
Perfect quiet Form returns their gaze.

Alexandra Chciuk-Celt

Asters
(Astern)

Asters—sweltering days,
old invocation, spells,
the gods keep in equipoise
for one hesitant hour the scales.

Once more those golden herds
of the heavens, the blossom, the light,
what is it old genesis broods,
under dying wings hatches out?

Once more the thing longed for in lack,
the frenzy, the roses' You—
Summer stood, leaning back,
and watched the swallows fly,

once more a divining mood
where certainty's vigil grows late:
the swallows dip down to the flood,
drinking transition and night.

                              Michael Hamburger

Asters

Asters—old incantations,
Steaming and spellbound days—
Just an hour's hesitation,
Gods holding down the scales.

Once again, herds are golden—
Flourishes, light, and skies.
What is Phoenix Past hatching
Under his wings as he dies?

Once again, you are roses—
I feel a yearning high—
Summer leaned back, a-watching
Swallows go flitting by . . .

One more stray supposition
Stumps the established guide:
Swallows skimming the waters,
Drinking in Night and Ride.

                    Alexandra Chciuk-Celt

Asters

Asters—smouldering days,
ancient conjuring, ban,
the gods, with some wavering delays,
halt the scales for an hour's span.

One last time the golden herd
heaven, the light, the bloom,
what emergence of yore, bestirred,
under dying wings brooding, does loom.

One final time the pining,
the passion, the roses' You—
while summer stood, reclining,
and watched what the swallows do.

One last time a bemusing
where certainty long has might:
the floods grazed by swallows cruising
imbibing flight and night.

Kerry Weinberg

Lost Identity
(Verlorenes Ich)

Lost ego, split by stratospheres,
victim of ion—lamb of the gamma ray,
particle, also field: chimeras of infinity
on Notre Dame, stony and gray.

The years hold neither snow nor fruit,
your days are passing without dawn or night,
they hold infinity—a menace—hidden:
The world as flight.

Where do you end, where do you camp,
where do your spheres extend—
Loss, gain: a game for beasts. Eternities:
your flight across their bars will never end.

Death in the jungle: the reason for creation.
Glance of the beast: stars are entrails.
Man, Catalaunian Plains, and battles of the nations,
slide down the gullet of the beast.

World thought to pieces. Space, and time,
and that which mankind wove and weighed,
they are but functions of eternities.
Religions lied.

Where to, where from—not night not morning,
no evoe, no requiem,
what you need is a borrowed slogan—
borrowed from whom?

Oh, when they all bowed toward one single center,
when even the thinkers only thought: the God,
when they branched out to lamb and shepherds,
blood of the chalice had purified them,

then all flowed from one wound;
all broke the bread and ate it in serenity—
distant, compelling hour of fulfillment
that once enclosed our lost identity.

Gertrude C. Schwebell

Chopin

His talk was fairly meager,
opinions were not his forte,
(opinions were just evasions),
when Delacroix started spinning theories
he grew uneasy, unable, for his part,
to justify the Nocturnes.

Tepid ladies' man;
shadows in Nohant,
where George Sand's children
received no paternal
advice from him.

His consumption the sort
with hemorrhages and protracted
clottings;
a death quieter
than by paroxysm,
quieter
than getting shot:
They shoved the piano (an Erard) by the door
and Delphine Potocka
sang him a *Lied* about violets
in his final hour.

He travelled to England with three pianos:
Pleyel, Erard, Broadwood,
evenings he played 15 minutes
for 20 guineas
at the Rothschilds, the Wellingtons, at Stafford House
to the applause of innumerable garters;
dimmed by fatigue and death's propinquity
he went home
to the Square d'Orléans.

Then he burned his rough drafts
and manuscripts, any
remnant, fragment, jotting
that might betray—
and said in the end:
"My attempts have been concluded
in accordance with my capacities."

The playing power of each finger
was to correspond to its build,
the fourth is the weakest
(mere Siamese to the middle).
They lay, when he began,
on e, f, g, a, c.

Whoever has heard
certain of his Preludes,
be it in country houses or
in the Alps or through
doors open, say,
on a sanatarium terrace,
will never forget them.

Never composed an opera,
no symphony,
just these tragic progressions
in artistic conviction
and with a tiny hand.

Richard Sieburth

Travel
(Reisen)

Do you think Zürich for instance
would be a town with more style?
Miracles galore and incense
To make your life worth while?

Or do you think Havana
White and hibiscus red
Would offer eternal manna
In your waste land for bread?

Zürich main streets, London mews,
Boulevards, lidos in plenty,
Even on Fifth Avenues,
Suddenly you feel empty.

What use does travel serve?
Not till too late do you see:
Stay put and quietly preserve
The self-sufficient me.

                    J. M. Ritchie

Travel

Do you think, for example, that Zurich
is a city more profound,
a place where wonders and blessings
can ever and always be found?

Do you think that from Havana,
hibiscus red and white,
there falls an eternal manna
to save you from your plight?

On station roads and *rue,*
on the boulevard, lido and lane,
even on fifth avenue,
emptiness hits you again.

Alas! to travel is futile.
Only late do you come to yourself.
Stay and preserve it calmly
that I that defines itself.

                    Franz Feige and Patricia Gleason

Partly-Partly
(Teils-Teils)

No Gainsboroughs hung in our parents' home
no Chopin was played
fine arts had no room in our thoughts
my father once went to a stage show
at the turn of the century
they played Wildenbruch's "Haubenlerche"
from that we drew our nourishment
that was all.

Now past history
gray hearts, gray hair
the garden now in Polish ownership
the graves partly-partly
but all Slavic.
Oder-Neisse Line
irrelevant for those in coffins
the children think of them
so do the spouses for a while
partly-partly
till they have to be on their way
Sela, end of psalm.

Still today in a metropolis
café terrace
summer stars,
from the next table
fine hotels in Frankfurt.
Compare,
the unsatisfied ladies
if their desire had weight
they would each weigh three centners.

But an atmosphere! Hot night
as in travel brochures and
the ladies step out from the illustrations:
unlikely beauties
long-legged, high waterfall
about their surrender
you cannot even permit yourself
to speculate.

Married couples fare poorly compared with that,
come off second-best, balls land in the net,
he smokes, she twiddles her rings,
altogether worth thinking about
relation of marriage to manly potency
paralysis or high drive.

Questions, questions! Reminiscences in a summer night
winked at, sketched out,
no Gainsboroughs hung in my parents' home
now everything dropped
partly-partly all of it
Sela, end of psalm.

Max Knight

Come—
(Kommt—)

Come, let's talk together,
Who talks cannot be dead,
The flames are already licking
High up about our head.

Come, let's say: those blue ones,
Come, let's say: that red,
We hearken, look, and listen,
Who talks cannot be dead.

Alone there in your desert,
Amidst your Gobi sands,
Alone: no swelling bosom,
No speech, no groping hands,

And close you see the cliffs now
As your frail bark sails ahead—
Come, unseal your lips now,
Who talks cannot be dead.

Robert M. Browning

People Met
(Menschen getroffen)

I have met people who,
if one asked them their names,
shyly—as though they couldn't presume
to lay claim to so much as an appellation—
answered "Miss Dennis," and then:
"like the Christian name," they wanted to make it easier,
not a difficult name like "Popiol" or "Babendererde"—
"like the Christian name"—don't burden your memory with it.

I have met people who
grew up with their parents and four
brothers and sister in one room,
at night, their fingers plugging their ears,
learned at the kitchen stove,
improved themselves, outwardly ladylike as countesses—
and inwardly gentle and diligent as Nausicaa,
bore the pure brows of angels.

I've often asked myself and found no answer,
where gentleness and goodness might come from,
don't know it even now, and it's time for me to go.

Michael Hamburger

People Met

I met people who
if one were to ask their name
would answer modestly
"Miss James"—as if they dared not even
claim their own name—and then:
"like the first name,"—they wanted to make it easier for you,
not a difficult name like "Popiol" or "Babendererde"—
"like the first name,"—please, don't burden your memory.

I met people who
grew up in one room
with their parents and four brothers and sisters,
and who, nights, fingers in ears,
learned at the kitchen stove,
rose in the world—outwardly beautiful and ladylike
        as a countess—
inwardly gentle and diligent as Nausicaä, and
with the pure brow of angels.

I have often asked myself but found no answer:
where do gentleness and goodness come from.
I do not know, even today—and now I must go.

Gertrude C. Schwebell

People Met

I have met people who, when asked what their names were,
Apologetically, as if they had no right to claim one's attention
Even with an appellation, would answer,
"Miss Vivian," then add, "Just like the Christian name";
They wanted to make things easier, no complicated names
Like Popkiss or Umpleby-Dunball—
"Just like the Christian name"—so please do not burden your
memory!

I have met people who grew up in a single room together with
Parents and four brothers and sisters; they studied by night,
Their fingers in their ears, beside the kitchen range;
They became eminent,
Outwardly beautiful, veritable *grandes dames,* and
Inwardly gentle and active as Nausicaa,
With brows clear as angels' brows.

Often I have asked myself, but found no answer,
Where gentleness and goodness can possibly come from;
Even today I can't tell, and it's time to be gone.

Christopher Middleton

No Mourning's Possible
(Kann keine Trauer sein)

In that small bed, a child's cot almost, Droste died,
(to be seen in her Meersburg museum),
on this sofa Hölderlin at a carpenter's, in his tower,
in Swiss hospital beds, probably, Rilke and Stefan George,
in Weimar the staring black eyes of Nietzsche
lay on a white pillow
up to the last look—
all lumber now or not extant at all,
indefinable, without quiddity,
in its painlessly timeless decay.

We bear inside us germs of all the gods,
the gene of death and the gene of lust—
who could divide them: the words and things,
who fuse them: the agonies and the frame
on which they end, boards with tear-runnels,
a pitiable home for a few brief hours.

No mourning's possible. Too far away
and too impalpable the bed, the tears,
neither No nor Yes,
our birth, the body's pangs and faith,
a surging, nameless, a scurrying,
superterrestial, stirring in our sleep,
it was that moved both bed and tears—
now go to sleep!

Michael Hamburger

Select Bibliography

Gottfried Benn. *Gesammelte Werke*. Edited by Dieter Wellershoff. 8 volumes. Wiesbaden, 1968.

———. Edited by Gerhard Schuster, in cooperation with Ilse Benn. 5 volumes. Stuttgart, 1986–.

———. Edited by Bruno Hillebrand. 5 volumes, paperback. Frankfurt/M., 1986–.

Lohner, Edgar. *Gottfried Benn Bibliographie 1912–1956*. Wiesbaden, 1958.

Adams, Marion. *Gottfried Benn's Critique of Substance*. Assen, 1969.

Alter, Reinhard. *Gottfried Benn: The Artist and Politics*. Bern, 1976.

Ashton, E. B. Introduction to *Primal Vision: Selected Writings of Gottfried Benn*. London, 1976.

Casey, Paul, and Timothy Casey. *The Galway Gottfried Benn Symposium*. Galway, 1987.

Casper, M. Kent. "The Circle and the Centre: Symbols of Totality in Gottfried Benn." *German Life and Letters* 26 (1972–73): 288–97.

Cuomo, Glenn. "Purging an 'Art-Bolshevist.' " *German Studies Review* 9/1 (1986): 85–105.

Eliot, T. S. *The Three Voices of Poetry*. London, 1955.

Hamburger, Michael. "Art and Nihilism: The Poetry of Gottfried Benn." *Encounter*, October 1954, pp. 49–59.

———. *Reason and Energy: Studies in German Literature*. Pp. 277–312. London, 1957.

Hannum, Hunter G. "Gottfried Benn's 'Gladiolen.' " *Modern Language Notes* 22 (1961): 167–80.

———. "Gottfried Benn's Music." *Germanic Review* 40 (1965): 225–39.

Hilton, Jan. "Gottfried Benn." *German Men of Letters* 3 (1964): 129–50.

Hohendahl, Peter Uwe. *Benn—Wirkung wider Willer.* Frankfurt/ M., 1971.

Jolas, Eugene. "Gottfried Benn." *Transition* 5 (1927):146–49.

Lennig, Walter. *Gottfried Benn.* Reinbek b. Hamburg, 1962.

Lohner, Edgar. "The Development of Gottfried Benn's Idea of Expression as Value." *German Quarterly* 26 (1953):39–54.

———. *Passion und Intellekt: Die Lyrik Gottfried Benns.* Darmstadt, 1961; paperback, Frankfurt/M., 1986.

Loose, Gerhard. "Gottfried Benn and the Problem of Art in Our Time." *Criticism* 4 (1962): 340–52.

Manyoni, Angelika. *Consistency of Phenotype.* Bern, 1983.

Ritchie, James McPherson. *Gottfried Benn: The Unreconstructed Expressionist.* London, 1972.

Schröder, Jürgen. *Gottfried Benn: Poesie und Sozialisation.* Stuttgart, 1978.

Spender, Stephen. "Doctor of Science, Patient of Poetry." *Noble Savage* 4 (1961).

Townson, Michael R. "The Montage-Technique in Gottfried Benn's Lyric." *Orbis Litterarum* 21 (1966): 154–80.

Weisstein, Ulrich. "Gottfried Benn and Expressionism." *The Folio* 19 (1954): 89–102.

Wellershoff, Dieter. *Gottfried Benn: Phänotyp dieser Stunde.* Berlin, 1958.

Wodtke, Friedrich Wilhelm. Introduction to *Gottfried Benn: Selected Poems.* Oxford, 1970.

Acknowledgments

The following material has been taken from *Primal Vision: Selected Writings of Gottfried Benn,* edited by E. B. Ashton. Copyright © 1971 by New Directions Publishing Corporation. Reprinted by permission of New Directions, New York, and Marion Boyars, London: Excerpts from the Introduction by E. B. Ashton, "The Birthday," "Alexander's March by Means of Flushes," "Primal Vision," excerpts from "The Way of an Intellectualist," "Wolf's Tavern," "Block II, Room 66," "Letter from Berlin, July 1948," "Art and the Third Reich," "Pallas," "Pessimism," "Future and Present," "Artists and Old Age," and the poems "Man and Woman Go through the Cancer Ward," "Night Café," "Songs," "Subway Train," "Icarus," "Who Are You," "Qui Sait," "Never More Lonely," "A Word," "Monologue," "Wave of the Night," "Chopin," "September," "Epilogue," "Fragments," "What's Bad," and "People Met."

Grateful acknowledgment is made to Ernst Klett Verlage GmbH U. Co. KG for permission to translate the following: "The Glass-Blower," "The Problem of Genius," "Can Poets Change the World," "After Nihilism," "Induced Life," and the poems "No Mourning Then," "The Late Ego," "Yesteryear," "And Yet, with Swords at the Ready," "Bistro," "What Are You?" "He Left the House," "Let's," "Travel," "Those Traits of Yours," "But They Are Human," "Half-and-Half," "Two Things Only," "Appendectomy," and "Tristesse."

Grateful acknowledgment is also made to Arche Verlag, Zurich, for permission to translate the following poems from *Statische Gedichte.* © 1948, 1983 by Verlags-A.G. Die Arche, Zurich: "Life—What a Vulgar Delusion!" "He Who's Alone," "Asters," "Turin," "Poem," "Forsaken I," "Those Traits of Yours," and "Quartenary."